# ARCHITECTURE DESCRIPTION LANGUAGES

## IFIP – The International Federation for Information Processing

IFIP was founded in 1960 under the auspices of UNESCO, following the First World Computer Congress held in Paris the previous year. An umbrella organization for societies working in information processing, IFIP's aim is two-fold: to support information processing within its member countries and to encourage technology transfer to developing nations. As its mission statement clearly states,

> *IFIP's mission is to be the leading, truly international, apolitical organization which encourages and assists in the development, exploitation and application of information technology for the benefit of all people.*

IFIP is a non-profitmaking organization, run almost solely by 2500 volunteers. It operates through a number of technical committees, which organize events and publications. IFIP's events range from an international congress to local seminars, but the most important are:

- The IFIP World Computer Congress, held every second year;
- Open conferences;
- Working conferences.

The flagship event is the IFIP World Computer Congress, at which both invited and contributed papers are presented. Contributed papers are rigorously refereed and the rejection rate is high.

As with the Congress, participation in the open conferences is open to all and papers may be invited or submitted. Again, submitted papers are stringently refereed.

The working conferences are structured differently. They are usually run by a working group and attendance is small and by invitation only. Their purpose is to create an atmosphere conducive to innovation and development. Refereeing is less rigorous and papers are subjected to extensive group discussion.

Publications arising from IFIP events vary. The papers presented at the IFIP World Computer Congress and at open conferences are published as conference proceedings, while the results of the working conferences are often published as collections of selected and edited papers.

Any national society whose primary activity is in information may apply to become a full member of IFIP, although full membership is restricted to one society per country. Full members are entitled to vote at the annual General Assembly, National societies preferring a less committed involvement may apply for associate or corresponding membership. Associate members enjoy the same benefits as full members, but without voting rights. Corresponding members are not represented in IFIP bodies. Affiliated membership is open to non-national societies, and individual and honorary membership schemes are also offered.

# ARCHITECTURE DESCRIPTION LANGUAGES

***IFIP TC-2 Workshop on Architecture Description Languages (WADL), World Computer Congress, Aug. 22-27, 2004, Toulouse, France***

*Edited by*

**Pierre Dissaux**
*TNI-Europe*
*France*

**Mamoun Filali-Amine (*Chair*)**
*IRIT/FERIA*
*France*

**Pierre Michel**
*ONERA/FERIA*
*France*

**François Vernadat**
*LAAS/FERIA*
*France*

Library of Congress Cataloging-in-Publication Data

A C.I.P. Catalogue record for this book is available from the Library of Congress.

***Architecture Description Languages*** Edited by Pierre Dissaux, Mamoun Filali-Amine, Pierre Michel and François Vernadat

p.cm. (The International Federation for Information Processing)

ISBN: (HB) 0-387-24589-8 / (eB00K) 0-387-24590-1 Printed on acid-free paper.



Printed in the United States of America.

9 8 7 6 5 4 3 2 1 SPIN 11391616 (HC) / 11391999 (eBook)
springeronline.com

# Contents

# Preface

These proceedings record the papers presented at the Workshop on Architecture Description Languages held in the city of Toulouse in the south of France.

The aim of an ADL (Architecture Description Language) is to formally describe software and hardware architectures. Usually, an ADL describes components, their interfaces, their structures, their interactions (structure of data flow and control flow) and the mappings to hardware systems. A major goal of such descriptions is to allow analysis with respect to several aspects like timing, safety, reliability, ... This workshop has provided a forum for practitioners and researchers to discuss recent development around ADLs. A feature of this workshop has been to brought different communities, from e.g., avionics and space embedded systems, automotive embedded systems, distributed systems, to confront their approaches, to discuss their emerging standards, and to share their respective knowledge.

Toulouse and Brest, September 2004

Pierre Dissaux, Mamoun Filali Amine, Pierre Michel, François Vernadat
Editors

# Program Committee

- Eric Conquet, ESA/ESTEC, France
- Anne-Marie Deplanche, IRCCYN, France
- Pierre Dissaux, TNI-Europe, France
- Jean-Pierre Elloy, IRCCYN, France
- Patrick Farail, EADS Airbus, France
- Jean-Marie Farines, DAS UFSC, Brazil
- Peter Feiler, Carnegie Mellon Univ./SEI, USA
- Mamoun Filali Amine, IRIT/FERIA, France
- Pierre Gaufillet, EADS Airbus, France
- Clegg Kester, Univ. of York, UK
- Bruce Lewis, US Army/ AMCOM, USA
- Pierre Michel, ONERA/FERIA, France
- Alek Radjenovic, Univ. of York, UK
- Françoise Simonot-Lion, LORIA, France
- François Terrier, CEA-LIST, France
- Jean-François Tilman, AXLOG Ingénierie, France
- François Vernadat, LAAS/FERIA, France
- Steve Vestal, Honeywell Laboratories, USA
- Sergio Yovine, VERIMAG, France
- Andre Windisch, EADS, Germany

# Referees

We are grateful for the following people who aided the program committees in the reviewing of papers.

| | | |
|---|---|---|
| Jean-Luc Béchennec | IRCCYN | France |
| Jean-Paul Bodeveix | IRIT/FERIA | France |
| Anne-Marie Déplanche | IRCCYN | France |
| Pierre Dissaux | TNI-Europe | France |
| Khalil Drira | LAAS | France |
| Jean-Pierre Elloy | IRCCYN | France |
| Patrick Farail | EADS Airbus | France |
| Jean-Marie Farines | DAS UFSC | Brazil |
| Peter Feiler | Carnegie Mellon Univ. /SEI | USA |
| Mamoun Filali | IRIT/FERIA | France |
| Pierre Gaufillet | EADS Airbus | France |
| Clegg Kester | Univ of York | UK |
| Bruce Lewis | US Army / AMCOM | USA |
| Christophe Lohr | Concordia University | Canada |
| Philippe Mauran | IRIT/FERIA | France |
| Pierre Michel | CERT/FERIA | France |
| Francisco Moo Mena | LAAS | France |
| Alek Radjenovic | Univ of York | UK |
| Xavier Rebeuf | LORIA | France |
| Pierre-Olivier Ribet | LAAS/FERIA | France |
| Pascal Sainrat | IRIT | France |
| Pierre de SaquiSannes | ENSICA | France |
| Françoise Simonot-Lion | LORIA | France |
| François Terrier | CEA-LIST | France |
| Jean-François Tilman | AXLOG Ingénierie | France |
| François Vernadat | LAAS/FERIA | France |
| Steve Vestal | Honeywell Laboratories | USA |
| Sergio Yovine | VERIMAG | France |
| Andre Windisch | EADS | Germany |

# TUTORIAL

# An Overview of the SAE Architecture Analysis & Design Language (AADL) Standard: A Basis for Model-Based Architecture-Driven Embedded Systems Engineering

Peter H. Feiler[1], Bruce Lewis[2], Steve Vestal[3] and Ed Colbert[4]
[1]*Software Engineering Institute, USA, phf@sei.cmu.edu*
[2]*US Army AMCOM, USA, bruce.lewis@sed.redstone.army.mil*
[3]*Honeywell Laboratories, USA, Steve.Vestal@honeywell.com*
[4]*Absolute Software, USA, colbert@abssw.com*

www.aadl.info *email: info@aadl.info*

**Abstract:** Architecture Description Languages provide significant opportunity for the incorporation of formal methods and engineering models into the analysis of software and system architectures. A standard is being developed for embedded real-time safety critical systems which will support the use of various formal approaches to analyze the impact of the composition of systems from hardware and software and which will allow the generation of system glue code with the performance qualities predicted. The SAE AADL standard (International Society for Automotive Engineers (SAE) Architecture Analysis & Design Language) is based on the MetaH language developed under DARPA and US Army funding and on the model driven architectural based approach demonstrated with this technology over the last 12 years. The SAE AADL standard is aimed at supporting avionics, space, automotive, robotics and other real-time concurrent processing domains including safety critical applications.

**Keywords:** Architecture Analysis & Design Language; AADL; architecture description language; computer architecture; computer modeling; computer analysis; embedded systems; model based development; SAE; software architecture; system architecture.

# 1. INTRODUCTION

The International Society for Automotive Engineers (SAE) Architecture Analysis & Design Language (AADL) is a textual and graphical language used to design and analyze the software and hardware architecture of real-time systems and their performance-critical characteristics. It is aimed at supporting the avionics, aerospace, and automotive industry. The language is used to describe the structure of such systems as an assembly of software components mapped onto an execution platform. The language can describe functional interfaces to components (such as data inputs and outputs) and performance-critical aspects of components (such as timing). The language can describe how components interact, such as how data inputs and outputs are connected, how and when components are executed, and how application software components are allocated to execution platform components. The language can also describe the dynamic behavior of the runtime architecture by supporting the modeling concept of operational modes and mode transitions. The language is designed to be extensible to accommodate analyses of additional runtime architectures that the core language does not completely support. Extensions can take the form of new properties and analysis specific notations that can be associated with components.

The AADL was developed under the auspices of the International Society for Automotive Engineers (SAE). The AADL is developed for embedded systems that have challenging resource (size, weight, power) constraints, that have challenging and strict real-time response requirements that must tolerate faults, that have specialized input/output hardware, and that must be certified to high levels of assurance. Intended fields of application are avionics systems, flight management, engine and power train control systems, certain medical devices, industrial process control equipment, and space applications. The AADL addresses system of systems architectures, supporting integration of embedded systems into higher level systems.

The language can describe important performance-critical aspects such as timing requirements, fault and error behaviors, time and space partitioning, and safety and certification properties. Such a description allows a system designer to perform analyses of the composed components and systems such as system schedulability, sizing analysis, and safety analysis. From these analyses, the designer can evaluate architectural tradeoffs and changes. Since the AADL supports multiple and extensible analysis approaches, it provides the ability to analyze the cross cutting impacts of change in the architecture in one specification using multiple analysis tools. The AADL specification language has been designed to be further used with proper tool support to generate the code needed to integrate the system components and build a system executive. Since the models and the architecture specification drive the design and implementation, they can be maintained to permit model driven architecture based changes throughout the system lifecycle.

## 2. Background

The AADL is based on experiences in the use of DARPA funded ADL efforts, in particular MetaH developed by Honeywell []. A number of organizations have used MetaH in prototypical system developments, including Boeing, US Army, and the SEI. The case study of a pilot application of the MetaH technology by the U.S. Army AMCOM SED laboratory to missile guidance systems produced some insights into the potential cost savings of an architecture-driven approach. An existing missile guidance system, implemented in Jovial, was reengineered to run on a new hardware platform and to fit into generic missile reference architecture []. As part of the reengineering effort the system was modularized and translated into Ada95. The task architecture consisting of 12-16 concurrent tasks was represented as a MetaH model and the implementation generated automatically from the MetaH model and the Ada95 coded application components. The resulting system consisted of 12,000 source lines of application component code, 3000 lines of MetaH executive generated from the MetaH model, and 3000 lines of code representing MetaH kernel services. The engineers doing the reengineering work made a conservative estimate of effort required to reengineer the system into a pure Ada95 implementation and validated the estimate with the prime contractor who implemented the missile. The cost savings of 40% (prime estimated 66%) was obtained for reengineering to a different language and platform, then the time critical software was ported to multiple processor/0S/compiler platforms at a cost savings of 90% per port.

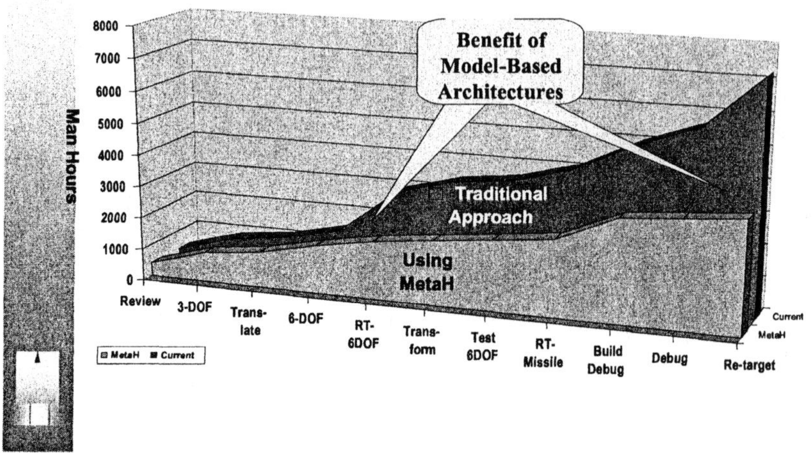


MetaH demonstrated the practicality of using an Architecture Description Language (ADL) as core modeling notation for providing analysis capabilities of several performance-critical quality attribute dimensions such as schedulability, dependability, and safety-critical concerns. The MetaH toolset demonstrated the capability of not only supporting system analysis, but also automatic generation of glue code in form of a system executive that performs all task binding, dispatching, and inter-task communication with application components as “plug-ins” into this infrastructure. This separation of concerns allows application developers to focus on domain functionality, while a software system architect can focus on achieving system-level performance-critical quality attributes.

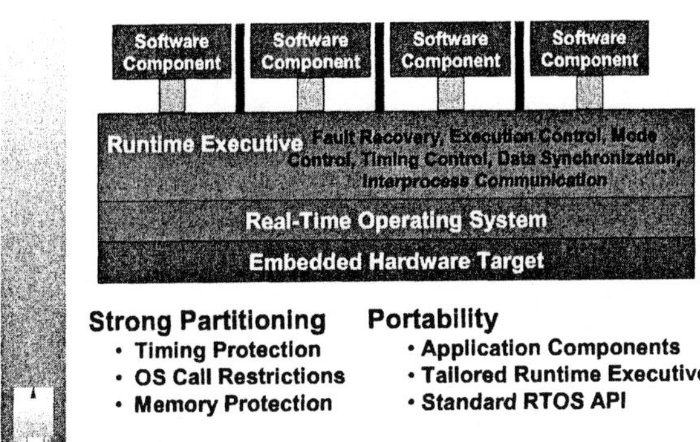


## 3. An Analyzable Software System Architecture Description Notation

The AADL has been designed to be a basis for model-based analysis and generation of embedded systems, i.e., embedded and system of systems engineering driven by an architecture that is reflected in the models and maintained throughout the system life cycle []. The notation has been designed as an extensible core language with well defined semantics and both a graphical and textual presentation. The core language supports modeling in several architecture views [7] and addresses timing and performance analyses through explicit modeling of application system and execution platform components and their binding as well as precisely defined concurrency and interaction semantics and timing/performance properties. The extension mechanisms permit properties to be introduced that are specific to additional architecture analyses in terms of other quality attributes such as reliability, security, etc, as were demonstrated with MetaH, and new analysis approaches. In this section we introduce to core language and in the next section we discuss the extension capability.

The focus of the AADL is to model the software system architecture in terms of an application system bound to an execution platform. The architecture is modeled in terms of hierarchies of components, whose interaction is represented by connections. Components have a component type that represents its externally visible interface and other characteristics, i.e., represents a component specification, and one or more implementations. A component implementation in the AADL may represent application source text and may be decomposed into an interconnected set of subcomponents that are instances of other component types and implementations. Generalization of components is supported in that component types and implementations can be expressed as extensions of other component types and implementations.

To support modeling of execution platforms four categories of components have been introduced: *processor* as a virtual machine that schedules and executes units of concurrent execution (threads) according to a specified scheduling protocol and may support space partitioning through protected address spaces; *memory* as a storage abstraction that can hold data and/or code; *bus* as a connector abstraction between execution platform components, and a *device* as an abstraction of an active component that an application system can interact with and a processor executing software may require access to via a bus. The execution platform components may represent hardware components or abstract execution platform components, whose implementations may represent virtual machines that are implemented in terms of another execution platform, with the bindings finally resolving to actual hardware. Each execution platform category has a number of predefined properties such as thread and process swap time or scheduling protocol for processors. The core AADL predefines such properties and an initial set of acceptable property value that can be extended. For example, new scheduling protocols can be introduced through a property extension mechanism.

Application system modeling is supported through two groups of component categories. The first group focuses on the runtime behavior of a system and consists of: *thread* as basic unit of concurrent execution which can be abstracted into *thread groups;* and *process* as unit of protected address space. Threads are contained in processes and have one of a set of predefined dispatch protocol property values or one introduced through the property extension mechanism. Predefined dispatch protocols include periodic, aperiodic, sporadic, and background. Threads have separate execution entrypoints into their associated source text for initialization, nominal execution, and recovery. In case of nominal execution server threads may have multiple entrypoints defined as server subprogram entrypoints. The process load, thread dispatch and scheduling semantics are defined using a hybrid automaton notation.

The second group focuses on the source text of a system and consists of: *package* as unit of source text; and *data* component as passive application data. The package category allows the modeler to represent the source text decomposition structure to a level of detail that is appropriate to the modeling effort. The data component category supports representing data types and class abstractions in the source text as necessary for architecture models. The data type is used to type ports (see below), to specify subprogram parameter types, and to type shared data component instances. The component type extension mechanism can model type inheritance. Subprogram features (see below) in component types can represent class methods and accessors of data component declared as sharable with a specified concurrency control protocol. Required access to sharable data component instances is specified in a *requires* subclause of a component type.

A final component category supports hierarchical composition and consists of: *system* as a unit whose implementations can contain execution platform components, application system components and other system instances.

The AADL supports modeling of three kinds of interactions between components: directional flow of data and/or control through data, event, and event data port connections; call/return interaction on subprogram entrypoints; and through access to a shared data component (see data component above).

Threads, processors, and devices, and their enclosing components (process and system) have in ports and out ports declared. Data ports communicate unqueued state data, event ports communicate events that are raised in their implementation, their associated source text, or actual hardware, and event data ports represent queued data whose arrival can have event semantics. Arrival of an event at a thread results in the dispatch of that thread – with semantics defined via property values and hybrid automata for event arrival while the thread is active. For data port connections data is communicated upon execution completion (immediate connection with the effect of mid-frame communication for periodic threads) or upon thread deadline (delayed connection with the effect of phase delay for periodic threads).

The data and event data ports appear to the application source text as data variables – in ports as data variables where input is found when a thread is dispatched, and out ports as variables into which output to be communicated to other components is placed for transfer at well-defined points. In other words, the application source text of a component has no knowledge of the components it interacts with. The interaction connection is defined as part of the AADL description, and appropriate runtime executive code can be generated for thread dispatching and communication.

Subprogram entrypoints are defined in component types as provided and required entrypoints. At the level of components representing source text they represent procedures/functions that are called sequentially. At the level of concurrent components they represent synchronous call/return between two concurrency units (client subprogram calling a server subprogram).

Components can have modes. Modes represent alternative configurations of the component implementation with only one mode being active at a time. At the level of system and process a mode represents possibly overlapping (sub-) sets of active threads and port connections, and alternative configurations of execution platform components, as well as alternative bindings of application components to execution platform components. Mode change behavior is specified as a state transition diagram whose states are the modes and the transitions are triggered by events. Thus, the AADL can model dynamically changing behavior of statically known thread and port communication topologies bound to statically known execution platform topologies. Modes can also be declared for sources text components. This permits mode-specific property values to be declared in situations where the thread and connection architecture does not change, but the thread internal behavior changes, e.g., it has different worst-case execution times under different modes. Such more detailed modeling of application systems allows for less conservative analysis such as schedulability analysis.

The AADL has the following basic fault handling model. Runtime faults may be handled within source text components through mechanisms that are part of the source language runtime environment For faults not handled at that level or propagated by the source text a thread is given an opportunity to recover and continue with the next dispatch through a recovery entrypoint. Thread unrecoverable errors are propagated as error events. The modeler of a particular application system indicates through event connections where the error event is propagated to, and mode change behavior descriptions indicate actions taken in response to error events.

The AADL also supports other behavior specifications. It supports specification of sequential execution paths within threads to represent control flow within a thread in more detail. It supports specification of expected invocation patterns on subprogram entrypoints that can be checked against actual invocations. It supports specification of expected event port trigger patterns for a port collection, i.e., a lower-level control flow protocol represented by a collection of event port connections that externally is viewed as a single event connection. It supports flow specification to support end-to-end flow analysis of data and control.

In summary, the core AADL supports modeling of application systems and execution platforms as interacting components with specific semantics and bindings. Such systems are configurable in that components have multiple implementations. Semantics defined as part of the component categories and their predefined properties address timing and resource consumption as well as interaction consistency in terms of matching port types and data communicated through the ports. Behavior descriptions allow for model checking of behaviors as well as mode(state)-specific analyses with less conservative results. The core language does not provide properties and semantics for all possible architecture analyses. Instead the AADL has been made extensible both in terms of language notation and in terms of standard annexes to accommodate further analyses. Annexes that will follow the initial core standard include language extensions such as ability to provide error modeling for various dependability analysis, a UML profile, an XML interchange format, and an Ada and C implementation annex. Additional annexes are planned for more detailed component behavior modeling, ARINC 653 and POSIX implementation, constraints etc.

## 4. An Extensible Software System Architecture Description Notation

The AADL has been made extensible in three respects. First, modelers can define an extensible set of component specifications in form of component types and implementations by making use of the extension mechanism discussed in the previous section. Second, the language itself can be extended through the ability to introduce new properties and extend the set of valid property values for existing properties. Third, the AADL draft standard includes its specification as a UML profile.

The AADL provides a library concept for organizing component type and implementation declarations. It provides a name scope, thus, facilitates independent development of major subsystems. Furthermore, the component extension mechanism allows modelers to define components and generalizations and specializations of other components.

The AADL currently supports the introduction of new properties extend the set of valid values, and associate them with existing component categories, ports, and connections through property extension sets. No specific notational capability is provided are part of the AADL to describe the semantic meaning of such properties, e.g., in terms of reliability characteristics. Instead, providers of such extension sets can use notations such as the hybrid automaton notation used in the definition of the core language, or resort to English text or other more precise notations to describe the formal model underlying a particular analysis to which the properties represent input.

In many cases it is desirable to express constraints on properties – such as a constraint that the sum of mass property values of any subcomponent with a mass does not exceed a certain maximum. We could consider extending the AADL to explicitly support a constraint language. At this time constraints can be introduced through properties with string values, whose meaning is only understood by constraint analysis tools.

The AADL can be viewed as a modeling notation that can be completed with notations tailored to the specific goals of a particular modeling view and analysis. Such complementary notations can be introduced through string-values properties as suggested above. Alternatively, additional modeling views and semantics addressing certain analyses can be expressed in terms of a UML sublanguage model. This approach is possible because we have developed a UML profile of the AADL as part of the draft standard.

AADL/UML Strategy

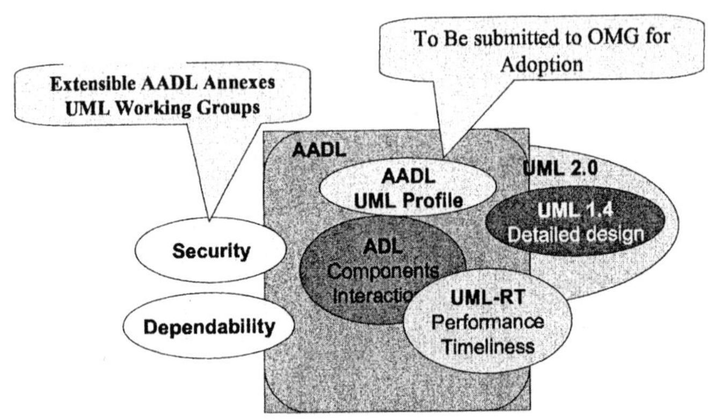


## 5. Status of the AADL as a Standard

The AADL standard has been in the works since 1999 with a balloted requirements document in 2000. The standard was approved for publication by the SAE in September of 2004. The specification of the AADL has been aligned with the OMG UML standard to benefit from its large practitioner base. The emerging UML2.0 standard is considered a partner in crime rather than competition. The UML profile of the AADL, which after being approved as an annex of the SAE standard, will be submitted for acceptance to the OMG to be part of their standard suite.

The standard provides a means for the commercial production of tools with a common AADL language interface. The UML profile, a specialization providing AADL semantics, will allow the application of formal analysis and code generation tools through a UML graphical specification, enabling the use of currently available UML tools for specification. We also will provide an XML specification for the AADL language now that the first version of the language standard is completed. These capabilities will provide an early interface for developing new analysis approaches.

The AADL Standardization Subcommittee also has a liaison relationship with a French research consortium, COTRE, headed by Airbus. COTRE has adopted the AADL for research into new tools, development and analysis methods to support aviation system development requirements. The AADL plays a significant role in a future software and systems development approach described by Airbus and COTRE in a recent paper[]. Other US and European companies and agencies are evaluating and experimenting with MetaH and the AADL.

Architecture based, model driven approaches are also beginning to appear in the general software engineering domain. UML 2.0, the Model Driven Architectures Initiative [], will provide a new layer to UML to directly support a generalized model driven architecture based approach. It is expected that multiple profiles for different domains will be defined as specializations of UML 2.0. UML 2.0 is expected to be released soon. The AADL UML profile will incorporate new architecture description capabilities from UML 2.0 when it is released.

**The Model Driven Architecture (MDA) Initiative**

- Based on the success of UML, the OMG has formulated a vision of a method of software development based on the use of models
- Key characteristic of MDA:
  - The focus and principal products of software development are models rather than programs
  - "The design is the implementation" (i.e. UML as both a modeling and an implementation language)
- UML plays a crucial role in MDA
  - Automatic code generation from UML models
  - Executable UML models
  - Requires a more precise definition of the semantics of UML (UML 2.0)

Source: Bran Selic, Rational

The University of Southern California, Center for Software Engineering, lead by Barry Boehm, has announced the development of Model-Based Architecting and Software Engineering (MBASE) approach []. This approach currently is being developed to be compatible with several Architecture Description Languages, one being the AADL.

## 6. Summary

The AADL has been designed to specifically support the development of large-scale systems through model-based architecture-driven software systems engineering by providing an analyzable architecture description language with well defined semantics. Its roots are in more than a decade's research in architecture description languages with an emphasis on concepts that address perfomance-critical embedded systems concerns, in particular timing and perfomance. The standard has been made extensible to permit inclusion of other perfomance-critical quality attribute concerns through annexes, without bloating the core standard. This permits new analyses to be supported in the future as they emerge from research, e.g., in the area of network security and intrusion management.

The AADL in a Nutshell

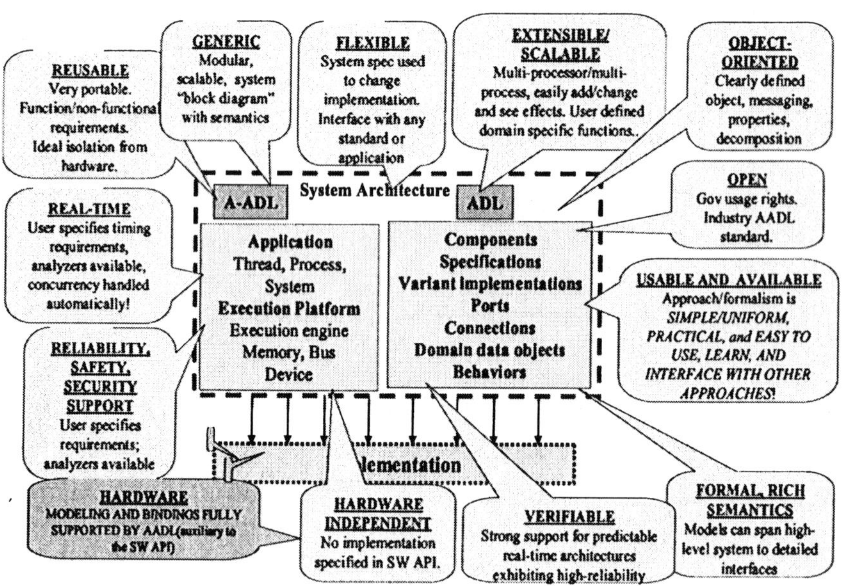


The SAE AADL provides an opportunity for the embedded real-time systems research community to have a direct impact on the practitioner community. As the AADL becomes the accepted means for modeling, analyzing, and integrating systems based on architectural models, it can become a vehicle for accelerated transition of research results in new analysis techniques by demonstrating the use of research theories in the context of the AADL/UML.

## References

1. Pam Binns, Matt Englehart, Mike Jackson and Steve Vestal, "Domain Specific Software Architectures for Guidance, Navigation and Control," Honeywell Technology Center,

Minneapolis, MN, International Journal of Software Engineering and Knowledge Engineering, Vol6, No. 2, 1996, pages 201-227.

2. Peter H. Feiler, Bruce Lewis, Steve Vestal, "Improving Predictability in Embedded Real-time Systems," Carnegie Mellon Software Engineering Institute, CMU/SEI-2000-SR-011, October 2000.
3. David J. McConnell, Bruce Lewis and Lisa Gray, "Reengineering a Single Threaded Embedded Missile application onto a Parallel Processing Platform using MetaH," 5th Workshop on Parallel and Distributed Real Time Systems, 1996.
4. Patrick Farail, Pierre Dissaux, "COTRE a Software Design Workshop", DASIA 2002, May 2002.
5. Bran Selic, "Performance Oriented UML", Tutorial, 3rd International Workshop On Software and Performance, July 2002.
6. Barry Boehm, Overview, Mini Tutorial, http://sunset.usc.edu/research/MBASE/
7. Paul Clements, et.al., "Documenting Software Architectures: Views and Beyond", Addison-Wesley, SEI Series in Software Engineering, 2002.

# SESSION 1: MODELS AND ANALYSIS

# DEPLOYING QoS CONTRACTS IN THE ARCHITECTURAL LEVEL

Sidney Ansaloni[1], Alexandre Sztajnberg[2], Romulo C. Cerqueira[1], Orlando Loques[1]
*[1]Instituto de Computação – Universidade Federal Fluminense (UFF), Rua Passo da Pátria – Niterói – RJ – Brasil; [2]Instituto de Matemática e Estatística – Universidade do Estado do Rio de Janeiro, Rua São Francisco Xavier, 524 / 6018-D – Maracanã – RJ - Brasil*

Abstract: This paper presents an approach to describe, deploy and manage software architectures having dynamic functional and non-functional requirements. The approach is centered on an ADL extended with high-level contracts, which are used to specify the non-functional requirements associated to the architecture of a given application. These contracts are also used to configure the infrastructure required to enforce the non-functional requirements and, during the running time, can be used to guide architecture adaptations, in order to keep them valid in face of changes in the supporting environment. The infrastructure required to manage the contracts follows an architectural pattern, which can be directly mapped to specific components included in a supporting reflective middleware. This allows designers to write a contract and to follow standard recipes to insert the extra code required to its enforcement in the supporting middleware.

Key words: QoS contracts ADL, architectural pattern, dynamic configuration

## 1. INTRODUCTION

The specification of QoS requirements and the implementation of the corresponding management strategies for the resource providers associated to the requirements are, generally, embedded in the application programming in an ad-hoc manner, mixed with the application's specific code. This lack of modularity makes evolution and code reuse difficult, also making difficult its verification and debugging. In this context, there is a growing interest for handling quality of services (QoS) aspects in a specific abstraction level[1, 2, 3]. This approach would allow to single out the resources to be used and the specific mechanisms of the native system that will be required by the application, and, if possible, turn automatic the configuration and management of those resources.

The traditional notion of QoS is bound to communication level performance. However, a more recent view of QoS includes characteristics associated to application's non-functional aspects, such as availability, reliability, security, real-time, persistency, coordination and debugging support. Such kind of aspect can be handled by reusable services provided by middleware infrastructures or native systems support. This makes feasible to design a software system based on its architectural description, which includes the functional components, the interactions among those components, and requirements regarding the behavior of system QoS resources. To this end, it has to be provided a means to specify those requirements in the context of the application's architecture description and, also, there has to be available an environment that allows to deploy those requirements over the system resources. In some applications, such environment has to include mechanisms to monitor the resources and to manage adaptations, according to the availability of those resources, in order to guaranty that the QoS requirements are met during run-time.

Among the available techniques to specify QoS constraints, we highlight the concept of contracts [4]. A QoS contract establishes a formal relationship between two parts that use or provide resources, where rights, obligations and negotiation rules over the used resources are expressed. For instance, a parallel computing application can have a QoS contract defining rules to replicate processing resources, in order to guaranty a maximum execution time constraint. According to the specified contract, the application can have its components parallelization degree automatically controlled by the supporting environment. Thus, when the time constraint is not being met by the present configuration, the number of replicas can be raised, if there are available processors [5].

In the previous context, this work presents the CR-RIO framework (*Contractual Reflective - Reconfigurable Interconnectable Objects*)[2,5] conceived to specify and support QoS contracts, associated to the architectural components of an application. The approach helps to achieve separation of concerns[6] facilitating the reuse of modules that implement the computation in other application systems, and allows the non-functional requirements to be handled separately during the system design process. The framework includes a contract description language, which allows the definition of a specialized view of a given software architecture. The supporting infrastructure required to impose the contracts during run-time follows an architectural pattern that can be implemented by a standard set of components included in a middleware. The results of our investigation point out that the code generation of these components can be automated, except some explicit parts of code related to specific contract and resources classes. In this way, contracts and their respective supporting infrastructures can be reused in different applications.

In the rest of this paper, we initially describe the key elements of the framework including the architecture description language with support to QoS contracts. Next, we present the supporting infrastructure and, based on an example we demonstrate the validity of the framework. Complementing the article we present some related proposals and provide some conclusions.

## 2. BASIC FRAMEWORK

The CR-RIO framework integrates the software architecture paradigm, which is centered in an architecture description language (ADL), with concepts such as reflection and dynamic adaptation capability[6], which are generally provided in an isolated fashion in middleware proposals described in the literature. This integration facilitates the achievement of separation of concerns, software component reuse and dynamic adaptation capability of applications. CR-RIO includes the following elements:

**CBabel**, an ADL used to describe the functional components of the application and the interconnection topology of those components, which follow the CR-RIO model. CBabel also caters for the description of non-functional aspects, such as coordination, distribution, planned reconfigurations and QoS. This set of features turns possible submitting CBabel descriptions to formal verification procedures[7]. A CBabel specification corresponds to a meta-description of an application that is available in a repository and is used to deploy the architecture in a given operating environment. In running time this meta-description provides the information required to manage architectural adaptations.

An **architecture-oriented component model**, that allows programming the software configuration of the application; (i) Modules, which encapsulate the application's functional aspects; (ii) Connectors, used in the architecture level to define relationships between modules; in the operation level connectors mediate the interaction between modules; and (iii) Ports, which identify access points through which modules and connectors provide or require services; ports are fundamental to allow component linking with low coupling.

A simple **software design methodology** that encourages the designer to follow a simple meta-level programming discipline, where functional aspects are concentrated in modules (base level) and non-functional aspects are encapsulated in connectors (meta-level). It is worth to point out that some QoS requirements can be directly mapped into connectors, which are equivalent to meta-level components, and can be configured in an application's architecture. For example, the access to real-time communication mechanisms, such as a real-time RMI[8], could be encapsulated into a connector and configured in different architectures.

The **Configurator**, a reflective element that provides services to instantiate, execute and manage applications with distributed configurations. The Configurator provides two APIs: configuration and architectural reflection, through which these services are used, and a persistency mechanism for the architecture meta-level description repository, where the two APIs reflect their operations. The configuration API allows to *instantiate, link, stop* and *replace* components of a running application. The architectural reflection API allows querying the repository. A specialized module of the application can consult the architecture's configuration and decide to make changes under certain conditions, say, in face of resource changes.

To specify non-functional aspects or quality of service (QoS) aspects related to operational requirements such as processing capacity, fault tolerance, real-time, information persistency, security or communication CBabel employs the concept of architectural contract. In our approach, an architectural contract is a description where two parts express their non-functional requirements, through services and parameters, negotiation rules and adaptation policies for different contexts. The CR-RIO framework provides the required infrastructure to impose and manage the contracts during run-time. Regarding QoS aspects we propose an architectural pattern that simplifies the design and coding of specific components of the infrastructure, consistently establishing the relationship between the Configurator and the QoS contract supporting entities.

## 3. THE QOS ARCHITECTURAL PATTERN

In our proposal a functional service of an application is considered a specialized activity, defined by a set of architectural components and theirs interconnection topologies; with requirements that generally do not admit negotiation[1]. Non-functional services are defined by restrictions to specific non-functional activities of an application, and can admit some negotiation including the used resources. A contract regulating non-function aspects can describe, at design time, the use of shared resources the application will make and acceptable variations regarding the availability of these resources. The contract will be imposed at run-time by an infrastructure composed by a set of components that implement the semantics of the contract.

## 3.1 The QoS Contract Language

Our proposal incorporates concepts from the QML (QoS Markup Language)[4], which were reformulated for the context of software architecture descriptions[2]. A QoS contract includes the following elements:

**QoS Categories** are related to specific non-functional aspects and described separately from the components. For example, if processing and communication performance characteristics are critical to an application, associated categories, *Processing* and *Transport*, could be described as in Figure 1.

```
01  QoScategory Processing {
02    utilization: decreasing numeric %;
03    clockFrequency: increasing numeric MHz;
04    priority: increasing numeric; }
05  QoScategory Transport {
06    delay: decreasing numeric ms;
07    bandwidth: increasing numeric Mbps; }
```

*Figure 1.* Processing and Transport QoS Categories

The Processing category (lines 1-5) represent a processing resource where the utilization property is the used percentage of the total CPU time (low values are preferred – decreasing), the *clockFrequency* property represents the processor's operating frequency (high values are preferred – increasing) and priority represents a priority for its utilization. The Transport category (lines 5-7) represents the information associated to transport resources used by clients and servers. The *bandwidth* property represents the available bandwidth for the client-server connection and the *delay* property represents the transmission delay of one bit between a client and the server. The use of those categories, and of the other elements of the language described next, is presented in Section 4.

A **QoS profile** quantifies the properties of a QoS Category. This quantification restricts each property according to its description, working as an instance of acceptable values for a given QoS Category. A component, or a part of an architecture, can define QoS profiles in order to constrain its operational context.

A set of **services** can be defined in a contract. In a service, QoS constraints that have to be applied in the architectural level are described, and can be associated to either (i) the application's components or (ii) the interaction mechanism used by these components. In that way, a service is differentiated from others by the desired/tolerated QoS levels required by the application, in a given operational context. A QoS constraint can be defined by associating a specific value of a property to an architecture declaration or associating a QoS profile to that declaration.

A **negotiation clause** describes a negotiation policy and acceptable operational contexts for the services described in a contract. As a default policy the clause establishes a preferred order for the utilization of the services. Initially the preferable service is used. According to the described in the clause, when a preferable service cannot be maintained anymore, the QoS supporting infrastructure tries to deploy a service less preferable, following the described order. The supporting infrastructure can deploy a more preferable service again if the necessary resources are again available.

## 3.2 Support Architecture

CBabel described architectures and QoS contracts are stored as meta-level information. Based on this information a set of middleware components (see Figure 4) composing a well-defined architectural pattern[2] is used to instantiate the application and to manage the contracts.

The **Global Contract Manager** (GCM) interprets a contract description and extracts its service negotiation state machine. When a negotiation is initiated the GCM identifies which service will be negotiated first and sends the configuration descriptions, related to each participating node, and the associated QoS profiles to the **Local Contract Managers** (LCM). Each LCM is responsible for interpreting the local configuration and activating a *Contractor* to perform actions such as resources reservation and monitoring requests. If the GCM receives a positive confirmation from all LCM involved, the service can be attended and the application can be instantiate with the required quality. If not, a new negotiation is attempted in order to deploy the next possible service. If all services in the negotiation clause are tried with no success, an *out-of-service* state is reached and a contract violation message is issued to the application level. The GCM can also initiate a new negotiation when it receives a notification informing that a preferred service became available again.

The **Contractor** has several responsibilities: (a) to translate the properties defined by the QoS profiles into services of the support system and convey the request of those services (with adequate parameters) to the QoS Agents; (b) when required, to map each defined interaction scheme (*link*) into a connector able to match the required QoS for the actual interaction, and (c) to receive *out-of-spec notifications* from the QoS Agents.

The information contained in a notification is compared against the profile and, depending on its internal programming the Contractor can try to make (local) adjustments to the resource that provides the service. For instance, the priority of a streamer could be raised in order to maintain a given frame generation rate. In a case where this is not possible an *out-of-profile* notification is sent to the LCM.

A **QoS Agent** wraps the access to system level mechanisms, providing adequate interfaces to perform resource requests, initializes local system services and monitors the actual values of the required properties. According to the thresholds to be monitored, registered by the Contractor, a QoS Agent can issue an *out-of-spec* notification indicating that a resource is not available or does not meet the specification defined in the profile.

# 4. EXAMPLE

During our research we developed some prototype examples to evaluate and refine the framework. A virtual terminal in a mobile machine was used to evaluate security and communication aspects in the context of a mobile network[9]. Specifically, a static contract was used to specify security protocol options (*telnet* or *ssh*, and cipher types) and a dynamic contract was used to specify communication channels that can be dynamically reconfigured (reconfiguration can be triggered by changes in available set of channels); in this example it was also demonstrated the composition of both contracts, which was immediately achieved joining theirs negotiation clauses. We developed in [5] the application with real-time requirements, mentioned in the introduction, an application with fault tolerance requirements, and the video on demand application to be presented in the next subsections.

## 4.1 Video on Demand (VoD)

The scenario of the application is comprised by a server, which stores a collection of video files in the MPEG-2 format, and by clients that connect themselves to the server and initialize a flow to receive and display a selected video. Each client can freeze or resume the video exhibition, in the same way it would be done if the video were locally stored. It is assumed that the clients can run on different platforms, from portable devices to workstations, in which the availability of resources such as CPU capacity and bandwidth can vary. In this context it is necessary to adapt the resources or the application's architecture configuration, depending on the specific operational environment, in order to have the video being exhibited with the expected quality.

The basic architecture of the example should fit two types of client: (i) high processing availability, with high-speed access to the server and (ii) medium processing availability, with dial-up modem access to the server. In principle, clients of type (i) have enough processing and communication resources to exhibit the video in the original MPEG-2 format. Clients of type (ii), with limited resources, can only exhibit the video in and alternative format, say H.261.

```
01  module Client_Server {
02      port provide, request;
03      module Client { out port request; } player;
04      module Server { in  port provide; } server;
05      instantiate server at serverHost;
06      instantiate player;
07      link player.request to server.provide;
08  } vod;
09  start vod;
```

*Figure 2.* VoD application Architecture Description

Figure 2 presents the CBabel description of the application's architecture, composed by a client (*player* - line 3) and a server (*server* – line 4), and their connection topology; communication is made effective through the player's *request* port and the server's *provide* port (lines 5-7). Note that this interconnection could be detailed, by defining a specific connector to mediate the client-server interaction, encapsulating the necessary communication mechanisms. However, as the non-functional restrictions include interaction aspects, the use of connectors in this architecture will be defined explicitly in a contract.

## 4.2 QoS Contract

The QoS contract of this example considers that two services can be used: (i) the exhibition of the video in the MPEG-2 format or (ii) in the H.261 format, according to the availability of resources at the specific client platform. To deploy any of these services in the client's node, the resources to be handled are those related to the host's processing characteristics and to the client-server communication channel properties.

The QoS categories for processing and transport, and their properties to specify the VoD application contract, are those presented previously in Figure 1. In the example it is considered that the client has to have a CPU with a minimum operating frequency of 700 MHz and a maximum of 50% of used CPU time to exhibit video in the MPEG-2 format. The exhibition of video with the H.261 format will demand from the CPU, by its turn, only a minimum frequency of 266 MHz and a maximum CPU time usage of 70%. In the example we are not considering static reservation of CPU time, in order to illustrate a contract renegotiation activity. Please note that in a dynamic context, even with CPU reservation, a contract could be invalidated by another contract with higher priority.

In the example, the MPEG-2 requires a bandwidth greater than 1.5 Mbps and a transport delay lower than 50 ms to sustain an acceptable video stream, while videos in H.261 format require a minimum bandwidth of 56 Kbps and can tolerate delays up to 200 ms. Other transport properties could be taken into account in this case, such as the *jitter* or data loss rate; for the sake of simplicity they were not included in the *Transport* QoS Category.

```
01  contract {
02     service {
03       instantiate player at clientHost with cpu_01;
04       link player to server by comTransport with network_01;
05     } MPEG_video;
06     service {
07       instantiate player at clientHost with cpu_02;
08       link player to server by H-261.comTransport
09                                          with network_02;
10     } H-261_video;
11     negotiation {
12       MPEG_video -> H-261_video;
13       H-261_video -> out_of_service;
14     }
15  } vod;
16  profile {
17     Processing.clockFrequency >= 700;
18     Processing.utilization <= 50;
19  } cpu_01;
20  profile {
21     Processing.clockFrequency >= 266;
22     Processing.utilization <= 70;
23  } cpu_02;
24  profile {
25     Transport.delay <= 50;
26     Transport.bandwidth >= 1.5;
27  } network_01;
28  profile {
29     Transport.delay <= 200;
30     Transport.bandwidth >= 0.056;        // 56 kbps
31  } network_02;
```

*Figure 3.* VoD application QoS Contract

Based on the previous requirements the application's contract can be described as in Figure 3. The *MPEG_video* service (lines 2-5) defines the QoS constraints for the architecture parts that participate in the MPEG video exhibition. The creation of a *player* component instance (line 3) in a client machine is associated to the *cpu_01* processing QoS profile. The interconnection of the *player* and *server* ports are bound to the *network_01* QoS profile (lines 25-27), being the communication provided by a connector that encapsulates the communication transport mechanism (line 4). The mentioned profiles specify, respectively, the constraints to the *Processing* and *Transport* QoS Categories properties, relevant to this contract. Thus, to create the player instance, the *clockFrequency* of the node has to be at least 266 MHz and then the CPU *utilization* has to be less than 70%. The *H-261_video* service description follows a similar procedure. The *cpu_02* (lines 20-23) and *network_02* (lines 28-31) profiles represent the requirements for the H.261 video exhibition. Note that, for this service, the interaction of the components is mediated by a connector that encapsulates the MPEG-2 to H-261 conversion mechanism. Additionally to the MPEG-2 and H.261, other formats could be supported by using specific decoders, encapsulated in connectors; e.g., the *bitmap* format that can be exhibited on PDAs and cell-phone video matrixes.

The negotiation clause of this contract (lines 11-14) defines the priority order between the services. The *MPEG_video* service has to be preferably provided in relation to the *H-261_video* service. If there are no resources available to attend any of these services, an *out-of-service* state is reached and the application cannot run.

## 4.3 Mapping the contract into the architectural pattern

The implementation of the QoS contract of the example-application using the proposed architectural pattern is depicted in Figure 4. Each participant node has a running instance of the *Local Contract Manager*, the specific *Contractor* for the VOD application and *QoS Agents* associated to the resources to be controlled in each specific platform. The *Configurator* (Section 2) and the *Global Contract Manage*r can be instantiated in a node dedicated to manage applications or in the same node were the application's server is running. The *H-261* connector only takes part of the configuration when the *H-261_video* service is deployed. It can also be observed that the *comTransport* connector has a distributed implementation.

The sequence diagram presented in Figure 5 depicts the interactions between the CR-RIO components to establish the MPEG_video service to a player running in a node, which is connected to the server through an Ethernet network. When starting the procedure to load the application the Configurator and the GCM are already running. As the first step, the GCM retrieves the associated QoS contract; all further actions are guided by this contract. Initially the GCM creates instances (create()) of the LCM in the nodes where the application components are to be instantiated. Next, it selects a service to be used (in this case, the MPEG_video) and initializes a negotiation activity, sending to the LCMs the information related to this service, including the associated QoS profiles (cpu_01 and network_01). Each LCM extracts from the received information the QoS characteristics that have to be considered and instantiates (*create()*) (a) the QoS Agents that provide the interfaces (management and event generation) to the resources used by the service, and (b) the application specific Contractor, that will interpret the service information and will interact with the QoS Agents to impose the desired properties.

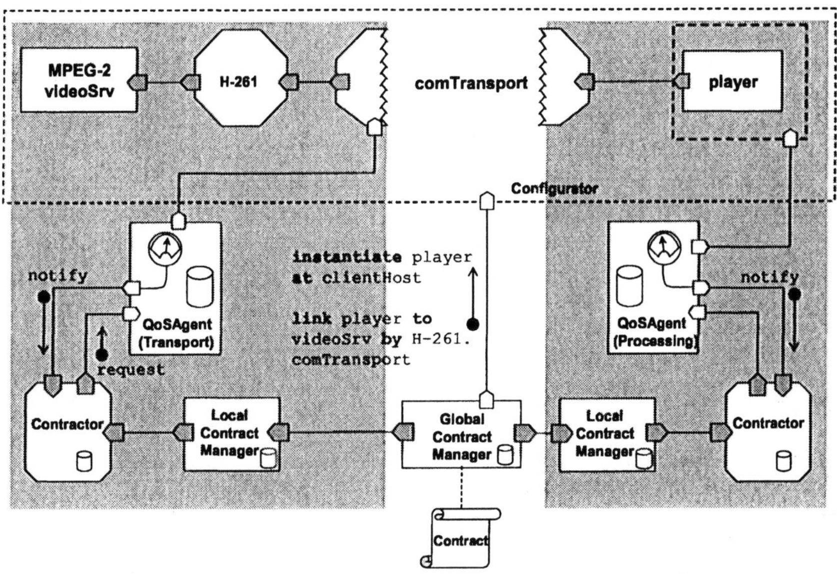


*Figure 4.* Mapping the VoD application contract in the architectural pattern

In the client node, the LCM identifies the processing resources that have to be managed (based on the `instantiate` ADL's primitive that creates an instance of the *player* module – QoS contract, line 3). In the server node, the local LCM identifies (based on the `link` ADL's primitive that interconnects the *player* module to the *server* module – QoS contract, line 4) that it will be responsible for the management of the transport resources (the adopted semantics is to assign to the server side the responsibility for managing QoS requirements that involves two peers). When the LCM instantiates a Contractor it also sends to it the profiles that have to be attended. In the sequence, the Contractor interacts with the QoS Agents to request resources and to receive relevant events regarding the status of the resources. In this example, the *Processing* QoS Agent verifies the operating frequency of the

CPU and is responsible for monitoring the CPU load (*utilization*). Also, observe that the client-server communication channel uses some kind of resource reservation put in effect through the *Transport* QoS Agent.

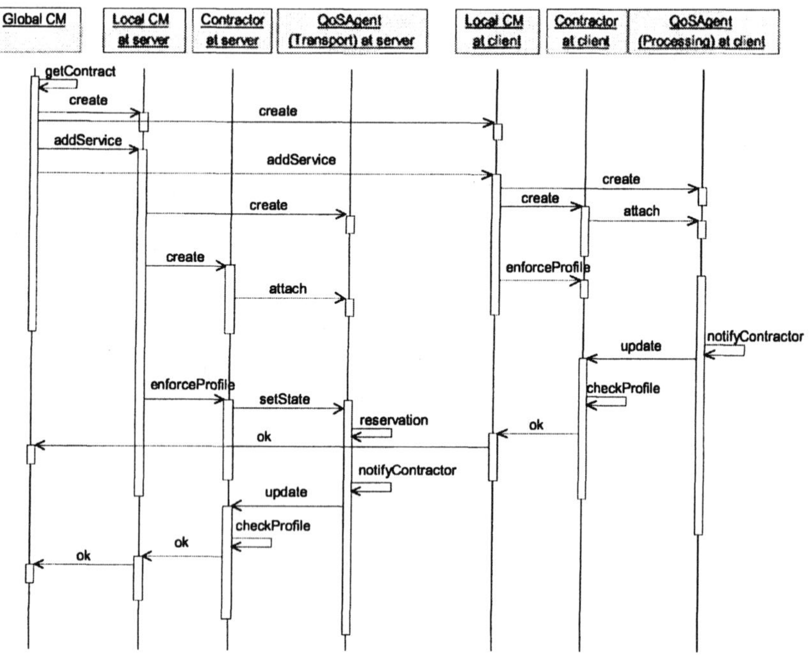


*Figure 5.* Establishing the MPEG_video service

After the initial phase, if the required QoS profiles were imposed, a Contractor notifies the success to its associated LCM that, by its turn, forwards a corresponding notification to the GCM. In the example, if all involved LCMs did return a positive confirmation, the GCM concludes that the negotiation was successful and that the *MPEG_video* service can be established. The next step is to instantiate the application's functional components in the context of the reserved resources and, then, to initialize its execution. This step is performed by the *Configurator* (Section 2) based on the *Architecture Configurator* design pattern[10]; see details in[5]. If during the negotiation any Contractor has a resource demand denied, or if it verifies that a QoS Agent notified an out of range value, an *out-of-profile* notification is sent to the LCM that, by its turn, sends an *out-of-service* notification to the GCM. In consequence the GCM selects the next service to be attempted, in this case the *H-261_video*, and a new negotiation cycle begins.

In steady state, if a significant change in the monitored values is detected, the QoS Agent notifies the registered Contractors invoking the *update()* method. If the reported values do not violate the active QoS profiles, nothing has to be done. If there is a violation, the Contractor can try to locally readapt the resource in order to keep the service; for instance, passing new parameters to the QoS Agent. If it is not possible to readapt, the Contractor sends an *out-of-profile* notification to the LCM and, in the sequence, another service can be negotiated. To exemplify the situation let's suppose that while the *MPEG_video* is operational, new processes are admitted to the client's node, diminishing the available processing power to the player. This would be captured by the *Processing* QoS Agent observing the increase of the value of the *utilization* property. Let's consider that the measured value overcomes the limit of 50% defined by the *cpu_01* profile, but is still lower than the 70% limit defined by the *cpu_02* profile.

The *Processing* QoS Agent notifies the Contractor triggering a new negotiation. The client's Contractor verifies that the property is out of the *cpu_01* profile specification and sends the respective LCM an *out-of-profile* notification. This information is then propagated to the GCM through an *out-of-service* notification. Then the GCM selects the H-261_video to be negotiated and sends the respective information as parameters invoking to the involved LCMs. Each LCM discontinues the current service and the procedures to impose the new service, bound by the *cpu_02* and *network_02* QoS profiles are performed (similarly as in the case to deploy the initial service). Several optimizations are feasible. For instance, when a Contractor sends an *out-of-profile* notification this could be followed by the set of QoS profiles that could be attended at that moment. Receiving this composed information the GCM could select the next service to be negotiated, immediately discarding the services with associated profiles out of the set. We are investigating the use of an event support service, with composition capability, to implement this optimization. A second optimization could be applied when a set of services is restricted to a given node. In this case the LCM of the given node could receive the information of all services and profiles related to the set and manage them locally.

A prototype of the VoD application is presented in[5]. The Java *Media Framework* was used to implement the functional modules. Some classes related to the video flow were encapsulated in connectors, e.g., those implementing RTP and the H.261 codec. The QoS architectural pattern was implemented as a set of classes integrated to the CR-RIO framework.

It was possible to identify that the implementations of the GCM and the LCM, directly related the application contract are reusable. The behavior of these elements is parameterized by the QoS contract of the specific application; in this level the manipulated information are symbolic. Each QoS Agent has dependencies related to the resource being managed. However, once implemented, an Agent can be reused in other applications that have operational requirements dependent on the same kind of resource.

The Contractor, by its turn, represents the *hot spot* of the pattern. Its implementation is dependent on the services and profiles to be imposed, and also dependent on the own resources to be managed via QoS Agents. The Contractor can also contain the code implementing specific policies to perform local adaptations, as discussed in the end of the last section.

## 5. RELATED WORKS

The reflective middleware approach[11] allows for the provided services to be configured to comply with the non-functional properties of the applications. However, the approach does not provide clear abstractions and mechanisms to help the use of such features in the design of the architectural level of an application. This leads to the middleware services being used in an *ad hoc* fashion, usually through pieces of code intertwined to the application's program. The Quality Connector pattern provides a methodology for the re-allocation of resources in response to context changes in the execution environment[12]. However, it requires access to the source code of every application and/or to the infrastructure's components in order to instrument them. Our approach, that includes configuration-programming mechanisms, is more transparent regarding the access to the source code of the application. The Quality Objects (QuO)[3] provides a framework for the development of distributed applications with QoS requirements, based on CORBA. In QuO, the specification of such requirements is associated to method invocations, through a contract description language, allowing only adaptations at this level. Our proposal considers services with differentiated quality in diverse levels, from the interface (or connection) level, in which services are encapsulated into connectors (similar to the QuO approach), to the architectural level, in which the service provision can involve the reconfiguration of the application's topology. The proposal described in[13] includes basic mechanisms to collect status information associated to non-functional services. It also suggests an approach to manage non-functional requirements in the architectural level, in a way quite similar to ours. CR-RIO complements this proposal providing an explicit methodology based on contracts and proposing extra mechanisms to deploy and manage these contracts. More details are available in[5].

## 6. CONCLUSION

We presented a unified approach to specify, deploy and manage applications having non-functional requirements. The approach helps to achieve separation of concerns and software reuse by allowing non-functional aspects of an application, such as QoS requirements, to be specified separately using high-level contracts expressed in an extended ADL. Being centered on an ADL-based configuration middleware the framework inherits all its well-known benefits, among them the capability of reconfiguration, which facilitates to execute dynamic architectural adaptations on behalf of a contract. Part of the coding, related to a non-functional requirement, can be encapsulated in connectors, which can be (re)configured during running time in order to cater for the impositions defined by the associated contract. The infrastructure required to enforce the contracts follows an architectural pattern that is implemented by a standard set of components of the middleware. In this pattern, each component performs a well-defined role in the support of the contract. We think that making these structures explicit and available to designers, the task of mapping architecture-level defined contracts to implementations can be simplified. The approach has been evaluated through several case studies that showed that the code of these supporting components can be automatically generated, excepting some localized pieces related to specificities of the particular QoS requirement under consideration. However, we should notice that the treatment of low-level details always has to be considered in any QoS aware application. Our approach can help to identify the intervening hot spots and to make adaptations more rapidly.

In our proposal, the composition of contracts can be specified combining in a unique clause the negotiation clauses of the involved contracts[9]. Contracts regarding different non-functional aspects (in the same or in different applications) can be orthogonal and cause no interference with each other; in this case, composing those contracts is immediate. In the general case, the composition process can lead to conflicts on the use of shared scarce resources. Conflicts can be handled applying a suitable decision policy to the set of involved contracts; already assigned resources could then be retaken in order to satisfy the preferred contracts.

Currently, we are investigating the specification of individual contracts for clients and servers[14]. This intends to allow each client to specify what it requires and each server to specify what it is committed to provide. This capability would permit to make decisions regarded to a component instantiation taking into account the availability of resources at its instantiation time. Besides providing the flexibility required to the support of dynamic architectures, this would allow managing conflicts through lower granularity interventions. We are also working towards giving a formal semantics to the QoS contracts, using Rewriting Logic, in the same line as presented in[7] for the CBabel ADL. With the results of that experience we plan to produce a set of guide-lines to allow the formal verification of the QoS contracts in the architectural level.

## ACKNOWLEDGMENTS

Orlando Loques is partially supported by CNPq (grant PDPG-TI 552137/2002) and Alexandre Sztajnberg is partially supported by CNPq (grant PDPG-TI 552192/2002 and Faperj APQ1 E26/171430-02).

## REFERENCES

1. Beugnard, A., Jézéquel, J.-M., Plouzeau, N., Watkins, D., "Making Components Contract Aware", IEEE Computer, 32(7), July, 1999.
2. Cerqueira, R. C., "A Methodology to Describe and Implement Contracts for Services with Differentiated Quality in Distributed Architectures ", Masters Dissertation, IC/UFF, 2002.
3. Loyall, J. P., Rubel, P., Atighetchi, M., Schantz, R., Zinky, J. "Emerging Patterns in Adaptive, Distributed Real-Time, Embedded Middleware", 9th Conference on Pattern Language of Programs, Monticello, Il., September, 2002.
4. Frolund, S. and Koistinen, J., "Quality-of-Service Specifications in Distributed Object Systems", Distributed Systems Engineering, IEE, No. 5, pp. 179-202, UK, 1998.
5. Ansaloni, S., "An Architectural Pattern to Describe and Implement Qos Contracts", Masters Dissertation, Instituto de Computação, UFF, May, 2003.
6. Loques, O., Sztajnberg, A., Leite, J., Lobosco, M., "On the Integration of Configuration and Meta-Level Programming Approaches", in Reflection and Software Engineering V. 1826, LNCS, pp. 191-210, Springer-Verlag, Heidelberg, Germany, June, 2000.
7. Braga, C. and Sztajnberg, A., "Towards a Rewriting Semantics to a Software Architecture Description Language", 6th Workshop on Formal Methods, Brasil, October, 2003.
8. Borg, A. and Wellings, A., "A Real-Time RMI Framework for the RTSJ", Proceedings of the15th Euromicro Conference on Real-Time Systems, Porto, Portugal, July, 2003.
9. Cerqueira , R. C., Ansaloni, S., Loques, O.G. and Sztajnberg, A., "Deploying Non-Functional Aspects by Contract", 2nd Workshop on Reflective and Adaptive Middleware, Middleware2003 Companion, pp.90-94, Rio de Janeiro, Brasil, June, 2003.
10. Carvalho, S. T, Lisbôa, J. and Loques, O, "A Design Pattern for Software Architecture Configuration", 2nd Latin American Conference on Pattern Languages of Programming, RJ, Brasil, August, 2002.
11. Kon, F. et alii, "The Case for Adaptive Middleware", Communications of the ACM, pp. 33-38, Vol. 45, No. 6, June, 2002.
12. Cross J.K. and Schmidt, D., "Quality Connector: A Pattern Language for Provisioning and Managing Quality-Constrained Services in Distributed Real-Time and Embedded Systems", 9th Conf. on Pattern Language of Programs, Monticello, Illinois, Sep., 2002.
13. Garlan, D., Schmerl, B. R. and Chang, J., "Using Gauges for Architecture-Based Monitoring and Adaptation", Work. Conference on Complex and Dynamic Systems Architecture, December, 2001.
14. Sztajnberg, A. and Loques, O., "Bringing QoS to the Architectural Level", ECOOP 2000 Workshop on QoS on Distributed Object Systems, Cannes.

# HIERARCHICAL COMPOSITION AND ABSTRACTION IN ARCHITECTURE MODELS

Pam Binns and Steve Vestal
*Honeywell Laboratories*
*Minneapolis, MN, USA*
*{pam.binns,steve.vestal}@honeywell.com* *

**Abstract** We present a compositional approach to generate linear hybrid automata timing models, and Markovian stochastic automata safety models, from an architecture specification. Formal models declared for components are composed to form an overall model for the system, where the composition rules depend on the semantics of the architecture specification. We further allow abstract models to be specified for a subsystem of components, where the abstract model may be substituted for the concrete model of that subsystem when composing the overall system model. We assume both abstract and concrete models are given, we address the problem of verifying that the abstractions yield safe if approximate results. An abstract model may be viewed as a formal subsystem specification used for both conformance checking and improving the tractability of system analysis.

**Keywords:** architecture description language, formal specification, hybrid automata, stochastic processes, schedulability modeling, reliability modeling, system safety

## 1. Introduction

Given a specification for the architecture of an embedded computer system, we want to generate and analyze formal models of system behavior. In this paper we discuss the generation and analysis of timing and safety models from specifications written in the SAE standard Architecture Analysis and Design Language (AADL) and its original research basis, MetaH[AADL 2004, MetaH 2000].

An architecture is often informally described as an assembly of connected components. Overall system behavior is determined by the interactions between components according to the way they are connected, which is to say system behavior is defined as a composition of the behaviors of its components. We will associate formal models with individual components in a specification. The formal models for a complete system are defined as compositions of the

*This work was supported by the US Air Force Office of Scientific Research under contract number F49620-97-C-0008.

individual component models. In this paper, we use a type of hybrid automaton to specify real-time component behaviors, and a type of stochastic automaton to specify component fault and error behaviors.

Architectures are specified hierarchically. Every component may have an internal implementation that may itself be specified as a set of connected subcomponents. Given a component that has an internal architecture, a formal model for that component can be generated by composing the models for its subcomponents. We call this the concrete model for that component. We may also directly associate an abstract model with a component that is intended to be a safe approximation for the concrete model. When generating a system model from an architecture specification, we thus have a choice for each component whether to use its concrete model or its abstract model. A different choice can be made for different components at different levels of the design hierarchy, so that a fairly large set of mixed-fidelity models is possible. Hierarchical abstraction can both improve understandability and enable tractable analysis for large and complex specifications.

We assume both concrete and abstract models are given, e.g. hand-developed. Our focus is on verifying that analyses performed when abstract subsystem models are substituted for concrete subsystem models are safe in some sense with respect to analyses of the fully detailed concrete models. In the case of our timing models, we show how to verify that classical periodic tasks are conservative approximations for hybrid automata used in the AADL standard to define thread semantics, or hybrid automata that model reusable middleware. In the case of our safety models, we explore the relationship between abstract and concrete stochastic automata models. We expect the effort required to develop pairs of abstract and concrete models to be justified by high degrees of reuse; and that many pairs of abstract and concrete models will be based on common and easily modified design patterns. An abstract model may be viewed as a formal specification that is also usable to improve the tractability of analysis.

## 2. Related Work

We borrow one of the fundamental ideas of process algebra[Milner 1989]: show that a large and complicated subsystem model can be replaced by a smaller and simpler subsystem model when performing overall system analysis. We permit the smaller simpler model to be an approximate abstraction rather than requiring some notion of equivalence. We deal with hybrid and stochastic automata rather than purely discrete models. We use automata rather than programming language models[Cousot 1977].

CHARON and Hybrid I/O Automata (HIOA) exhibit many of these concepts[Alur et. al. 2001, Lynch et. al. 2003]. The notion of abstraction used in this paper also involves containment of reachable states or traces. We allow looser definitions than the CHARON notion of refinement or the HIOA notion of implementation, for example we allow the sets of abstract and concrete variables to differ. We allow fairly arbitrary abstractions to be specified and focus on verifying that they are adequate for the purpose at hand. CHARON and HIOA use more traditional ways to compose automata based on shared variables and/or shared events, whereas we use a scheduler function to compose models of real-time tasks that interact by contending for shared processors.

Markov (and more general stochastic) processes are well known to exhibit the state space explosion when trying to solve large models of complex systems. This served to motivate the desire to use more computationally tractable abstractions. Early work established necessary and sufficient conditions for when abstractions of Markov chains were again Markov [Kemeny and Snell 1976]. Considerable effort has been spent in developing efficient algorithms to find tractable Markov abstractions (*e.g.* [Derisavi et al. 2003a]). Other researchers have sought abstractions for which the solution is exact when the concrete model is a semi-Markov processes, which is more expressive than a Markov process[Bradley et al. 2003]. When a Markov process has no tractable abstraction that is again Markov, techniques for finding approximate abstractions might be useful [Lefebvre 2002].

From a computer science perspective, process specifications typically begin with models of concurrent automata, to which various stochastic semantics have been applied. Considerable work has gone into linking conditions for when variants of stochastic automata are analyzable as Markov chains (*e.g* [Brinksma and Hermanns 2001, Desharnais et al. 2003]). Software tools have been developed to support specification of numerous modeling formalisms and abstractions coupled with a collection of optimized solution techniques for evaluating them (*e.g.* [Derisavi et al. 2003b]).

## 3. Timing Models

Classical real-time scheduling theory deals with the scheduling and analysis of repetitively dispatched tasks[Liu and Deitel 2000]. The time between dispatches is fixed (periodic tasks) or has a lower bound (sporadic tasks). There is an upper bound on the compute time at each dispatch (often called the worst-case execution time). The theory provides algorithms for optimal (in some sense) uni-processor scheduling and for tractable schedulability analysis of large sets of tasks. However, classical real-time scheduling theory deals with only very restricted forms of internal task behaviors or interactions between tasks (beyond contention for a shared processor resource). For example, tasks in an actual system may exist in a number of discrete states, e.g. halted, initializing, suspended, computing, recovering.

Hybrid automata can model more complex dynamical systems[Alur et. al. 1994]. A hybrid automaton is a classical finite state automaton plus a set of real-valued variables. The variable values may change continuously in a fixed location (a fixed discrete state), and may change discontinuously (may be assigned) at discrete transitions between locations. The allowed transitions may depend on the variable values (edge guards may be predicates over variables). These additional behaviors are specified by annotating the edges and locations of the classical finite state automaton with various kinds of constraints. In this paper we limit our attention to linear hybrid automata, where constraints are expressed using linear functions. A state of a hybrid automaton consists of a location together with a real value for each variable. We use ***polyhedron*** to refer to a set of possible real values for the variables (e.g. specified as a system of linear inequalities), and use ***region*** to refer to a location plus a polyhedron. Composition rules exist to define semantics for sets of concurrent hybrid automata.

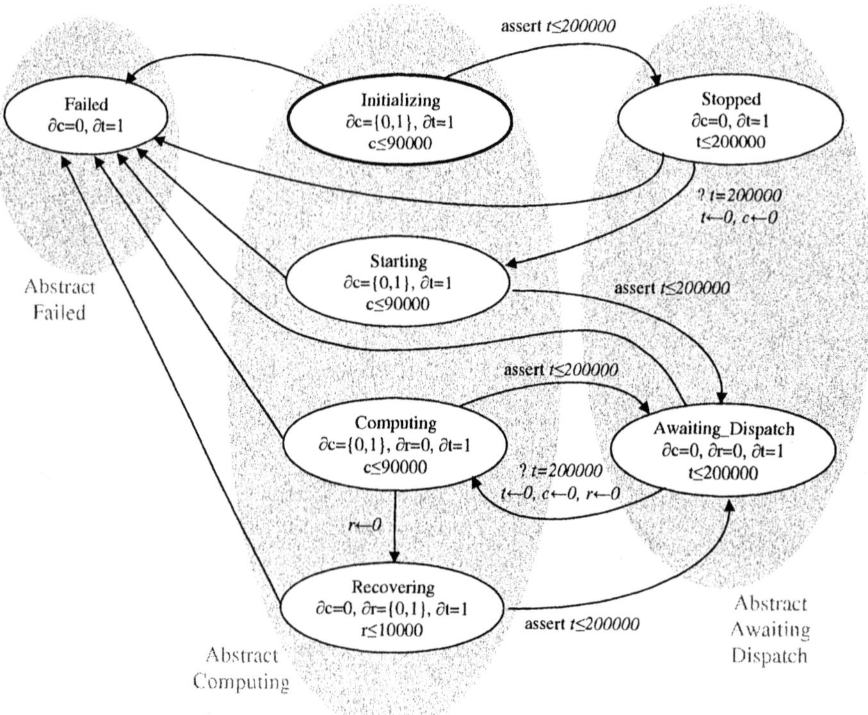


*Figure 1.* Concrete Hybrid Automata Model $T$ for a MetaH Periodic Task

Certain AADL thread semantics are defined in the standard using a hybrid automata notation[AADL 2004]. We have automatically generated linear hybrid automata models for the portions of the MetaH middleware that perform preemptive scheduling and enforce time partitioning[Vestal 2000]. Figure 1 shows a hybrid automata model $T$ for a periodic task. This model was automatically generated from the MetaH middleware code, i.e. it shows task behavior actually implemented by the middleware (excluding stopping and restarting at dynamic architecture reconfigurations). We use $\delta x$ as an abbreviation for $\delta x/\delta t$. The choice for $\delta c = \{0, 1\}$ is made as follows.

We do not use shared variables or shared edge labels (synchronized transitions) to compose multiple automata. Instead, we use a scheduling function that defines the rates at which compute times accumulate as a function of the current set of task locations (e.g. as a function of which tasks are in ready states)[Vestal 2000]. Let $\bar{l} =< l_{1i}, l_{2j}, ... >$ be a location vector for a system of automata, i.e. $l_{1i}$ is a location from automaton $T_1$, $l_{2j}$ is a location from automaton $T_2$, etc. A scheduler function $< \delta v_1, \delta v_2, ... >= S(< l_{1i}, l_{2j}, ... >)$ (also written $\delta\bar{v} = S(\bar{l})$) defines the variable rate vector as a function of the system location vector. In our example, the scheduler function always sets $\delta t = 1$ for timers $t$, and sets $\delta c_i = 1$ if task $i$ is executing and $\delta c_i = 0$ if task $i$ is preempted for that system location (for that set of contending ready tasks).

Unfortunately, analyzing schedulability by model-checking systems of hybrid automata is not currently very tractable. We have done this for pairs of different kinds of tasks during the MetaH middleware verification exercise, but revolutionary advances in hybrid automata model-checking are needed to consistently analyze even a dozen non-trivial concurrent task models. We instead explore how to verify that a complex hybrid automaton task model (such as one defined in the AADL standard) can be safely approximated by a classical real-time task model for the purpose of schedulability analysis.

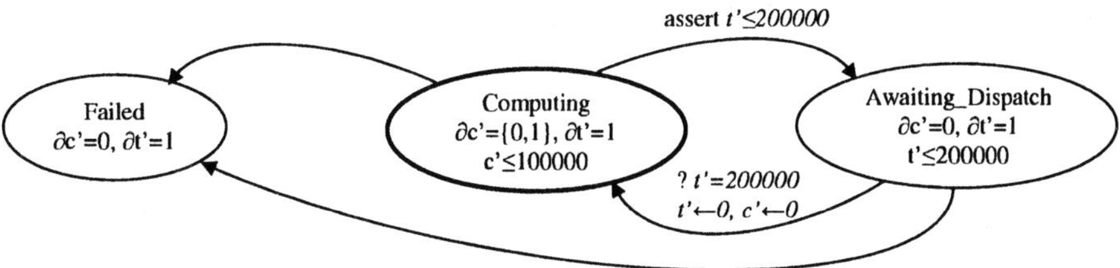


*Figure 2.* Abstract Hybrid Automata Model $T'$ for a MetaH Periodic Task

Figure 2 shows an abstract hybrid automaton specification $T'$ for a periodic task having a period of 200000 time units and a worst-case compute time of 100000 units. We assert this formally specifies a classical periodic real-time task, slightly extended by the addition of a Failed state. We define a mapping between this abstract automaton and the concrete automaton of Figure 1 as follows.

We define a many-to-one mapping of concrete to abstract locations, $l' = a(l)$ for abstract location $l'$ and concrete location $l$. Every initial concrete location must map to an initial abstract location. Our example mapping is illustrated in Figure 1 using shaded ovals to represent the abstract locations to which the concrete locations are mapped. We define the value of each abstract variable as a linear function of the concrete variables, $v'_i = f_i(v_1, v_2, ...)$ for each abstract variable $v'_i$ and concrete variables $v_j$ (also written $\bar{v}' = \bar{f}(\bar{v})$) . For our example, $t' = t$ and $c' = c + r$. Each initial valuation for the concrete variables must map to an initial valuation for the abstract variables.

Assume we are given a system of abstract tasks $T'_1, ..., T'_i, ...$ having an abstract scheduler function $\delta\bar{v}' = S'(\bar{l}')$. We can view this as an abstract specification for scheduling a system of tasks. We can modify this system by replacing some particular $T'_i$ with a concrete $T_i$, with suitable changes to the domain and range of the scheduler function.

We constrain the modified scheduler function $S$ obtained from the abstract $S'$ so that all concrete locations that map to the same abstract location are equivalently scheduled, and concrete scheduler rates are consistent with abstract scheduler rates. Assume that, due to the replacement of $T'_i$ by $T_i$, abstract variable $v'_i$ is removed from the range of $S$ and concrete variables $v_{i1}, ...$ where $v'_i = f_i(v_{i1}, ...)$ are added. For unreplaced abstract variables $v'_j$, $\delta v'_j = S'_j(< ..., l', ... >) = S_j(< ..., l, ... >)$ whenever $a(l) = l'$. For substituted variables, $\delta v'_i = S'_i(< ..., l', ... >) = \delta f_i(v_{i1}, ...)$ with $\delta v_{ij} = S_{ij}(< ..., l, ... >)$ whenever $a(l) = l'$.

We assert that the original abstract system can be analyzed using a classical schedulability analysis algorithm appropriate to the abstract scheduling function $S'$. If the reachable regions of the modified system are contained in those of the original abstract system (after applying the variable abstraction function) for all feasibly scheduled abstract systems, we assert that the abstract system is a safe approximation for the modified system for the purpose of schedulability analysis.

To formalize the notion of containment in the presence of variable abstraction, let $P'^{\downarrow}$ be the system of linear inequalities obtained from an abstract $P'$ by substituting for each abstract variable $v'_i$ its linear abstraction function $f_i(v_1, v_2, ...)$. Only concrete variables appear in $P'^{\downarrow}$. We say that concrete $P$ is contained in abstract $P'$ if $P \subseteq P'^{\downarrow}$

We verify by model-checking that a modified $S$ derived as explained above from a feasible abstract scheduler $S'$ will always feasibly schedule $T_i$. First, for our example pair of abstract and concrete models we restrict our attention to schedulers that are functionally equivalent to the set of constant rate schedulers $S'(..., \texttt{Computing}'_i, ...) \geq 1/2$, i.e. an abstract scheduling function is feasible for this example if it allocates at least 50% of the processor to $T'_i$ between its release time and deadline while $T'_i$ is in its compute state. Second, we construct a specific $S$ that satisfies the conditions above, one that sets $\delta c = 1/2$ and $\delta r = 0$ in all concrete states that map to the abstract computing, except $\delta r = 1/2$

d $\delta c = 0$ in the recovering state. For our MetaH example, both abstract and concrete scheduler functions are preemptive fixed priority schedulers. (Note that, as one might expect, a number of concrete schedulers could be defined that satisfy the above conditions on the relation between abstract and concrete scheduler functions.)

Using these abstract and concrete scheduler functions, we applied a region enumeration tool to both an abstract and a concrete task model. Then, for each reachable concrete region $(l, P)$ where $l$ is a concrete location and $P$ a polyhedron in the concrete variable space, the tool verified that there was some reachable abstract region $(l', P')$ such that $l' = a(l)$ and $P \subseteq P'^{\downarrow}$. Note this is a conservative containment test, sufficient but not necessary, because in principle $P$ might be contained in a union of abstract polyhedra but not in any single abstract polyhedron.

The condition that $S$ is indistinguishable from $S'$ for all concrete locations that map to the same abstract location means the scheduling of a given task model is the same regardless of whether it is being composed with abstract or with concrete models. We can thus make this substitution for any arbitrary subset of tasks to produce mixed-fidelity models that range from all abstract to all concrete.

This worked for our example concrete MetaH task model by design, in the sense that the task scheduling implementation was designed to present a classical real-time workload. This enabled accurate schedulability analysis for implemented systems, at least to the degree we could verify the implementation satisfied the abstraction (subsequent hybrid system model generation and checking revealed some implementation defects[Vestal 2000]). The advent of hybrid automata methods (largely occuring after the original MetaH design) and abstraction methods (such as those presented here) can hopefully enable more rigorous and defect-free development in the future.

Abstraction methods such as that presented here might be used to produce mixed-fidelity hybrid automata models that are more tractable to model-check. Our earlier experience suggests that expanding only two or three out of a dozen abstract tasks into their fully detailed concrete models might yield a tractably analyzeable model[Vestal 2000]. This might be useful, for example, to verify some complex interaction protocol between a pair of tasks.

Our use of model-checking to verify containment of concrete behavior within abstract behavior required us to constrain the class of abstract and concrete schedulers and the mapping between them. It would be useful to verify that the abstraction is a safe approximation for the concrete for broad classes of abstract and concrete schedulers and mappings. For example, it might be possible to permit a (mapped) concrete scheduler rate to exceed the abstract rate under certain circumstances. This might make it easier to deal with things like different scheduling priorities for different concrete locations, or bounded blocking times, which would be of significant practical utility. It might also be possible to prove more complex cases of containment using an explicit detailed abstraction mapping between concrete and abstract invariants and edges (including guards and assignments), rather than model-checking with constrained scheduler functions.

## 4. Safety Models

We now revisit the same general problem addressed in the previous section, but rather for safety models than for timing models. The AADL Error Modeling Annex defines language features to specify stochastic models for fault, error and failure behaviors in embedded computer architectures[AADL 2004]. A stochastic automaton approach is used[Brinksma and Hermanns 2001] for specification. The rules for composing individual component stochastic automata depend on the specified architectural structure, i.e. depend on the possible error propagation paths between components that interface to or depend on each other. Propagation modifiers can be specified to make propagation conditional, which allows consensus and voting protocols to be modeled.

An error model for a system specified as a nested hierarchy of components can be obtained by composing the error models for its subcomponents according to the rules of the language. However, another option is made available: the user can specify a subsystem error model that may optionally be substituted as an abstraction for the concrete compositional model. Propagation modifiers can also map one error into another. This makes it easier to compose legacy models or models developed at different levels of abstraction. (Legality rules are included in the annex to enable automatic verification of error model compatibility within an overall architecture specification, or identify places where such mappings are needed.)

The remainder of this section is organized as follows. We introduce Markov processes, the modeling language to which stochastic automata specifications are translated before solving the system. We suggest rules to preserve safety properties when going from concrete (larger) steady state Markov models to abstract (smaller) steady state stochastic models. Abstractions of several steady state Markov models are presented. Steady state analyses are computationally much simpler to find than transient analyses.

We show that the transition rate assignment in the abstract model is uniquely determined by the transition rates of the concrete model when the abstraction is "lumpable". When the abstraction is not lumpable, rate assignments in an abstract model need not be uniquely determined. We discuss selection criteria for "reasonable" assignments from an engineering perspective when possibly infinite (beyond a constant rescaling of all transition rates) assignments will satisfy the constraints of the abstract model. For safety analyses, transient solutions are generally required. We discuss conditions for preserving safety in transient models. We close with an illustration of how Markov chains are composed at the (AADL) specification level.

## 4.1 Brief Markov Process Introduction

The reader is assumed to be familiar with Continuous Time Markov Chains (CTMCs) at an introductory text level (e.g. [Hoel et. al. 1972]). We use standard notation for describing CTMCs, which unfortunately has some overlap with hybrid systems notation. Hopefully the context will make clear the use. The notation we use to specify and solve CTMCs is compactly defined in Table 1. When considering limiting distributions, we assume there are no death states and the limiting distribution does not depend on the initial distribution. That is, we assume the CTMC is ergodic and regular.

| Notation | Description |
|---|---|
| $\delta$ | A finite discrete set of systen states. Typically, $\delta = \{1, 2, ..., m\}$. |
| $x, y$ | Elements in $\delta$. $x, y \in \delta$. |
| $X(t)$ | System state at time $t \geq 0$. $X(t) \in \delta$ for all $t \geq 0$. |
| $q_{xy}$ | Instantaneous rate of change from state $x$ to $y$ for $x \neq y$. The set $\{q_{xy}\}$ describes the infinitesimal generators of the CTMC. For $x = y$, $q_{xx} = -q_x = -\sum_{y \in \delta - \{x\}} q_{xy}$. In practice, $q_{xy}$ is known or must be approximated (*e.g.* the failure rate of a component, perhaps given by a vendor specification). |
| $\mathbf{A}$ | The infinitesimal generator matrix. Denote $(\mathbf{A})_{ij} = q_{ij}$. |
| $q_x$ | The transition rate out of state $x$. For a CTMC, this means the probability that a process in state $x$ will remain in state $x$ for a time greater than $t$ is $e^{-q_x t}$. If $x$ is a death state (with no transitions leaving $x$), then $q_x = 0$. |
| $D$ | A diagonal matrix, with $D_{xx} = q_x$ and $D_{xy} = 0$ for $x \neq y$. |
| $Q_{xy}$ | The probability of transition from state $x$ directly to state $y$ given the system is about to transition out of $x \neq y$. $Q_{xy} = q_{xy}/q_x$ for $x \neq y$. |
| $P_{xy}(t)$ | The probability that $X(t) = y$ given that $X(0) = x$. Or, the probability that a process $X$ in state $x$ will be in state $y$ after $t$ time has elapsed. |
| $\pi$ | The steady state distribution. That is $\pi = (\pi_1, \pi_2, ..., \pi_m)$, where $\pi_x = \lim_{t \to \infty} P(X(t) = x)$. For a CTMC, $\pi$ satisfies $\pi \mathbf{A} = 0$. For a Discrete Time MC (DTMC), $\pi$ satisfies $\pi Q = \pi$. Also require $\sum_{j=1}^{m} \pi_j = 1$, to fully constrain the model. |

*Table 1.* Continuous Time Markov Chain (CTMC) Notation

## 4.2 Examples of Concrete Continuous Time Markov Chain Models

We give three Markov models used in subsequent examples. Models are concrete when no further detail is captured in any of the states or transitions.

The model shown in Figure 3 is the simplest possible Markov process that can represent a single repairable component (SRC). The right hand side shows standard notation. The left hand side is an equivalent, yet more compact representation that we adopt. In Figure 3, $\delta = \{1, 2\}$. When in the operational state (1), faults occur at rate $\lambda$, when the process transitions to the failed state (2). The failed system returns to operational when the repair event has been effected, which occurs at rate $\mu$. When repairs are not instantaneous, the repair completion time is equated with the repair event epoch. Table 2 summarizes

*Figure 3.* Failure/Repair Transition Notation and SRC Model

these transitions and gives the steady state distribution.

| $x \in \delta$ | $(x, y)$ | $q_{xx}$ | $q_{xy}$ | $\pi_x$ |
|---|---|---|---|---|
| 1 | $(1, 2)$ | $-\lambda$ | $\lambda$ | $\mu \cdot (\mu + \lambda)^{-1}$ |
| 2 | $(2, 1)$ | $-\mu$ | $\mu$ | $\lambda \cdot (\mu + \lambda)^{-1}$ |

*Table 2.* Single Repairable Component Markov Process Specification

For our second example, we consider an abstraction that aggregates a sequence of events, which may be desirable in practice. Figure 4 show a process consisting of a sequence of four events reduced to three events.

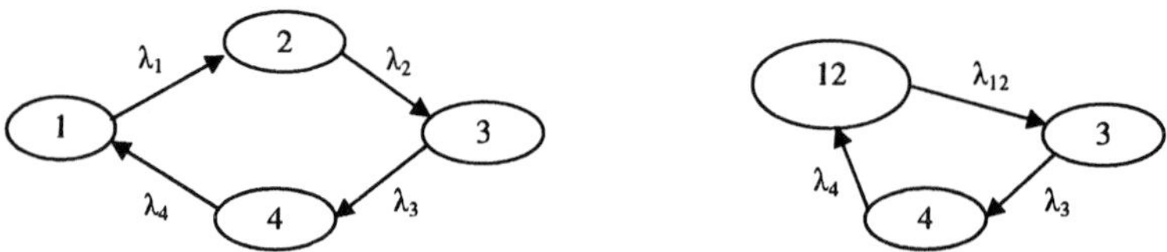


*Figure 4.* Markov Cycle Models (Right abstracts Left)

The last example is a triple modular redundancy (TMR) system with three independent and identical components, $C_1, C_2$, and $C_3$. Components are either working or failed, with failure and repair rates $\lambda$ and $\mu$, respectively. System state is defined by the state of all components, with "operational" states as two or more components are working. Figure 5 and Table 3 show the TMR Markov process, parameters, and steady state solution.

**4.3 Safe Abstractions of Concrete Models**

Superscripts $a$ and $c$ are used to distinguish between abstract and concrete models. For example $\delta^a$ and $\delta^c$ denote abstract and concrete states, respectively. To ensure safety properties, we propose two rules for defining abstract models in terms of concrete models.

(1) To ensure that concrete states are not split and distributed among multiple abstract states, we recommend that the concrete states are partitioned where

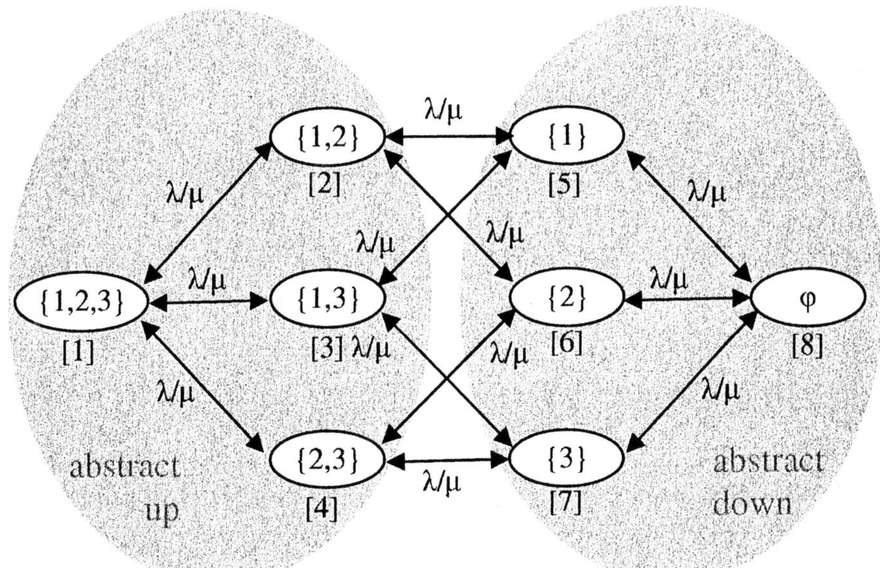


*Figure 5.* Markov TMR Model

| op comps | state $x$ | $q_x$ | up? | $\pi_x$ | Abs 1 | Abs 2 |
|---|---|---|---|---|---|---|
| $\{1,2,3\}$ | 1 | $-3\lambda$ | yes | $\mu^3 \cdot (\mu+\lambda)^{-3}$ | $P_1^{a1}$ | $P_1^{a2}$ |
| $\{1,2\}$ | 2 | $-(2\lambda+\mu)$ | yes | $(\mu^2\lambda) \cdot (\mu+\lambda)^{-3}$ | $P_2^{a1}$ | |
| $\{2,3\}$ | 3 | $-(2\lambda+\mu)$ | yes | $(\mu^2\lambda) \cdot (\mu+\lambda)^{-3}$ | | |
| $\{1,3\}$ | 4 | $-(2\lambda+\mu)$ | yes | $(\mu^2\lambda) \cdot (\mu+\lambda)^{-3}$ | | |
| $\{1\}$ | 5 | $-(\lambda+2\mu)$ | no | $(\mu\lambda^2) \cdot (\mu+\lambda)^{-3}$ | $P_3^{a1}$ | $P_2^{a2}$ |
| $\{2\}$ | 6 | $-(\lambda+2\mu)$ | no | $(\mu\lambda^2) \cdot (\mu+\lambda)^{-3}$ | | |
| $\{3\}$ | 7 | $-(\lambda+2\mu)$ | no | $(\mu\lambda^2) \cdot (\mu+\lambda)^{-3}$ | | |
| $\emptyset$ | 8 | $-3\mu$ | no | $\lambda^3 \cdot (\mu+\lambda)^{-3}$ | $P_4^{a1}$ | |

*Table 3.* TMR Markov process specification for Figure 5

each partition corresponds to a single abstract state. When $\delta^a = \{1^a, 2^a, ..., m^a\}$ then a partition on $\delta^c = \bigcup_{i=1}^{m^a} P_i^c$ is defined so that $j^a \equiv \{x | x \in P_j^c\}$ and $j^a \cap i^a = \emptyset$ for $j^a \neq i^a$. For a "safe" steady state abstraction, assign probabilities to the abstract states by:

$$\text{For } x \in \delta^a, \text{ assign } \pi_x^a = \sum_j \pi_j^c, \text{ where } j \in P_x^c \cap \delta^c.$$

When error states are aggregated in an abstraction, this assignment ensures that the probability of the error in the abstraction is not reduced.

This state aggregation (or partitioning) rule is consistent with the abstraction model of heirarchical decompositions. It is also intuitive when system states correspond to the (discrete) operational condition of physical components. For dependent faults an abstraction that "splits probabilities" across states might result in a better approximation. Further investigation is needed to determine if this heirarchical decomposition rule eliminates a number of useful abstractions.

(2) We further suggest that a one step transition from $x \in \delta^a$ to $y \in \delta^a$, $q^a_{xy} > 0$ only if there exists some $x' \in P^c_x \subset \delta^c$ and some $y' \in P^c_y \subset \delta^c$ such that $q^c_{x'y'} > 0$. This preserves a notional mapping from the abstract model to the system through the established mapping from the concrete model to the system. More importantly, it implies that errors in the abstract model cannot propagate in ways that were not specified in the concrete model.

**4.4 Transition Rate Assignments for Safe Abstractions**

We give three examples of safe steady state probability assignments for abstractions using the two step process in Section 4.3. We investigate the relationship between safe probabilities and rate assignments.

The right side of Figure 4 shows an abstraction of a four cycle model which merely collapses two states into one. Equation 1 gives the steady state solution of the concrete cyclic model in Figure 4.

$$\pi^c \quad = (\pi^c_1, \pi^c_2, \pi^c_3, \pi^c_4) \quad = \frac{(\lambda^c_2\lambda^c_3\lambda^c_4, \lambda^c_1\lambda^c_3\lambda^c_4, \lambda^c_1\lambda^c_2\lambda^c_4, \lambda^c_1\lambda^c_2\lambda^c_3)}{\lambda^c_2\lambda^c_3\lambda^c_4 + \lambda^c_1\lambda^c_3\lambda^c_4 + \lambda^c_1\lambda^c_2\lambda^c_4 + \lambda^c_1\lambda^c_2\lambda^c_3} \tag{1}$$

For the reduced model on the right of Figure 4, a similar computation gives $\pi^a = (\pi^a_{12}, \pi^a_3, \pi^a_4)$ in terms of transition rates $\lambda^a_{12}$, $\lambda^a_3$ and $\lambda^a_4$. A solution that preserves exiting transition rates in non-aggregated states of $\mathbf{A}^a$ is

$$\lambda^a_{12} = (\lambda^c_1\lambda^c_2)(\lambda^c_1 + \lambda^c_2)^{-1}; \quad \lambda^a_3 = \lambda^c_3; \quad \text{and } \lambda^a_4 = \lambda^c_4. \tag{2}$$

The solution in Equation 2 is not unique (four concrete parameters define three abstract parameters).

For the TMR example of Figure 5 we consider two abstractions. The two right most columns of Table 3 define the abstraction partitions. Abstraction 1, which defines abstract states by the number of operational components is shown in Figure 6. Section 4.5 shows this is a lumpable abstraction with unique

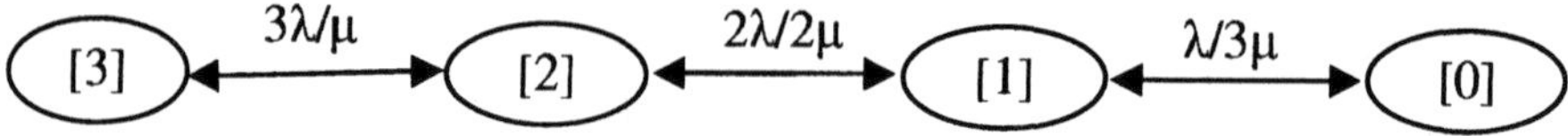


*Figure 6.* Number of Operational Components TMR Abstraction

(relative to the concrete model) transition rates, and how to compute them.

A courser abstraction of the TMR model is simply the two state model, $\delta^a = \{1, 2\} = \{\text{up}, \text{down}\}$. This abstraction is shown with shading in Figure 5 and also in the right most column of Table 3. When approximated by a

Markov process, this abstraction is represented in Figure 3. Equation 3 is the result of equating the two formulations for $\pi^a$, which does not have a unique assignment. The abstract model parameters must sastisfy

$$\lambda^a/\mu^a = (\lambda^c/\mu^c)^2 \cdot (\lambda^c + 3\mu^c)/(3\lambda^c + \mu^c) \tag{3}$$

In general, partitioned (abstract) processes are not Markovian, in which case the rate assignment need not be uniquely determined. The question is which assignment of values produces the best results from an engineering perspective. Is it preferable to hold constant the flow in, the flow out, the ratio of the flow in to the flow out, or some other property? One can envision practical circumstances which would favor each of these decisions.

### 4.5 Lumpability, Safe Abstractions and Rate Assignments

We define necessary and sufficient conditions for when the partitioned abstraction is again Markovian. Our discussion of strong lumpability for DTMCs follows the presentation in [Kemeny and Snell 1976].

Consider a partition $P$ on $\delta$ with $k < m$ elements. Define $U_{k,m}$ and $V_{m,k}$ according to $P$ as follows. The $j^{th}$ row of $U$ puts a probability distribution on the elements in $P_j$. For example, if $P_j$ contains $b_j$ states over which the uniform distribution is to be placed, then

$$U_{j,s} = \begin{cases} 1/b_j & \text{for } s \in P_j \\ 0 & \text{otherwise} \end{cases} \tag{4}$$

The rows of a matrix $V$ define the partition to which the state belongs. *I.e.*

$$V_{s,j} = \begin{cases} 1 & \text{for } s \in P_j \\ 0 & \text{otherwise} \end{cases} \tag{5}$$

Theorem 1 gives conditions for strong lumpability with respect to partition $P$ of a Discrete Time Markov Chain (DTMC).

THEOREM 1 (DTMC STRONG LUMPABILITY) *Let $P$ be a partition for the DTMC with state space $\delta$ and transition matrix $Q$. Let $U$ and $V$ be matrices defined by Equations 4 and 5 with respect to $P$. The DTMC is said to be strongly lumpable with respect to $P$ if and only if*

$$VUQV = QV.$$

*For a proof, see Theorems 6.3.4 and 6.3.5 of [Kemeny and Snell 1976].*

Theorem 2 is an easily obtained analog for conditions of strong lumpability in a Continuous Time Markov Chain (CTMC).

THEOREM 2 (CTMC STRONG LUMPABILITY) *Let $P$ be a partition for the CTMC with finite state space $\delta$ and infinitesimal generator matrix $A$. Let $U$ and $V$ be matrices defined by Equations 4 and 5 with respect to $P$. The CTMC is said to be strongly lumpable with respect to $P$ if*

$$VUD^{-1}AV = D^{-1}AV$$

*where $D = -diag(A)$. That is, $D$ is a diagonal matrix with $(D)_{ii} = -(A)_{ii}$.*

*To show this result, note that the DTMC transition matrix $Q = D^{-1}A + I$. An application of Theorem 1 gives*

$$VU(D^{-1}A + I)V = (D^{-1}A + I)V.$$

*Since $UV = I$, the result follows.*

The rates for the abstract model are found by computing $A^a = UA^cV$. An algorithm for finding the coursest (*i.e.* the most abstract) strongly lumpable model is given in [Derisavi et al. 2003a]. This algorithm has computational complexity $O(|Q^c| \cdot \log_2(|\delta^c|))$ and space $O(|Q^c| + |\delta^c|)$, where $|Q^c|$ is the number of positive transitions in the concrete model.

Weak lumpability occurs when the lumped process is Markov when starting from some (but not all) initial distributions ([Kemeny and Snell 1976]). Work has been done linking both strong and weak lumpability MP results to the same properties in stochastic automata(*e.g.* [Brinksma and Hermanns 2001]).

Investigation as to whether lumpable partitions create natural and useful abstractions for system models is needed. When an abstraction is not lumpable, a measure of "near lumpability" has been proposed as a measure of the quality of the approximation.

## 4.6 Time Dependent or Transient Solutions

For a time dependent analysis, we define safety for an abstract model with partition $P$ as follows. Let $x \in P_s \subset \delta^c$ be a non-fault or safe set of states and $y \in P_f \subset \delta^c$ be a "fault occurence" set of states. The abstraction is said to be safe in the time interval $[0, T]$

$$P_{s^a}(X^a(t) = f^a) \geq P_x(X(t) \in P_f) \; \forall \, x \in P_s \text{ and } \forall \, t \in [0, T]. \quad (6)$$

In words, we require for all $t \in [0, T]$ that when starting in safe abstract state $s^a$, the probability of reaching abstract fault state $f^a$ is at least as great as the probability of reaching any state in partition $P_f$ when starting from in any state in partition $P_s$ in the concrete model.

When the concrete Markov process is started in steady state $\pi^c$, then for every time $t > 0$ and for all $x \in \delta^c$, the $P_\pi(X(t) = x) = \pi_x$. When the abstraction is strongly lumpable (hence Markovian), the requirements of Equation 6 are satisfied because probabilities sum within partitions and the distribution of time to transition from all states in a partition to another partition is the same.

We are not sufficiently familiar with the literature to be able to report whether a transition assignment that can satisfy the requirements of Equation 6 exists for an arbitrary complex fault model with a non-lumpable abstraction. Perhaps an equally important question is how those conditions might be applicable for guiding the development of practical fault models.

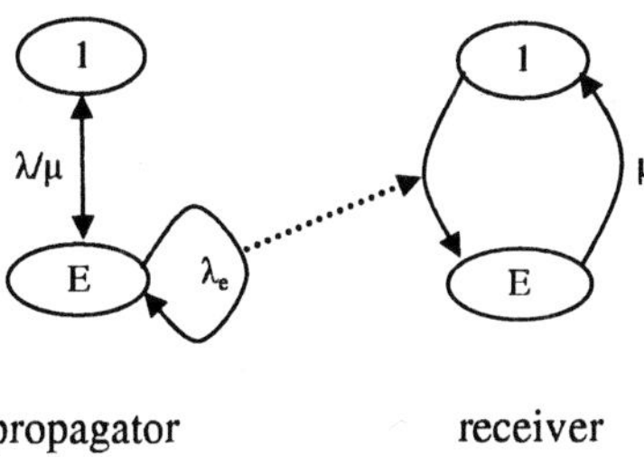


*Figure 7.* Error Propagation Between Markov Models

### 4.7 Composing Concurrent Models

Figure 7 illustrates the basic idea behind composing multiple Markov chain component models, one Markov Chain per component. The user may distinguish selected states as error propagating states, which is modeled as a self-transition with a given error propagation rate. For an error that may propagate from one component to another (determined by the architecture specification), the rate of a transition in the receiving model is determined by the rate of the propagating transition rather than a rate specified in the receiving model. A fundamental result of stochastic process algebras is that, under suitable restrictions, such rendezvous between concurrent stochastic processes have Poisson rates. Once this rate has been determined it can be used for the rate within the receiving model, and the methods of the preceeding sections applied to verify an abstraction. Similarly, self-transitions can be added to an abstract model to define propagation rates to be used in other receiving models.

The AADL Error Model Annex includes a way to define guards on error transitions to model things like voting and consensus protocols. In other words, additional language features and semantics are included to compactly specify complex event propagation conditions. More research is needed to determine when high level abstractions are closely approximated by the generated Markov abstractions.

## 5. Future Work

We have given only two examples of techniques that can be used to demonstrate that an abstract model can safely (in some sense) be substituted for a more complex concrete model when generating hybrid and stochastic automata models from architecture specifications. Preliminary approaches for linking MetaH/AADL safety specifications with concrete and abstract Markov models with solvers have been reported [Binns et al. 2000]. A more complete toolbox is needed. Also, more complex notions of abstraction may be useful, for example conformance relations[Krichen and Tripakis 2004].

## References

[AADL 2004] SAE AS5506, *Architecture Analysis and Design Language*, Society of Automotive Engineers, Warrendale, PA, 2004.

[MetaH 2000] *MetaH User's Guide*, Honeywell Technology Center, 3660 Technology Drive, Minneapolis, MN, www.htc.honeywell.com/metah.

[Alur et. al. 2001] R. Alur, T. Dang, J. Esposito, R. Fierro, Y. Hur, F. Ivančić, V. Kumar, I. Lee, R. Mishra, G. Pappas and O. Sokolsky, "Hierarchical Hybrid Modeling of Embedded Systems," EMSOFT 2001, Springer Verlag LNCS 2211, 2001.

[Alur et. al. 1994] R. Alur, C. Courcoubetis, N. Halbwachs, T. A. Henzinger, R.-H. Ho, X. Nicollin, A. Olivero, J. Sifakis and S. Yovine, "The Algorithmic Analysis of Hybrid Systems," *International Conference on Analysis and Optimization of Discrete Event Systems*, LNCIS 199, Springer-Verlag, 1994.

[Binns et al. 2000] P. Binns, S. Vestal, W. Sanders, J. Doyle, and D. Deavours, "MetaH/Mobius Integration Report", Customer Report for DARPA's Evolutionary Design of Complex Systems (EDCS) Program, Honeywell Labs, April 2000.

[Bradley et al. 2003] Jeremy Bradley, Nicholas Dingle, and William Knottenbelt, *International Symposium on Performance Evaluation of Computer and Telecommunication Systems* (SPECTS), July 2003

[Brinksma and Hermanns 2001] Ed Brinksma and Holger Hermanns, "Process Algebra and Markov Chains," Springer LNCS 2090, *European Educational Forum: School on Formal Methods and Performance Analysis*, 2001.

[Cousot 1977] P. Cousot and R. Cousot, "Abstract interpretation: a unified lattice model for static analysis of programs by construction or approximation of fixpoints," Sixth Annual Symposium on Principles of Programming Languages, Los Angeles, California, 1977.

[Derisavi et al. 2003a] S. Derisavi, H. Hermanns, and W. H. Sanders, "Optimal State-Space Lumping in Markov Chains," *Information Processing Letters*, vol. 87, no. 6, September 30, 2003,

[Derisavi et al. 2003b] S. Derisavi, P. Kemper, W. Sanders, and T. Courtney, *Performance Evaluation,* Volume 54(2), October 2003

[Desharnais et al. 2003] J. Desharnais, V. Gupta, R. Jagadeesan, and P. Panagaden, "Metrics for Labelled Markov Processes," to appear *Theoretical Computer Science*, Elsevier

[Hoel et. al. 1972] Paul G. Hoel, Sidney C. Port, and Charles J. Stone, *Introduction to Stochastic Processes*, Houghton Mifflin Company, USA, 1972.

[Kemeny and Snell 1976] John G. Kemeny and J. Laurie Snell, *Finite Markov Chains*, Springer-Verlag, 1976.

[Krichen and Tripakis 2004] Moez Krichen and Stavros Tripakis, "Black-box Conformance Testing for Real-Time Systems," SPIN'04 Workshop on Model Checking Software, LNCS 2989, 2004.

[Lefebvre 2002] Yannick Lefebvre, "Approximate aggregation and applications to reliability," *Third International Conference on Mathematical Methods on Reliability (MMR)*, 2002

[Liu and Deitel 2000] J. Liu and P. Deitel, *Real-Time Systems*, Prentice-Hall, New Jersey, 2000

[Lynch et. al. 2003] Nancy Lynch, Roberto Segala and Frits Vaandrager, "Hybrid I/O Automata," *Technical Report MIT-LCS-TR-827d*, MIT Laboratory for Computer Science, Cambridge, MA, Jan. 13, 2003; and *Information and Computation*, 185(1), Aug. 2003

[Milner 1989] Robin Milner, *Communication and Concurrency*, Prentice Hall, UK, 1989

[Vestal 2000a] Steve Vestal, "Formal Verification of the MetaH Executive Using Linear Hybrid Automata," *Real-Time Applications Symposium*, June 2000.

[Vestal 2000] Steve Vestal, "Modeling and Verification of Real-Time Software Using Extended Linear Hybrid Automata," *NASA Langley Formal Methods Workshop*, June 2000.

# PATTERN-BASED ANALYSIS OF AN EMBEDDED REAL-TIME SYSTEM ARCHITECTURE

Peter H. Feiler, David P. Gluch, John J. Hudak, Bruce A. Lewis
*Software Engineering Institute (SEI), Embry-Riddle University, US Army AMRDEC*

Abstract: The emerging Society of Automotive Engineers (SAE) Architecture Analysis & Design Language (AADL) standard is an architecture modeling language for real-time, fault-tolerant, scalable, embedded, multiprocessor systems. It enables the development and predictable integration of highly evolvable systems as well as analysis of existing systems. This paper discusses the role and benefits of using the AADL in the process of analyzing an existing avionics system. We use the AADL to describe architecture patterns in the system being analyzed and to identify potentially systemic issues in the system. We discuss some of the findings related to timing, scheduling, and fault tolerance and the benefits of the use of the AADL. Additionally we highlight the benefits of working with architecture abstractions that are reflected in the AADL notation, in particular the separation of architecture design decisions from implementation decisions. Such a light-weight architecture analysis is typically followed by a full-scale AADL model of the system with required and actual timing, performance, and reliability figures, and its analysis to determine whether the requirements are met.

Key words: software architecture, real-time, embedded, model-based system engineering, standard

## 1. INTRODUCTION

The SAE Architecture Analysis & Design Language (AADL) (AS2C, 2004) has been developed for embedded real-time systems that have challenging resource (size, weight, power) constraints, requirements for real-time response, fault tolerance, and specialized input/output hardware, and that must be certified to high levels of assurance. Intended fields of application are avionics systems, flight management systems, space applications, automotive applications such as engine and power train control systems, robotics applications, industrial process control equipment, and medical devices. The AADL was developed under the auspices of the International Society for Automotive Engineers (SAE) in their Avionics Systems Division (ASD) and has passed ballot (AADL, 2004). For more information on the AADL the reader is referred to www.aadl.info.

The AADL can be used as an embedded system engineering tool in two ways: analysis of architecture patterns identified in real systems to discover potentially systemic issues, and analysis of a full-scale system model with quantified system properties and generation of a model-specific runtime system (Feiler et.al., 2003). The SEI has applied the AADL to analyze an existing avionics system design as AADL patterns. The results of this work are summarized in this paper and described in more detail in (Feiler et.al., 2004). The cost-effectiveness of using MetaH, the precursor to AADL, for precise modeling, early analysis, and auto-generation of a system implementation is discussed in (Feiler et.al., 2000).

An avionics system typically consists of a collection of hardware and software that controls the flight, navigation, radio communication, and in the case of military aircraft, the targeting and weapons systems. Early generations of digital avionics systems consisted of embedded controllers executing on specialized hardware. As general purpose processors became faster, controllers were implemented with application software executing with a static timeline and shared variable architecture. Use of shared variables minimized the memory footprint and resulted in efficient communication between components within a controller. This approach led to an efficient implementation with deterministic execution behavior, but resulted in a software runtime architecture that was carefully crafted and difficult to change.

In this paper we focus on the use of the AADL as an effective tool for initial analysis of embedded systems for potential problem spots. We have analyzed the architecture of an avionics system that is being modernized. The analysis has focused on different aspects of the embedded system architecture and identify potentially unanticipated side effects: the migration from a statically scheduled system to a preemptively scheduled system to improve resource utilization and create a flexible architecture, the impact of this change in task scheduling on task communication via shared variables, scheduling of system partitions as virtual processors, management of end-to-end latency, and modeling of redundancy in a fault tolerant architecture. We will examine each of these issues in the next sections.

## 2. PREEMPTIVE SCHEDULING AND PORT COMMUNICATION

In the following discussion, we will focus on a flight manager subsystem executing within one of the system partitions. This subsystem consists of several components that process signal data in a certain order, with some components operating at 20Hz while other components operate at lower rates.

The system is being migrated from a cyclic executive to the use of preemptive fixed priority scheduling to achieve better resource utilization and a more flexible system design. Preemptive fixed-priority scheduling is offered as a solution to improving resource utilization of processors and to increase the flexibility of evolving embedded systems while ensuring that deadlines are met. In particular, if used with Rate-Monotonic Analysis (RMA) (Klein et.al., 1993) a system design can be analyzed at design time to determine whether all deadlines will be met despite the fact that tasks can preempt each other.

Inter-partition communication port communication between threads is performed via message ports, while communication within threads is based on shared variables. The shared variable approach was retained to accommodate legacy components and to achieve highly efficient communication.

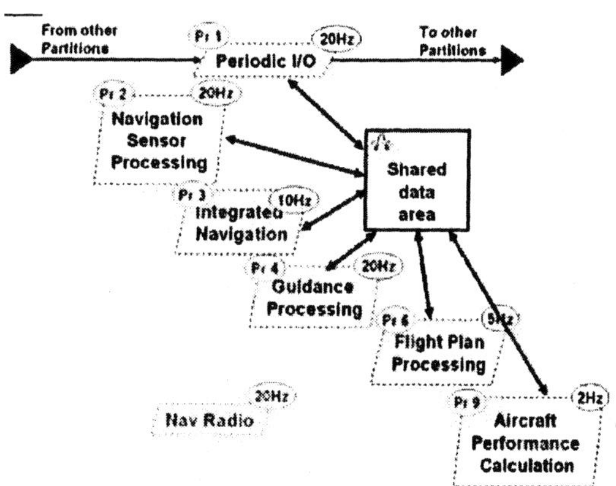


*Figure 1.* Preemptive Scheduling With Priority Assignment

A naïve way of introducing preemptive scheduling into this example is to turn each task into a separate thread. To ensure the desired flow of data between components, priorities are assigned to the threads according to the desired execution order. We have modeled this design using AADL (shown in Figure 1). The intended task execution order is from the top to the bottom. The task priority is indicated with Pr i, where a smaller i represents a higher priority.

Since AADL supports scheduling schemes based on RMA, it is natural to examine the resulting model from an RMA perspective. Thus, it is apparent that the manual priority assignment result in potential priority inversion, i.e., a lower rate thread has a higher priority than a higher rate thread. For example, the lower-rate Integrated Navigation task is given a higher priority than the higher-rate Guidance Processing task. This potential priority inversion does not occur if all threads can complete their execution in a minor frame, i.e., they have a pre-period deadline corresponding to the highest rate thread. A consequence of this assumption is that no thread is preempted and thread execution is the same as that of a static timeline. In other words, assigning priorities to enforce an execution order incurs the runtime overhead of preemptive scheduling without obtaining the benefits of improved resource utilization and flexibility.

In summary, development of AADL models with an RMA-based fixed priority scheme provides properties for specifying the period, deadline, and worst-case execution time, but not for assigning priority. Thus, priority inversion cannot be introduced. If AADL is used to model existing implementations that do not use the RMA approach, then the red flag of priority inversion in the RMA framework can be provided as a consistency check in AADL models with explicit priority assignment.

The AADL promotes port-based communication between all application threads, both within and across partitions. Furthermore, it distinguishes between queued message communication and unqueued state communication. Finally, the AADL distinguishes between immediate (mid-frame) and delayed (phase-delayed) communication of state data between periodic threads in a deterministic manner. Such communication semantics can also be found in real-time OS standards such as OSEK (OSEK, 2003). In this section, we model communication within the flight manager partition through ports and discuss the issue of efficient communication implementations.

The AADL-based model of the flight manager is shown in Figure 2. All data communication is modeled by ports (black triangles) and connections; there is no need for shared data and coordinating concurrent access through locks. No task priorities have been specified by the modeler. They are determined according to the scheduling protocol; in the case of rate monotonic scheduling, according to the thread periods.

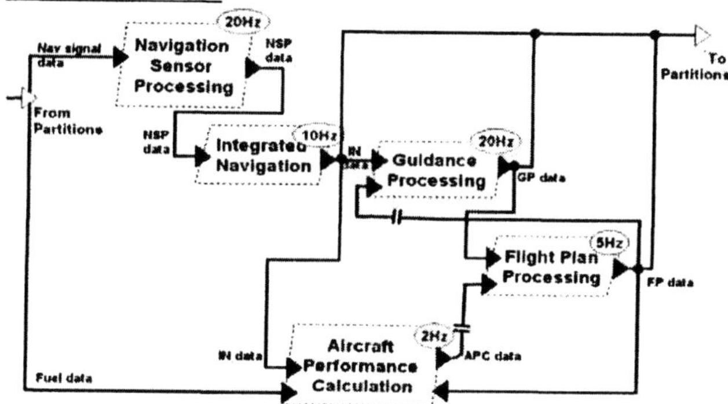


*Figure 2.* Port & Connection Based AADL Model of the Flight Manager

The model indicates which connections are *immediate* (solid line) and which are *delayed* (solid line with crossing double line). Cyclic sequences of immediate connections are not permitted since they cannot be achieved. Such cycles can be detected by an analysis tool. If the application developer documented an acceptable phase delay for a task (in a port property) the degree of actual phase delay can be calculated and compared against the acceptable value.

Note that the periodic I/O task of Figure 1 is not represented explicitly in Figure 2. The periodic I/O task achieves two objectives: it groups several data items together and sends them as a composite data item, i.e., the values of several output ports are sent together; it always sends the data phase delayed at the start of the next period. In the AADL, these two concerns are modeled separately. Time-consistent data transfer of multiple *out data ports* is modeled by an aggregate data port (shown as hollow triangle), and as phase delay as a delayed connection. The application developer now has the choice of transferring the data immediately or delayed, by choosing the appropriate connection symbol.

The following observations can be made about the use of AADL. The AADL separates runtime architecture design decisions from implementation decisions, and application component development from architecture design. At the same time, it precisely specifies temporal properties of both task execution and communication in such a way that application developers (control engineers) can develop their components against documented assumptions regarding sampling rates, phase delay of data, and processing rates. The semantics of AADL periodic thread execution and data port connections assure deterministic and consistent data communication. At the same time, implementation of task dispatching and communication can be delegated to tools. Such tools can generate task dispatch and communication code that correctly implements the intended temporal semantics. In addition, they can produce highly efficient implementations by taking advantage of information and analysis results from the AADL model.

Separation of architecture design from implementation concerns allows a software system engineer to investigate alternatives that improve the performance characteristics of an embedded system in cooperation with control engineers. One example is control engineers analyzing the sensitivity of their controllers to variations in phase delay, while software system engineers identify improvements in resource utilization. Another example is sensitivity analysis by control engineers to changes in sampling and execution rates, while system engineers investigate the impact of rate changes on schedulability and resource utilization.

## 3. HIDDEN TIMING SIDE EFFECTS OF PARTITION SCHEDULING

Partitions provide time and space partitioning between software components. In doing so they ensure that malfunctioning components in one partition cannot affect the execution of components in other components. This concept is at the heart of the ARINC653 standard for avionics systems (ARINC653, 1997). Partitions are placed in a particular order on the static partition scheduling timeline of a processor. Partitions may have to be rearranged on the timeline or reassigned to other processors to accommodate new tasks and partitions and to balance the load across processors. Such rearrangements of partitions are a delicate undertaking and may have hidden side effects. This section focuses on the effects of such rearrangements on inter-partition communications within and across processors.

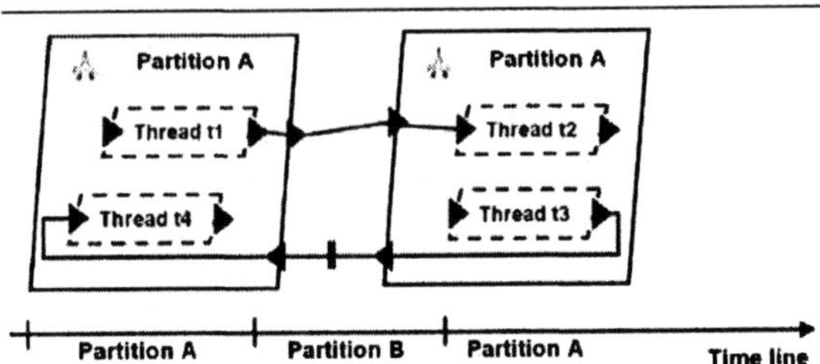


*Figure 3.* Partition Schedule & Communication

Let us first examine the issue for inter-partition communication within a processor. We have a static timeline with partition A executing before partition B for the same time frame, followed by the execution of partition A in the next time frame, as shown in Figure 3. Partition A has two threads $t_1$ and $t_4$ that can be executed in either order. Partition B similarly has two tasks $t_2$ and $t_3$. If a thread $t_1$ in partition A sends data to a thread $t_2$ in partition B, the data is transferred mid-frame, i.e., within the same time frame. If thread $t_3$ sends data to thread $t_4$, the data arrives at $t_4$ at the next time frame, i.e., phase delayed (shown as an explicitly marked delayed connection). In other words, the partition order affects the timing of communication.

Modeling inter-partition communication in the AADL helps uncover a potentially undesirable side effect of rearranging the partition schedule. From an application perspective, flow between components is modeled as mid-frame (immediate) or phase-delayed (delayed) connections. These timing characteristics place a constraint on the possible partition orderings on the static partition execution timeline. Thus, a system engineer rearranging the partition timeline is made aware of such conflicts within the AADL description.

In the case of an immediate connection, the recipient partition must be placed after the sending partition. Note that there cannot be immediate connections from any thread in partition B to any thread in partition A if there is an immediate connection from a thread in partition A to a thread in partition B (i.e., if partition A's execution must precede partition B's execution). This can be easily detected through analysis of the AADL model. Note that if a design is over-constrained, no partition order can satisfy the specified communication delay characteristics.

Both the application engineer and the system engineer can contribute to relaxing the constraints on partition ordering. The application engineer can design the system to only use delayed inter-partition communication. This is effectively the case in the system design of Figure 1 by the periodic I/O task performing all inter-partition communication at the beginning of partition execution. An application developer can also specify that a component is insensitive to (a certain variation in) phase delay, i.e., that the connection could be either immediate or delayed, if the receiving component can handle variation in phase delay. The system engineer can provide an implementation of delayed inter-partition communication by transferring data just before a partition dispatch as part of the runtime system functionality, thus, relieving the application developer from repeatedly implementing the periodic I/O task. By doing so, the application architecture is insulated from partition ordering changes.

If we have a partitioned system that is distributed across multiple processors, the alignment of the static partition timelines on those processors determines whether communication is immediate or phase delayed. An AADL model of the application system will specify the desired communication timing characteristics, thereby placing constraints on the ordering of tasks on partitions across all processors. Techniques for relaxing the constraints on a partition rely on the assumption that the system is synchronous, i.e., that the processors operate on a single global clock.

Processors in such a system may be connected via an aperiodic bus with data transferred immediately (with a well defined maximum communication time), or via a periodic bus with data transferred at a rate determined by the bus itself. A periodic bus samples the data stream to be transferred and introduces a phase delay determined by the bus rate. This means that all connections that are bound to the bus must be delayed connections. In other words, only partitions with delayed data port connections can be placed on different processors that are connected physically by a periodic bus. This can be checked by analyzing the AADL model.

In a time-triggered architecture (TTA) (TTA, 2003) the bus is periodic and drives the scheduling of tasks on different processors. Thus, it acts as a global clock that manages any clock drift of individual processors. In that case, one can attempt to align the schedule of partitions across processors under AADL's immediate connection constraints. Again, the AADL model permits quick identification of over constraints due to immediate connections, e.g., identification of immediate connections between two independent pairs of threads in two different partitions.

If a distributed system is asynchronous, i.e., if each processor operates on a local clock, clock drift can occur. Two partitions with an immediate connection on different processors may have overlapping execution times and the ordering may change over time. In other words, their execution times relative to each other may vary over time, resulting in a varying sampling phase delay for the recipient. A periodic I/O task solution, as shown in Figure 1, does not eliminate the non-determinism in phase delay due to clock drift. However, it does address the issue of time-consistent transfer of aggregate data, i.e., the transfer of data as a single unit that is consistent with respect to the execution of multiple sending threads in a given partition. As mentioned earlier, the AADL provides an aggregate data port for this purpose.

In summary, the ordering of partitions in a partition schedule potentially can affect the timing characteristics of connections. AADL models with immediate and delayed connections explicitly document the desired timing characteristics of data transfer. They act as constraints on the placement of partitions on their static timeline. This allows us to determine whether a feasible partition ordering exists. The constraints can be relaxed by the AADL runtime system supporting delayed connections, independent of partition scheduling order, and by the application developer investigating the impact of a change of immediate connection requirements to delayed connection requirements or the sensitivity of application components to variation in phase delay. The aggregate data port concept in the AADL contributes to addressing asynchronous distributed system issues by providing time-consistent data transfer.

## 4. END-TO-END LATENCY

The avionics system has a number of flows, namely, signal streams that require periodic processing and aperiodic command processing flows such as the flow of control information from sensors to actuators and changing the Navigation Radio channel. A critical requirement for these flows is to meet the maximum latency requirements. This end-to-end latency analysis can be based on deadline and worst-case execution time of individual steps in the flow executed by threads and on the worst-case latency specified for the transfer of information from one step to the next. We can separately determine whether threads meet their deadline given their worst-case execution times for a given processor binding, and whether the bus can schedule the transfer of data for those connections that must communicate via the bus within their transfer latency limits. In this section we focus on end-to-end latency analysis on the assumption that the thread execution and data transfer performance properties have been validated.

AADL supports the declaration of flows as flow specifications, i.e., as externally observable flows through components, as flow paths, i.e., the realization of the specified flows, and end-to-end flows, i.e., flow paths with specific start and end points. Such flows are represented as sequences of connections and threads. From their timing characteristics as periodic threads with a given period, delayed and immediate connections, and whether connections are bound to periodic buses, we can derive the end-to-end latency. Worst-case latency of a flow is effectively the cumulative latency along the path of a flow, i.e., latency due to execution (competition for execution resources), communication (competition for the bus as resource), and sampling or pacing (delay due to dispatch delay and/or queuing delay). This can be based on the maximum execution latency and maximum communication latency figures. We can also consider average case end-to-end latency for those flows where it is acceptable.

When dealing with flows there are two major concerns: adjusting the end-to-end latency to meet requirements, and understanding the interaction between multiple flows, in particular at their merge points. When actual end-to-end latency does not meet the requirements, a typical response is to ask application developers to make their code run more efficiently. However, this may be futile because certain latency contributors are inherent in the system or application architecture and are insensitive to a reduction in actual execution time by a thread. For example, consider output that is to be communicated over a periodic bus. Having a source thread execute faster to output a little earlier will not result in improvement unless the change crosses a period boundary of the bus sampling. Similarly, a periodic thread receiving data through a data port connection does not receive the data earlier if the sending thread is also periodic, since the data transfer semantics in that case are defined by the AADL to be deterministic.

The representation of an application architecture in the AADL, with timing characteristics for both threads and connections and an explicit specification of flows, allows us to quickly identify the key contributors to end-to-end latency. In the previous sections, we have encouraged the consideration of delayed connections between threads to improve processor utilization and reduce constraints on partition scheduling order. These are decisions that can be revisited to reduce end-to-end latency. We may also eliminate sampling latencies if delayed connections can be turned into immediate connections. We can examine latency contributors due to the binding of the application system to the execution platform. For example, we can consider placing processing steps in a critical flow on the same processor. We can examine latency contributors due to allocation of application components into partitions. For example, we can consider collocating two sequential processing steps in the same partition.

A key issue with multiple flows is the interaction of their latency characteristics. If we have a periodic thread receiving data from an aperiodic thread, the actual completion time of the sending thread relative to the dispatch of the receiving periodic thread determines which value is accessible to the receiving thread. Variation in actual completion time may result in either the old or the new value being accessible, i.e., data latency may non-deterministically vary by a period. This potential non-determinism can be identified through analysis and recorded as a property in the AADL model. Note that the semantics of immediate and delayed data port connections have been defined in the AADL such that neither immediate nor delayed data port communication between periodic threads introduces latency non-determinism.

Non-determinism in latency can result in potentially undesirable consequences. For example non-deterministic variation in phase delay has the effect of an oscillating target position resulting in a blurred display. In general, whenever two data streams merge and one data stream has non-deterministic latency there is a potential problem. In actual systems, the merge point is often a controller. In that case, any oscillation observed by the control engineer may be perceived as noise in the sensor data, which the control engineer may compensate for by adjustments in the controller.

In summary, an AADL model specifies timing characteristics for both the execution of threads and the transfer of data between threads. The AADL supports the specification of end-to-end flows as well as flow specifications through individual components as part of their interface specification. As a result the worst-case end-to-end latency of an end-to-end flow specified for a system can be determined in terms of the expected worst-case latency specified as part of the flow specification of each subsystem. In particular, this permits end-to-end latency analysis early in development to identify potential problem spots when subsystem implementations may not have been completed yet. As the implementation of the system gets refined the latency analysis results can become less conservative to reflect the full implementation.

## 5. REDUNDANCY IN APPLICATION ARCHITECTURES

Many embedded real-time systems have a requirement for high dependability. Dependability is the ability of a system to continue to produce the desired service to the user when the system is exposed to undesirable conditions (LaPrie, 2002). One method to increase computer systems' dependability is through redundancy of hardware, software or both. The AADL contains constructs that allow the developer to clearly represent and subsequently model the redundant artifacts at various levels of abstraction. In this section, we focus on the dependability aspects of a system and how general fault tolerant approaches can be supported by the AADL.

A typical diagram of such a software architecture mapped onto the hardware is shown in Figure 4. Multiple instances of hardware and software are shown with little or no indication as to the intended functional redundancy. This results in speculation about the intended behavior of the system under fault conditions. Such information tends to be spread throughout the design document. For example, there are four MFD processors, four DMs, and four WAMs. Are they one operational unit with three spares, two operational units each with its own spare, or four fully functional operational units? What is the mechanism by which failures are detected? What is the mechanism by which failover is achieved? Does each replicated unit perform failover switching separately, or are groups of replicated tasks switched together? What data is necessary, if any, for state space preservation? What are the data sources that feed the redundant entities? Answers to these types of questions could not be ascertained from the architectural drawings. Reading through software design documentation uncovered some useful information, but not enough to completely model the system. It is in this setting that the AADL abstractions help guide us to a clear understanding of the fault tolerant aspects of the system.

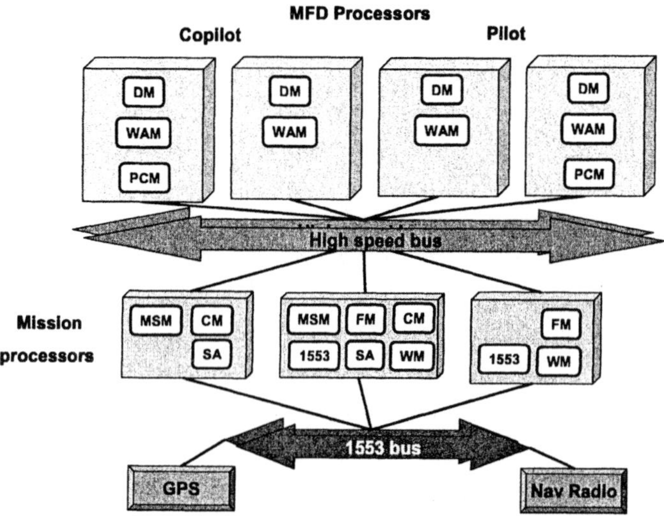


*Figure 4.* Typical Documentation of Avionics System Architecture

Analysis of this architecture from a dependability perspective begins with understanding what is being replicated. The intentions of the redundancy design can be expressed as a set of properties on the basic system architecture. In Figure 5 we are showing the above system as an AADL model. The logical grouping capability is used to clearly indicate which logical units are treated as redundant units. The degree of redundancy is indicated through a property shown visually in an oval decorator icon. Specific choices of redundancy mechanisms, such as master/slave, and the form of replication, are indicated through properties pre-declared as part of the AADL core language. Collocation constraints of components on processors and memory as well as connections over buses are similarly specified through properties.

Specific redundancy mechanisms can also be modeled in AADL as separate patterns. Figure 6 illustrates the master-slave pattern we found documented for several subsystems, each written with their own words and limited precision. This made it difficult to discern whether a single master-slave mechanism and protocol was used or whether different subsystems had variations. Questions that should be answerable from a design document include: Are both the master and slave active? What is the operational scenario for failover? Is state information exchanged between the redundant components? Who decides whether a component failed?

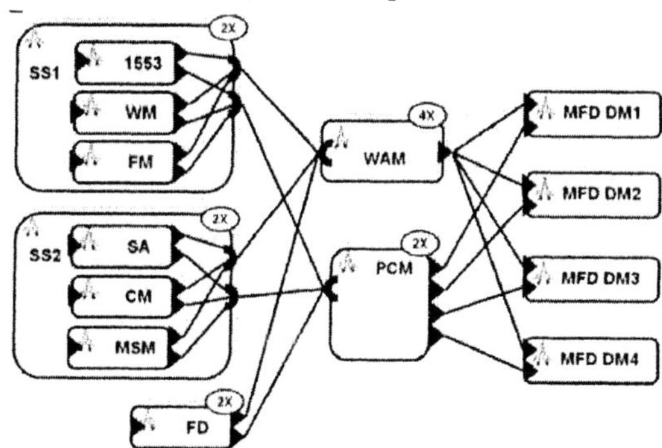


*Figure 5.* AADL Representation of Avionics System Redundancy

We use the AADL mode concept to model alternative fault tolerant system configurations. Figure 6 shows the replicated subsystem PCM as PCM.rep1 and PCM.rep2 contained in PCM, which takes on the role of SS1 (Figure 5). The left hand side illustrates the different mode configurations of the master-slave pattern. In Master mode, PCM.rep1 is active, receives input, and provides output (shown in black). PCM.rep2 (the slave copy) is not active and does not receive input nor produce output (shown in grey). In Slave mode the opposite is the case. The right-hand side of Figure 6 illustrates a hot-standby Master-Slave pattern of a stateful application component. In this case both copies of the component are supplied with input and both process the data. However, the output of only one copy is made available to the component output. The state of the component is modeled with the data component construct and is shown as exchanged between the components. This exchange can be specified to occur while operating in a mode, or on a mode transition. The figure also shows an Observer thread that receives the output from both copies and decides whether to operate in Master or Slave mode. The data is specified to be received by the observer thread at the next period. If a mode switch is necessary, it requests any necessary mode change by raising an appropriate event through the respective event out port (shown as a double arrow head). This event is routed to the appropriate mode transition in the mode state transition diagram. If the event arrives at an outgoing transition of the current mode, a mode switch is initiated.

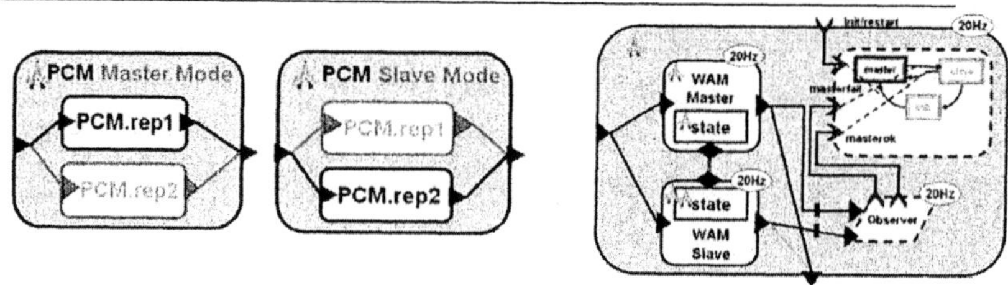


*Figure 6.* Hot Standby Master-Slave Mode Logic

In summary, the AADL allows the aggregation of application and execution platform components into a system hierarchy. Properties can be associated with components to specify the degree and form of desired redundancy. Redundancy protocols can be modeled in the AADL utilizing modes, mode transitions, routing of events that reflect detected faults to appropriate mode transitions. Binding constraints address collocation restrictions of replicated components. Error models support stochastic modeling of fault occurrences for reliability analysis.

# 6. CONCLUSION

In this paper, we have analyzed an existing avionics system to show use of the SAE AADL, an emerging international standard for modeling the system architecture of embedded real-time systems. The AADL focuses on modeling task and communication architectures by modeling application system architectures as threads, processes, and aggregates thereof, and by modeling their interactions as port connections, synchronous subprogram calls, or concurrency controlled access to shared data. An application system architecture is then mapped onto an execution platform to support analysis of runtime system properties such as schedulability and reliability.

In the process of applying the AADL in the analysis of an existing avionics system, we were led to modeling the system so that implementation decisions were separated from architecture decisions. In particular, we were able to model the system interactions purely in the form of port communication, although the actual system is implemented with communication through shared variables. The use of the AADL abstractions allowed us to quickly identify potential issues with the shared variable communication solution within partitions.

The AADL model and its support for characterizing timing for both threads and connections allowed us to establish a framework for negotiating tradeoffs in resource demand between the application developer (typically, a control engineer) and the system engineer who is responsible for integrating the application components into an operational system. The characterization of connections as immediate and delayed also allowed us to identify issues with respect to partition ordering on the static partition scheduling timeline and permitted us to perform end-to-end latency analysis effectively.

Finally, the use of the AADL modeling capability allowed us to describe the redundancy aspects of the system architecture and to address fault tolerance concisely. By focusing on separation of concerns, we were able to describe the application system perspective, the realization of the chosen redundancy protocol, and the mapping onto the execution platform as three views.

## 7. REFERENCES

AS2C, 2004, SAE AS-2c Subcommittee "Scope of the SAE AADL Standard". Excerpt from draft standard document. http://www.aadl.info

AADL, 2004, Society of Automotive Engineers (SAE) Avionics Systems Division (ASD) AS-2C Subcommittee. "Avionics Architecture Description Language Standard." Draft v0.99. May 2004.

Feiler et.al., 2003, P. Feiler, B. Lewis, S. Vestal, "The SAE AADL Standard: A Basis for Model-Based Architecture-Driven Embedded Systems Engineering", Workshop on Model-Driven Embedded Systems, Real-Time Application Systems (RTAS) Conference, May 2003. See publications at http://www.aadl.info.

Feiler et.al., 2000, P. Feiler, B. Lewis, S. Vestal, "Improving Predictability in Embedded Real-time Systems" Software Engineering Institute, Special Report, CMU/SEI-2000-SR-01.

Feiler et.al., 2004, P. Feiler, D. Gluch, B. Lewis, J. Hudak, "Embedded System Architecture Analysis Using SAE AADL" Software Engineering Institute Technical Note CMU/SEI-2004-TN005, April 2004.

Klein, et.al., 1993, M. H. Klein, T. Ralya, B. Pollak, R. Obenza, M. Gonzalez Harbour, "A Practitioner's Handbook for Real-Time Analysis: Guide to Rate Monotonic Analysis for Real-Time Systems," Kluwer Academic Publishers.

OSEK, 2003, Open systems and the corresponding interfaces for automotive electronics, OSEK, http://www.osek-vdx.org (2003).

ARINC653, 1997, "Avionics Application Software Standard Interface", ARINC Specification 653, Airlines Electronic Engineering Committee, Aeronautical Radio Inc., 1997.

TTA, 2003, "TTA: Time-Triggered Architecture". http://www.tttech.com/ and http://www.vmars.tuwien.ac.at/projects/tta/

LaPrie, 2002, J.C. LaPrie (editor), "Dependability: Basic Concepts and Terminology", Springer Verlag (publisher), November 2002, ISBN: 037822968.

# AN ADL CENTRIC APPROACH FOR THE FORMAL DESIGN OF REAL-TIME SYSTEMS

Sébastien Faucou, Anne-Marie Déplanche, Yvon Trinquet
*Institut de Recherche en Communications et Cybernétique de Nantes - UMR 6597 CNRS, École Centrale de Nantes, École des Mines de Nantes, Universit de Nantes France*
firstname.name@irccyn.ec-nantes.fr

**Abstract** This paper presents the REACT project, dedicated to real-time system design. REACT aims at combining into an architectural design process some formal modelling and verification techniques and providing those corresponding tools. It emphasizes on the ADL of REACT (CLARA), and the validation of functional architectures using formal techniques.

**Keywords:** ADL, real-time systems, architecture design process, formal validation

## 1. Introduction

The increasing complexity of real-time systems (as regards not only their functionality but also their hardware and software components and the interactions and mappings between these components) in domains such as in-vehicle embedded electronic, robotics, field-devices control, or avionic leads to attach more and more importance to their architectural design step. *Architectural design* is not only about specifying (or even choosing) and assembling (logical, software, hardware, ...) components together so as to create a coherent and functionally correct system. It has also to make sure that some other extra-functional[1] requirements such as timeliness, reliability, safety, costs, etc. will eventually be met by the system under operation. Introducing V&V activities as soon as possible in the development process of computer-based control systems is now a widely accepted need. This implies several important consider-

[1]As in (ARTIST, 2003), we use extra-functional instead of non-functional. Indeed, the timing constraints for instance, are part of the definition of the functionalities of a real-time system and thus should not be qualified as "non-functional".

ations: (i) designers must have available a way (a language) to describe (to model) the system architecture (its constitutive parts and relations) at different levels of abstraction; (ii) verification tools for system analysis and stating on its performances from the architectural level (and still after) have to be provided; (iii) the architectural design process (transformation(s) from the functional architecture up to the runtime configuration) has to be integrated to form a continuous and traceable chain, even an automatic one. It should guarantee that the (functional and extra-functional) properties stated at the upper levels are always met at the lower levels.

The objectives of our present work are to combine into an architectural design process some formal modelling and verification techniques. The strong dependency between embedded software and its execution platform requires us to focus on techniques that take into account the operational characteristics of the system, so as to reason on its extra-functional properties. REACT, "REal-time Application Configuration Tool", is the name we gave to this project and to the corresponding toolkit we are thinking of building.

Real-time systems that are aimed, are embedded ones, using some RTOS or middleware as runtime platform. They may be distributed. However we only consider situations where the system hardware is already defined (either a ready-to-use commercial platform or a reused yet designed one): hardware architecture design or co-design are out of concern.

In this paper, we present only a few constitutive parts of REACT: its architecture description language CLARA[2]and the validation of functional architectures. It is built as follows: in section 2, we give an overview of the development process, from the high level design to the binary code synthesis. In section 3, we introduce CLARA, the ADL that we use to perform the description of embedded software systems. In section 4, we discuss the validation of architecture descriptions with regards to some functional and extra-functional properties.

## 2. Design process

The REACT project aims at offering a set of formal modelling and verification facilities in an unified framework for the rigorous architectural design of real-time systems. It does not cover the whole development process: we consider that the specifications are given. Our main goal is to produce an operational architecture that has been validated

[2]CLARA: Configuration LAnguage for Real-time Application (Durand, 1998).

against some functional and extra-functional requirements (especially timeliness). Before to present the process, we define some vocabulary:

We call *functional architecture* (FA) the structure of the system in terms of its *functions*, their behaviours, and the control and data flows between them (*function* denotes a logical computation block that has not to be refined at this design level).

We call *runtime platform* (RP) the hardware and low-level software layer (RTOS, device drivers, middlewares, communication protocols) that are used for the deployment of the application. All these elements are seen as a platform, accessible through a set of runtime services.

We call *operational architecture* (OA) the result of the mapping of the FA onto the RP. The functions are allocated to tasks and the tasks are allocated to processing nodes. The control flows and data flows are translated into appropriate invocations of RP services. At last, the configuration of the RP (e.g. priorities of the tasks and messages) is given.

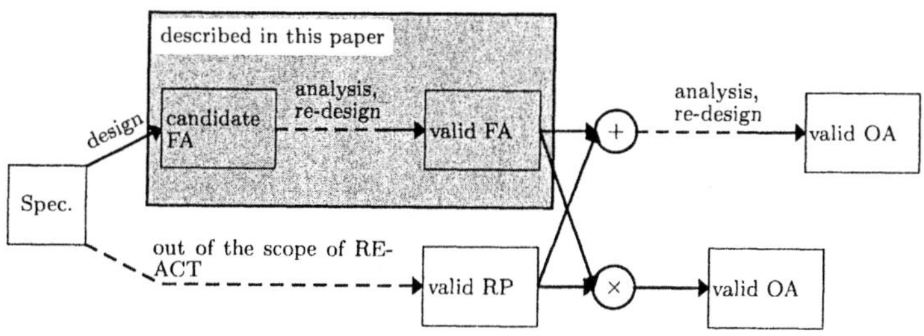


*Figure 1.* Overview of the design process of REACT.

As an entry point of REACT, we have defined an ADL, CLARA, dedicated to the description of the FA of reactive systems. It provides also some support for specifying timing constraints and properties. Thus, the design process (see fig.1) starts with the description of a candidate FA, which needs to be validated. For this purpose, we use Petri net (PN) theory to assess safety properties (eg. deadlock freedom). We also propose a high level consistency analysis of the timing constraints and properties (assessment of a necessary condition over the existence of a valid implementation). Given the results of these analyses, the designer can either validate the candidate and go on, or design a new one (generally not from scratch). As an output of these steps, a valid FA is defined, together with a set of timing constraints and properties that may be consistent. A complete illustration of this part of the process is given in the paper.

As stated in the introduction, we consider that the RP is already defined. To achieve the mapping of the FA onto the RP so as to produce an OA, we have explored a first direction and are presently working on a second one. We present both approaches hereafter (due to space limitation, they won't be discussed any further in this paper).

With the first approach (operator + on fig. 1, see (Faucou, 2002)), the mapping is made so as to "preserve the structure" of the FA. It targets especially the OSEK/VDX-based RP[3]. The active components are mapped onto OSEK tasks that interact, according to the connections described in the FA, through the services of a "CLARA middleware" (the configuration of which is extracted from the FA). The assignment of the tasks to the computing nodes and the configuration of the RP have to be done by the system architect. Such a mapping allows to preserve traceability between the levels (the FA and the OA). Nevertheless, it can potentially produce OA with a complex execution structure involving a lot of inter-task communications, the behaviour of which being hardly analysable. On the one hand, we have developed a simulation approach that takes into account the effective operational behaviour of the RP (including the middleware, OS and communication protocol). It is thus possible to observe for instance the impact of ISR executions on the scheduling of the tasks. It is also a good framework to play the "what-if?" game in order to tune the OA. On the other hand, we are studying the use of an extension of Time Petri Nets (TPN) to real-time scheduling (SETPN from (Roux and Déplanche, 2002)). These two approaches are supplementary.

The second approach (operator × on fig. 1) aims at defining algorithms and tools to generate a "valid by construction" OA ("valid" in reference to timeliness). Similar works are being presently driven in the "model integrated computing" community (Kodase et al., 2003). We target RP using fixed priority task scheduling and CAN protocol (ISO, 2003). To achieve our goal, we have identified several intermediate steps. In a first time, end-to-end control flows (transactions) are extracted from the FA. They give a precedence relationship between user-defined functions. In a second time, a task set is composed by grouping the user-defined functions (using some heuristics) of a transaction. This task set is the input of a tool that tries to find an allocation of tasks to processing nodes and priorities to tasks and messages, so that the resulting OA meets all the end-to-end timing constraints (the tool combines constraint programming and schedulability analysis (Cambazard et al., 2004)). For

[3]OSEK/VDX is a set of specifications for a real-time runtime platform dedicated to in-vehicle embedded systems. Homepage: `http://www.osek-vdx.org`.

more complex properties, it is possible to use (for instance) SETPN analysis.

The logical follow-up of the works exposed above concerns code synthesis: given a set of files containing the source code of user-defined functions and the description of a valid OA, synthesise the code of the tasks, as well as the configuration files for the RTOS and communication protocols. A tool has also to be developed to ensure the compliance between the code of the user-defined functions and their model (used for the design of the OA). Presently, these problems are not explored within REACT.

In the next sections, we illustrate the process exposed here, from the first design of the FA to its validation.

## 3. CLARA: the ADL

According to (Medvidovic and Taylor, 2000), an ADL is a language that provides features for modeling a software system's conceptual architecture. Classically, its building blocks are *components*, *connectors* and *configurations*. Within the context of REACT, we have defined an ADL, CLARA, to describe the functional architecture of reactive systems (Durand, 1998). CLARA stands for "Configuration LAnguage for Real-time Applications".

While defining CLARA, we paid a special attention to the description of the control flows. Compared to other ADLs, it allows to express complex synchronisation and activation laws. It provides also some support for the description of the behaviour of the components and for the expression of real-time requirements (timing constraints) and properties (time budgets).

We illustrate[4] the concepts and abstractions of CLARA through the design of the FA of a small reactive embedded system (see shaded frames). The parts of the text related to this design are embedded within coloured panels. Moreover, to facilitate the global understanding, we give on fig. 2 its final functional architecture.

### 3.1 The components

Five component families are proposed: activity, occurrence generator, shared resource, shared variable and system. Within each of the four first families, the architect must define at first a set of types that will be used (through instantiation) in the description.

[4] CLARA has both a textual and a graphical syntax. In this paper, we use mainly the graphical one.

**Terms of the problem:** We consider a simple feedback control loop: two sensors measure the value of the controlled variable (its value is not spatially homogeneous) and an actuator sets the manipulated variable to the computed value. Moreover, the state of the controlled process has to be displayed to an operator (HMI).
The control loop must be triggered every $10ms$, with an end-to-end deadline equal to the period (stringent constraint). The HMI must be updated every $20ms$, with a deadline equal to the period (soft constraint: a period on two can be missed).

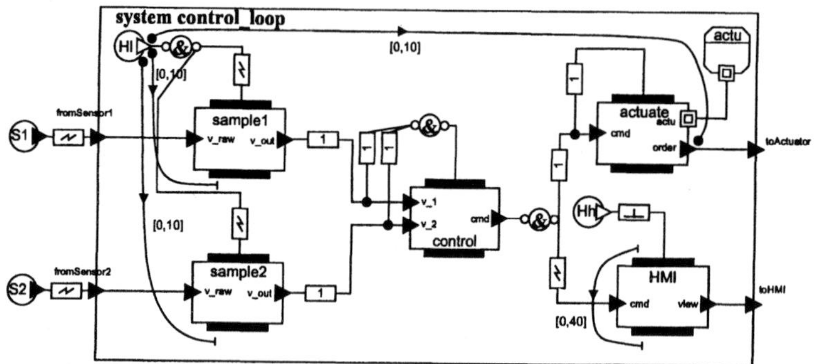


*Figure 2.* Description of the control loop in CLARA

The *activity* family denotes active components. It can be either *atomic* or *composed* (in our example, we only use atomic activities). For short, atomic activities are the basic building blocks of the architecture and composed activities introduce abstraction levels through hierarchy and encapsulation.

An activity has two interfaces: control and interaction. The *control interface* has only two ports: *start* (input port) and *end* (output port). *start* is used to attach an activation law; *end* is used to signal the end of the execution. From a behavioural point of view, they control the transition from "not operational" to "operational" state [5]. The *interaction interface* is a user-defined set of directed exchange ports (to transfer data or signals) and a set of access ports (to access shared resources or variables). The graphical representation of an activity is given figure 3: cmd and order are data exchange ports, actu is a resource access port.

When it becomes operational, an (atomic) activity executes a finite sequence (fig. 4). The actions can be user functions for which an execution time budget [6] has to be given (a closed interval that will be used for

[5]The execution of an activity instance is not reentrant.

[6]If it is planned to use an heterogeneous runtime platform, budgets are couples (function, processor).

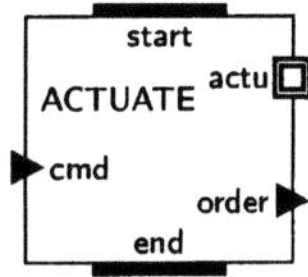


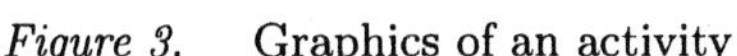

*Figure 3.* Graphics of an activity

```
name ACTUATE;
sequence {
read(cmd);
access(actu.get);
call(translate_command,0.5,1);
access(actu.release);
write(order);
}
```

*Figure 4.* Behaviour of an activity

verification purpose[7]). To ensure consistency between the model and the implementation, the budget becomes a requirement (i.e. the "Best Case Execution Time" and the "Worst Case Execution Time" of the function must be within the interval). Other actions are invocations of interaction services (eg. *read(cmd)* or *access(actu.get)*). The invocation of the control services (on port *start* and *end*) are implicit.

All control and interaction service invocations are synchronous. They can be blocking, depending on the behaviour of the connector attached to the port (see below). This enforces the designer to give a complete specification of the application control flows.

**Specification of the activities:** The FA contains 5 (atomic) activity (see fig. 2):

- sample1 and sample2 (two instances of the same type) read the controlled variable value on v_raw, translate it into a computation-friendly format and write the result on v_out;
- control computes the command from two values (read on v_1 and v_2) and writes the result on cmd;
- actuate controls the actuator. It reads the command on cmd, translates it into an actuator-friendly format and writes the result on order;
- HMI produces (a part of) a synoptic of the controlled process and sends it to an external display equipment. It reads the newly computed command on cmd and writes the new view on view.

The *occurrence generator* (OG) family denotes data or signal sources, which can be part of the system or its environment. Their interface is made of a single output signal or data port (signal ports are white triangles, data ports are black ones). The associated graphics is a circle containing the name of the instance and an output port. An OG can be periodic or sporadic. A periodic OG can only produce signals. Its behaviour is defined through its *period* attribute (cycle time). A sporadic OG can produce signals or data. Its behaviour is given as a sequence

[7]Closed intervals implicitly forbid the use of blocking calls in user functions.

of dates (resp. a sequence of couples (date, value)) that denotes the absolute signal production dates (resp. the absolute data production dates and the data values).

**Specification of the OG:** The control loop has a period of 10ms: it is measured by a periodic OG *Hl*. The HMI has a period of 40ms: the periods being different, we will use another periodic OG (*Hh*).
Furthermore, there are two sporadic data sources in the environment (one for each sensor) modelled by *S1* and *S2*. We don't define their behaviour and we don't need it (for much of the analysis work to perform) because the control flows of the control loop are not synchronised with the production dates of these OG.

The *shared resources* and *shared variables* denote "passive" entities. Their interface is composed of a single access port (containing subports *get* and *release* for resources and *read* and *write* for variables). The graphics are an oval for a resource and an octagon for a variable, decorated with the instance name and the access port. The access policy is an attribute. The set of predefined values contains mutual exclusion, write exclusive / read many, etc.

**Specification of the shared resources:** We use a shared resource to control the access to the actuator (access policy: mutex; name: actu). Although it is not shared by several activities, it is included: (i) to illustrate the concept of shared resource in CLARA, (ii) to reference its name in the description of the behaviour of actuate, (iii) to anticipate further extensions of the architecture (for instance adding an activity that uses the same actuator).

The last component family is the *system* family, used to define the boundaries and the interface of the control system under design. Each architecture contains exactly one system component. In fig. 2, the system is named *system_control_loop*.

## 3.2 The links

In CLARA, a *link*[8] is used to connect a set of output ports to a set of input ports. Beyond to specify which components interact, it states the interaction policies that are used in terms of control flow between the "producers" and the "consumers". A link is built from a set of basic building blocks that allow the specification of very simple as well

[8] In the literature, "connector" is used rather than "link" . However, as "connector" denotes a specific CLARA object, we use "link".

as very complex policies [9]. These blocks are: protocols, connectors and operators (not used in this paper).

A *protocol* has a producer hook and a consumer hook. Each one is associated to a service (production or consumption) and is attached to one (and only one) connector (see below). A protocol synchronises its producers with its consumers according to a specific policy. At the present time, a set of pre-defined protocols is proposed: rendez-vous, transient, blackboard, blackboard with consumption and mailbox. Graphically, it is a small rectangle with a specific symbol inside. The example uses: mailbox (symbol: a number that is the size of the box), blackboard (symbol: a lightning) and transient (symbol: a peak in the middle of a flat line).

A *connector* connects ports to protocol hooks. A simple connector is just a wire (concerning both graphics and behaviour). For more complex connexions, complex connectors have been defined:

- conjunctive connectors (a circled &) for "1 port to n hooks": production (resp. consumption) requests are broadcasted to all protocols; a single acknowledgement is delivered to the caller when all protocols have acknowledged.
- selective connectors (a circled vertical dash) for "n ports to 1 hook": each production (resp. consumption) request is delivered to the protocol and the acknowledgement is sent to the original caller (concurrent requests are serialised).
- hybrid connector, which is (graphics and behaviour) the "merging" of a conjunctive connector and a selective connector.

## 3.3 The configurations

In the ADL ontology, a configuration is a bipartite graph of components and connectors that describes (a part of) the architecture of the system. The system of fig. 2 is a configuration. As CLARA targets real-time reactive systems, it supports the expression of real-time constraints at the configuration level. More configuration-level facilities might be offered in the future, depending on the needs detected during the on-going case-studies.

A real-time constraint is expressed on events that are observable at the architecture level: production or access request and acknowledgement. A constraint can be:

[9]There is a list of link patterns that are forbidden because they lead to structural deadlocks.

**Specification of the links:** At first, we specify the data exchange links.

- from sample_1.v_out to control.v_1 (simple link): we use a 1-mailbox protocol: every produced value must be consumed before the delivery of the next one. We do the same with sample_2.
- from control.cmd to actuate.cmd and HMI.cmd (complex link, conjunctive connector on producer side): on the one hand, actuate must consume every command (before the production of the next one) so we use a 1-mailbox protocol; on the other hand, HMI reads the value "when it wants" and is allowed to loose some occurrences so we use a blackboard protocol.

Then we specify the activation laws.

- Hl output signal activates sample_1 and sample_2 (complex link, conjunctive connector on producer side): a blackboard is used and a timing constraint will require that every occurrence is consumed; control is activated each time there are new values on v_1 and v_2 (complex link, conjunctive connector on consumer side); actuate is activated each time there is a new value on cmd (simple link).
- Hh output signal activates HMI (simple link): a transient protocol (without memory) is used. Thus, some occurrences can be lost (HMI must be waiting for the signal to catch it). A timing constraint will require that two consecutive occurrences are not lost.

At last, we specify that the system asynchronously reads the values produced by S1 and S2, using blackboard protocols.

- absolute: the first occurrence of an event must occur in [dmin, dmax] where dmin and dmax are dates;
- relative: the delay between two consecutive occurrences of an event must me in [dmin,dmax] where dmin and dmax are delay;
- causal: the delay between the $i^{th}$ occurrence of a source event and the $i^{th}$ occurrence of a target event must be in [dmin, dmax] where dmin and dmax are delay.

The graphic is a curved line between the involved ports. At the extremities of the line, a bullet denotes a req (request) event, a dash denotes a ack (acknowledgement) event. The interval labels the line. For causality constraint, an arrow indicates the direction. This notation is sufficient for end-to-end deadlines and simple real-time constraints and can be used by non specialists. However, it lacks the expressiveness of TCTL, the possibility to express probabilistic QoS requirements, ...

## 4. Validation of the functional architecture

An architecture provides with a comprehensive description of the system. This description must be validated before to engage the next design

**Expression of the timing constraints:** There are three constraints:

- the control loop execution must complete at most $10ms$ after its last activation (stringent constraint). This is a causality constraint between Hl.out.req and actuate.order.req;
- to avoid the lost of occurrences of the control loop clock, the execution of sample1 and sample2 must complete at most 10ms after the clock period: two causality constraints between Hl.out.req and sample1.end.cnf and between Hl.out.req and sample2.end.cnf;
- the HMI activity must not lost two consecutive occurrences of Hh.out. We translate this constraint as a deadline on its execution: once operational, it must finish before $40ms$ (twice the period of Hh). A deadline is a causality constraint between start.cnf and end.cnf.

step. For critical system, the use of formal methods in the validation process is mandatory. These methods can be used only if (a subset of) the ADL has a formal semantics. Moreover, it makes sense only if a rigorous approach is followed for the continuation of the design process, to ensure that the successive refinement steps (up to the binary code) preserve the properties stated at the upper level. The operational semantics of CLARA is given by means of (time) Petri nets (TPN). We will first introduce (informally) this semantics and expose how a CLARA architecture is translated into a TPN model. Then, we will show some analysis possibilities on our example. For PN, useful definitions and theory can be found in (Murata, 1989). For TPN, see (Berthomieu and Diaz, 1991).

## 4.1 TPN model of a CLARA architecture

The translation from a CLARA description to a TPN is done in two steps. At first, every entity (activities, shared variables, protocols, connectors, etc.) is associated to a TPN pattern. If the behaviour of the entity is predefined or defined through simple parameters (e.g. shared resources), a predefined pattern is used. For more complex entities (activities and aperiodic occurrence generators), a pattern is generated from the textual behaviour description. Then, a global TPN is built by merging the elementary patterns, according to the composition rules specified in the CLARA description. A prototype tool has been designed that performs the translation (the TPN follows the input format of ROMEO[10]).

[10]ROMEO: `http://www.irccyn.ec-nantes.fr/d/en/equipes/TempsReel/logs/software-2-romeo`

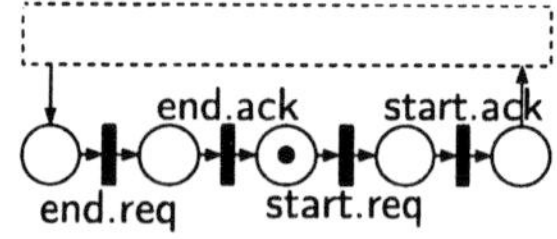


*Figure 5.* Control interface

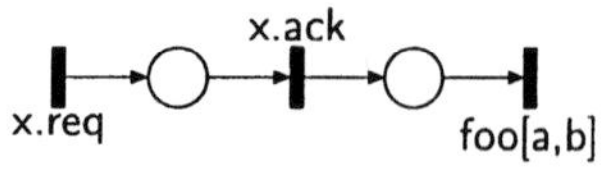

*Figure 6.* **read**(x); **call**(foo,a,b)

Fig. 5 shows the TPN pattern associated to an activity. The visible transitions model the (implicit) interaction on the start and end ports. The dashed box is to be replaced by a pattern corresponding to the activity behaviour (see fig. 6): an interaction on port x gives rise to a pair of transitions (x.req: interaction request and x.ack: interaction acknowledgement); the invocation of the user-defined function foo gives rise to a single timed transition foo[a,b] where [a,b] is the time budget allocated to the function foo.

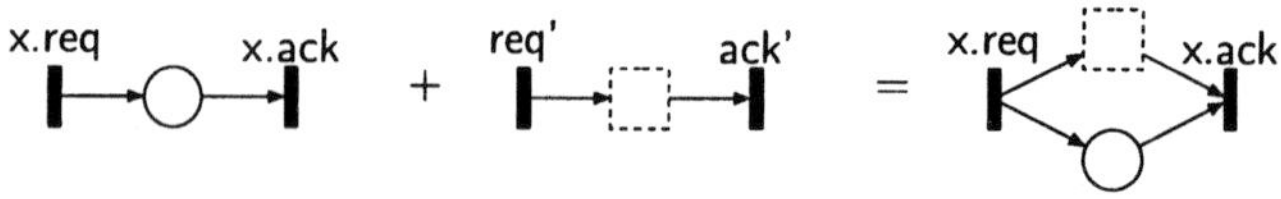

*Figure 7.* Connection of a port to a link

Fig. 7 illustrates the merging step. The x.req and x.ack transitions are respectively merged with transition req' and ack' of the connector attached to port x. The same mechanism is used to make the connections between all the entities.

The TPN corresponding to our example has 91 places and 71 transitions. This is obviously "big". This is a consequence of the "naïve" translation performed by the tool. Indeed, most of the places and transitions are withdrawn by the usual static reduction rules (Murata, 1989) applied before analysis (presently, the reduction is handmade).

## 4.2 Validation of the candidate design

At this design level, the validation concerns some functional properties and the consistency between the timing constraints and the allocated time budgets. To achieve these goals, we use presently the tools ROMEO, CADP[11] and TINA[12]. ROMEO computes (among other things) the marking graph of a PN. TINA computes (among other things) its structural properties. CADP allows to perform a wide set

[11]CADP: http://www.inrialpes.fr/vasy/cadp/

[12]TINA: http://www.laas.fr/tina/

of analysis on labelled transition systems (ROMEO and TINA can output the marking graph of a PN in CADP format).

At first, the timing informations are discarded and we consider the classical PN theory. The goal is to state properties on the FA that will be verified by any further correct refinement (a system the behaviour of which is simulated by our PN for the events that are observable at the FA level). This "weak" equivalence relation limits us to the analysis of safety properties. As an example, we will use deadlock freedom analysis.

Then, the usual reduction rules are applied onto the PN. It does not only reduce the size of the model but also produces a bounded PN (clock modeling produces unbounded marking when the time is not taken into account). Notice that this transformation preserves: liveness, safeness and boundedness (for the places still present in the reduced model). Concerning our example, the reduced PN has only 42 places and 25 transitions. Its marking graph has 26,124 states and 136,204 transitions. There is no deadlock state. Some more complex properties might be verified using CADP model-checking facilities (e.g. "for each pair of input value, there is exactly one actuation"). They can be carried along the design process as long as they can be expressed as safety properties.

We will now use the structural analysis of the PN, performed by TINA. We expect our system to have two periodic end-to-end transactions: control loop and HMI update. To validate this assumption, we look after the T-semi-flow generating sets (a positive T-semi-flow denotes a cyclic behaviour of the system). Five positive T-semi-flow generating sets exist. All of them are feasible (i.e. there exists at least one run from the initial state whose firing vector corresponds). Three of them are artefacts of the model; The two others correspond respectively to the cyclic execution of the control-loop transaction and the HMI transaction. If we let aside the artefacts,the description corresponds to our expectations. The artefacts are caused by the modelling of periodic occurrence generators: as we do not take time into account, the "y.expire" transitions (corresponding to the clock expiration) can be fired from any marking. If we try to remove the artefacts by controlling the transitions, we reduce the set of possible implementations (the behaviour of which will be simulated by the model): we would make the strong hypothesis that some part of the transaction is always executed within one period of the occurrence generator. Such a reduction of the design space is obviously not desirable at the FA level since it could potentially exclude all the valid solutions.

Let's consider the consistency between the timing constraints and the time budgets. It is clear that -at this level- it is not possible to assess the timing correctness: it cannot be done without taking into account the operational characteristics (mapping of functions to tasks, of tasks

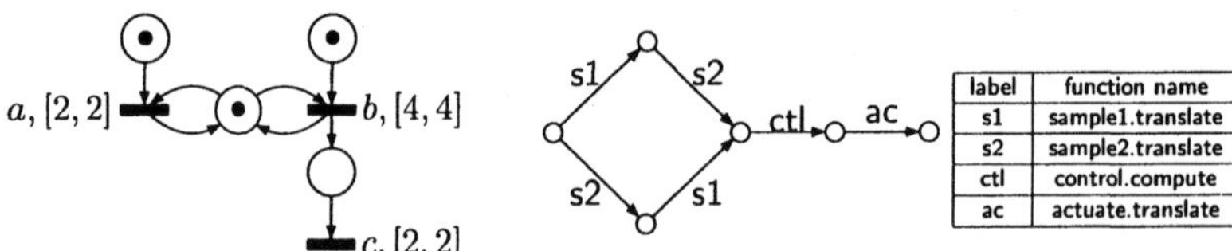


| label | function name |
|---|---|
| s1 | sample1.translate |
| s2 | sample2.translate |
| ctl | control.compute |
| ac | actuate.translate |

*Figure 8.* *Figure 9.*

to nodes, scheduling policies and parameters, etc.). However, a first analysis can be driven to check that there may be an implementation, with these time budgets, that could meet the constraints (*i.e.* we check a necessary condition). We have to find a "best case" for the execution time of the sequence (of transitions) bounded by $e_s$ (the "starting" event of the constraint) and $e_c$ (the "closing" event). "Best" means that every possible implementation will produce highest or equal execution times.

First, notice that the study of the state class graph of the TPN doesn't give us a best case from an operational point of view. To get convinced, consider a system with two concurrent tasks $T_1$ and $T_2$. $T_1$ executes the action $a$ and completes. $T_2$ executes $b$ then $c$ and completes. Actions $a$ and $b$ need a shared resource and are mutually exclusive. The TPN of fig. 8 is a model of this system (where one can see the execution time of each action). If the deadline of $T_1$ is 10 and the deadline of $T_2$ is 7, the analysis will show that $T_1$ always meets its deadline whereas $T_2$ always misses its deadline. Nevertheless, this system is schedulable, e.g. with a fixed priority scheduler and $prio(T_2) > prio(T_1)$.

Let's go back to our consistency checking. Because we don't know the operational characteristics of the system, the only information that we can take into account is the precedence relation between the executions of the user-defined functions of a same transaction and their execution time budgets. Thus, we must extract the graph of the precedence relation from the PN marking graph. Then, the edges corresponding to the invocation of user-defined functions (involved in the constrained transaction) are weighted with the upper bounds of the function time budgets. If no information is known about the RP, we have to compute the value of the longest path in the graph (to take into account an optimistic true parallelism). In case of a mono-processor RP (we consider this hypothesis for our example), we just have to sum up the weights (the execution sequence is a sequential chain) and compare the result to the upper bound of the constraint. Any implementation for which the computation times actually reach the upper bounds of the execution time budget will inevitably executes this sequence of functions with a *higher or equal* execution time (in the implementation, the execution will be delayed at least by the overhead of the RTOS services, and may be by the network and/or the execution of some transactions of higher priority). Thus, timing consistency between constraints and budgets occurs *when the value of the path is less or equal than the upper bound of the constraint.*

For our example, the work is trivial for three of the constraints (they involve only one atomic activity and thus no concurrency). For the fourth one (between, HI.out.req and actuate.order.ack), the problem is a bit more complex. Even if it can be done "by hand", we illustrate how to use tools to automate the work.

First, we know that the control loop transaction is cyclic and has no transitional mode. Thus, we can limit our study to the paths in the marking graph that correspond to the first instance of the transaction (any further instance will exactly have the same set of runs). At first, we hide all the labels that are not useful (i.e. not corresponding to $e_s$, $e_c$ or any function of the transaction where $e_s$ is the source event and $e_c$ the closing event of the constrained sequence). Then, we extract the paths that match $i^*.e_s.(\sim e_s \& \sim e_c)^*.e_c$ (a path starting with a sequence of silent actions, then $e_s$, then any action that is not $e_s$ and not $e_c$, then $e_c$) using CADP. We forbid the paths containing more than one occurrence of $e_s$ in order to eliminate the interference of some other instance of the transaction. From this set of paths, we obtain the labelled transition system (LTS) shown on fig. 9. The length of the chain is 6 ms and the upper constraint is 10 ms. We conclude that the solution space may contain some valid implementations.

We now have a candidate FA, together with a set of extra-functional characteristics, that have been validated. We have shown that it will not deadlock and that the values of the extra-functional properties seem to be consistent.

As stated in section 2, the next step is to map the candidate FA onto the RP, so as to obtain a candidate OA. This candidate OA has to be validated too, especially with regards to extra-functional properties that can be assessed only at this level. However, due to space limitation, we will not detail this stage in this paper.

## 5. Conclusion

In this paper, we have described the goals of the REACT project. We have exposed (i) the process that it adopts for the architectural design of real-time systems; (ii) its ADL CLARA; (iii) the validation of CLARA architectures through formal analysis techniques.

In ( Faucou et al., 2004) (extended version of this paper), a comparison is done between CLARA and some related projects (all of them being discussed in other papers included in this volume): MetaH/AADL ( Binns and Vestal, 2001), COTRE (Farines et al., 2003) and EAST ( Debruyne et al., 2004). Although the development of REACT is certainly less ahead than these projects, we have highlighted some of its specificities. Hence, the link mechanism of CLARA allows to easily describe complex multi-components synchronisation patterns and enforces the designer to specify and validate the control flows at the architecture level (obviously a good practice for real-time system design) . Moreover, compared to MetaH/AADL or Cotre, REACT can be used at a higher design level (FA rather than SA). This allows us to investigate the synthesis of "valid by construction" operational architecture and to propose in the future a coherent and automated toolset for the rigorous design of real-time systems.

## References

ARTIST (2003). Component-based Design and Integration Platforms. Technical Report W1.A2.N1.Y1, ARTIST - Advanced Real-Time Systems - IST project.

Berthomieu, B. and Diaz, M. (1991). Modeling and verifications of time dependent systems using time Petri nets. *IEEE TSE*, 17(3).

Binns, P. and Vestal, S. (2001). Formalizing software architectures for embedded systems. In *EMSOFT 2001*, volume 2211 of *LNCS*. Springer.

Cambazard, H. et al. (2004). Decomposition and learning for a hard real-time task allocating problem. In *CORS/INFORMS Joint International Meeting.*

Debruyne, V. et al. (2004). EAST-ADL, an Architecture Description Language, Validation and Verification Aspects. In *IFIP 2004 WADL.*

Durand, E. (1998). *Description et vérification d'architectures d'application temps réel: CLARA et les réseaux de Petri temporels.* PhD thesis, École Centrale de Nantes.

Farines, J. et al. (2003). The COTRE project: rigorous software development for real-time systems in avionics. In *27th IFAC/IFIP/IEEE WRTP'03.*

Faucou, S. (2002). *Description et construction d'architectures opérationnelles validées temporellement.* PhD thesis, Université de Nantes.

Faucou, S. et al. (2004). REACT: an ADL centric approach for the rigorous design of real-time embedded systems. Technical report, IRCCyN. (to be published).

ISO (2003). *ISO 11898 : Road Vehicles - Controller area network (CAN).* ISO.

Kodase, S. et al. (2003). Transforming Structural Model to Runtime Model of Embedded Software with Real-time Constraints. In *DATE'03 Designer's Forum.*

Medvidovic, N. and Taylor, R. (2000). A Classification and Comparison Framework for Software Architecture Description Languages. *IEEE TSE*, 26(1).

Murata, T. (1989). Petri Nets: Properties, Analysis and Applications. *Proc. of the IEEE*, 77(1).

Roux, O. and Déplanche, A. (2002). A T-time Petri net extension for real-time task scheduling modeling. *European Journal of Automation (APII-JESA)*, 36(7).

# SESSION 2: SPECIFICATION AND DESIGN

# SAFARCHIE STUDIO: ArgoUML EXTENSIONS TO BUILD SAFE ARCHITECTURES

Olivier Barais - Laurence Duchien
*Université des Sciences et Technologies de Lille*
*Laboratoire LIFL (UMR 8022), Projet INRIA-FUTURS JACQUARD*
*Fr 59655 Villeneuve d'Ascq Cedex*
{barais,duchien}@lifl.fr

**Abstract** Nowadays, no standard and universal definition of software architecture was accepted by all the community. Various points of view on different studies bring to several approaches. These approaches focus on only one or two concerns such as component interfaces specification, behavioral analysis or software reconfiguration. This paper argues that, in order to accrue the true benefits of software architecture approaches, one may need to use an architecture centric approach with a global reasoning: From software architecture design to software architecture management to software architecture building, deployment and refinement. However, these different concerns of a software architecture definition must be in consistency. For this reason, we based our approach on architecture types that are points of reference at each step of our reasoning. We offer with SafArchie Studio, a first architecture centric approach based on three-view perspective and driven by the component life cycle.

**Keywords:** Software Architecture, Tools

## 1. Introduction

Nowadays, industrial component platforms such as CCM[22], EJB[11] give first means for assembling and deploying components on distributed environments. Academic approaches with ArchJava[2] or Fractal[7] provide more structural elements as composite or connector for precisely defining an abstract architecture and transforming it on deployed and running code. However, facing the difficulties to define correct and safety software architectures, more abstract software architecture models were proposed. They are commonly gathered under the label of ADL for Architecture Description Languages. They come with powerful methods and tools of specification and analysis for high-level designs.

In other hand, since several years, software engineering community promotes model based engineering. New industrial components platforms should allow programmers to easily create distributed software by a composition of components[13] [26]. Nevertheless the re-usability implied by this view seems to be skewed. Platforms are in constant improvement and the re-usability is actually impossible. Therefore, the software engineering community should abstract essential concepts from the platforms. The OMG (Object Management Group) tries to resolve this new challenge by MDA (Model Driven Architecture) [25] approach. In this context, architecture languages become one of building steps mainstays. They define models and tools to build platforms independent, reusable, safe software architecture.

We propose SafArchie, an architecture centric approach for helping architects, designer and developers in the composition of components at each step of the life cycle of applications. Built from a set of models for putting in evidence some properties according to the component life cycle, SafArchie Studio assists the software architecture specification. We based our tool tool on architecture types that we instantiate and deploy on abstract platform. SafArchie integrates results from component frameworks and models based engineering in a powerful ergonomic tool. This tool aims to increase software architecture reasoning in front of component based design and programming on platforms such as CCM, ArchJava, or Fractal.

This paper follows the reasoning about building new software architecture. The first section is an overview of SafArchie approach. It defines the three-view perspective approach leaded by component life cycle. In the second section, we present the design perspective based on architecture types. We propose a reasoning on this design and a new ArgoUML[27] diagram to create this specification. Section 4 defines the deployment perspective, the first physical abstraction model and the mapping to it. The end of section 4 specifies the execution perspective. Some next steps of this work and next features of the SafArchie studio are defined. The section 5 presents related works on software architecture from which we build SafArchie Studio. Finally, the last section gives a conclusion of this work.

## 2. Overview of SafArchie approach

### 2.1 A three-view perspective approach

Software architecture defines component instances, their interfaces, their structures, their interactions and the mappings to hardware systems. It represents a static view at a given moment. However, at the run-time, this architecture will be dynamic[4]. For example, component instances and bindings can appear and disappear. In ubiquitous computing domain, run-time environment can also change in accordance with the context.

Defining architecture should consider all facets of the application life. Component approaches provide lots of information in relation with the component life cycle and this information should clarify the architecture. SafArchie works on three-view perspectives depending on the component life cycle: Design perspective, deployment perspective, and run-time perspective. For each perspective, we define a meta-model for clarifying its concepts.

The *design perspective* defines *architecture type* by a set of constraints respected by an architecture. These constraints represent invariants for software architecture such as component interfaces, relations and interactions between components, but also component structure and behavior specifications. From this architecture type, we check the structural and behavioral conformities between components constraints. Therefore *Design perspective* defines consistent architecture types. By this way, architect guarantees architecture consistency.

The second perspective, called *deployment perspective*, ensures an initial position for a logical architecture on top of a physical architecture. For this perspective we need three models. The first one, the instance model (called *logical architecture*) is a graph of connected component instances. The second one, the *physical architecture*, consists of an abstract representation of physical platforms. Finally the last one specifies the mapping of a logical architecture to an abstract physical architecture.

Finally the last perspective, *run-time perspective*, consists of a supervision of software architecture. This work still in progress builds framework to follow the evolution of a software architecture at run-time.

SafArchie Studio is an extension of ArgoUML tool. We maintain the consistency among the models thanks to a common abstract component model that unifies the common definition and an architecture type model that helps in conformity check at each step of life cycle. We present this component model in the next sub-section.

## 2.2 SafArchie common abstract component model

Our representation of a component and of relations between components is closely related to ArchJava component model [1]. A component is a grey box defined by its structure and its interfaces. Components can be composed and must be as generic as possible for easily reusing in different contexts. They communicate through ports by provided or required operations. A component is defined by two parts. Firstly, the communication part represents the component interfaces defined by a set of ports. Secondly, the internal part corresponds to the component implementation. In the internal part, only public *attributes* are visible, the component implementation component is hidden. A component can only communicate with its environment through explicitly declared ports.

A *port* is an access point on the component. It represents a logical communication way. Each port defines two sets of operations, *provided* or *required* operations.

An *operation* represents an action of a component. A provided operation can be invoked by a client component. Conversely, the required operations can be processed by a server component. They make explicit dependencies. These dependencies are resolved at the composition time. Operations are defined like methods in Object Oriented Programming (OOP) with a signature with name, parameters, result, and exceptions. An operation can be released by a remote procedure call or a sent message.

Finally, as in ArchJava or Fractal component models, our component model is hierarchical. A component can be a *composite* or a primitive. A composite contains delegation ports, component children and *bindings* between these component children. The ports of a composite are only delegated, i.e. they reference a component child port. The composite reifies the software architecture configuration.

# 3. Modelling software architecture types

In architecture definition, first steps of architect abstract global structures of the future application by the definition of component assemblies. First, we define concept of architecture type for helping architect in its first design steps. Second, we clarify this architecture by structural and behavioral contracts. Therefore, checking contracts makes architecture safe. Finally, we integrate our approach in ArgoUML.

## 3.1 Type of architecture definition

As in type definition in programming language, an *architecture type* defines a set of possible values that must be respected by software architectures. Defined constraints deal with component interfaces and identify relations and interactions between these component interfaces. Therefore, an architecture type represents a static view of a software architecture. It also clarifies component structure or behavior specification. From these architecture types, we will check the structural and behavioral compatibilities between components by set of identified invariants.

An architecture type is composed of six main elements: Component type, composite type, bindings, port type, operation, and attribute (see Figure 1).

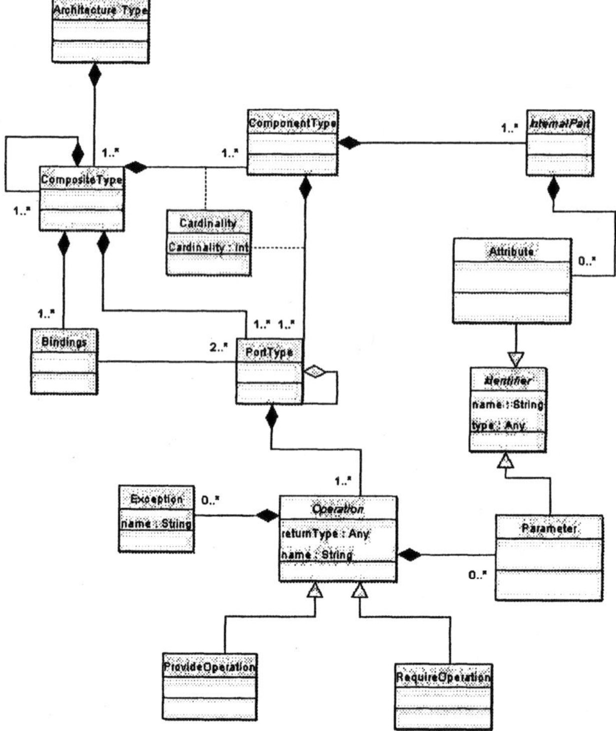


*Figure 1.* Architecture type meta-model

Designing a *port type* consists of identification of a set of operations that the port should provide or require (see Figure 1). A port type corresponds to a set of operation signatures and their gathering together is guided by the application design. *Component type* defines all port types of the component and the minimum and maximum cardinalities for each one (see Figure 1).

*Composite type* also identifies all the component types that it should contain and the minimum and maximum cardinalities for each one (see Figure 1). It defines the interactions between these component types through the *binding* concept. Then, a binding identifies a possible interaction between two port types belonging to component types.

By this way, software architecture type is a set of structured constraints in terms of composite type, component type, and port type. Each typed software architecture should respect these constraints.

**Example** We illustrate our type model with an example describing the architecture type of a replicated calculator. This architecture type has two primitive component types bound into one composite type (see Figure 2). The component type **A** provides one service of calculator through a port type **P**. Each instance of **A** could have only one port **P**. The specification defines the cardinality between the component type **A** and the Port **P**.

The component type **B** is a proxy. It receives some requests and chooses the provider for the service. It has two port types: **(P,Q)**: the first to communicate with the client, the second to interact with the service provider.

Finally, the composite type **C** has one binding and one delegated port type . The composite environment communicates with component type **B** through this latter. The binding models the communication capabilities between **A** and **B**. The composite could have several instances of **A** but only one instance of **B**.

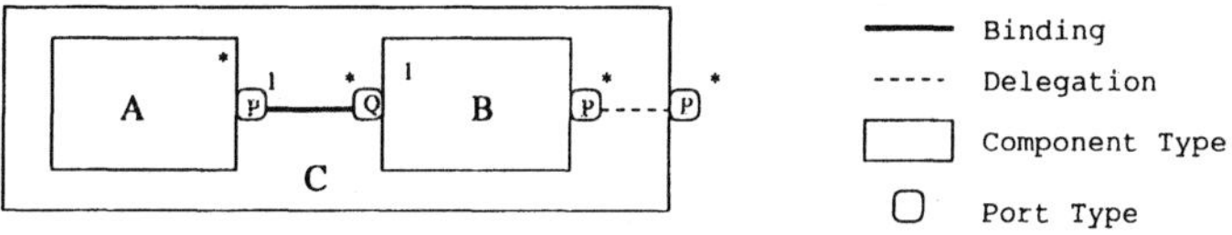


*Figure 2.* Architecture type example

## 3.2 Design software architecture by contracts

All the constraints defined by the composite type, the component type and the port type are structural and architectural. With this framework we will assist the components composition. For example, from an architecture type, we could decide the binding of two port types if all the operations provided by the first port type are required by the other and vice-versa. However this type checking often used in Object Oriented Programming has already shown its limits [15]. The compatibility between two operation prototypes could not guarantee their correct use. That is why, in SafArchie, we add a visible part of a black box component in order to simplify the components integration.

```
            provide Boolean withdraw(String clientID, Integer price)
            Context Bank::Auth::withdraw(clientID:String,
price:Integer):Boolean
            pre:  price > 5
            post:  self.accountValue > 0
```

*Figure 3.* Pre and post condition example

These specification enrichments are commonly used in *Design by Contract* software development techniques. They ensure high-quality software architecture. They guarantee every component of a system lives up to its expectations [20]. In SafArchie architecture type meta-model, we identify two contracts. The first contract is a set of constraints on the operation, called *assertion contracts.* It adds *pre* and *post* conditions in an operation to guarantee its correct using context. The second contract, called *behavioral contracts*, specifies the external behavior of a component type.

### 3.2.1 Assertion contracts.

In some case, an operation could be invoked and processed only if its context is valid. The context of a component is described from attribute values, parameter values but also architectural constraints like the presence or the lack of a binding. An assertion is a boolean expression about the state of a software system. In a valid software system, all assertions evaluate to true.

Architect can define two classes of assertion. First, *preconditions* define the context that must hold before an operation can be invoked. They are evaluated just before an operation execution. Precondition involves component state and operation parameters. They specify obligations that a software client component must meet before invoking a particular operation of the component. Second, *postconditions* specify conditions that must hold after an operation completes. Consequently, postconditions must be true after the operation execution. Postconditions on a provided operation involve the old system state, the new system state, the operation parameters, and the operation's return value. Postconditions on a required operation involve only the operation's return value. They define the guarantees that a software component makes to its clients. If a postcondition is violated, the supplier component does not work correctly.

For example, in a provided operation *withdraw* of component type *Bank*, we can specify that the first parameter should be upper than 5. Therefore, if a client asks a debit lower than five, an exception will be risen. Architects can also define a postcondition to ensure that the *Bank* attribute, called *accountValue*, will be always positive (see Figure 3).

### 3.2.2 Behavioral contracts.

The structural description of an architecture type does not allow a complete efficient re-use. Indeed, the component integration requires a well understand-

```
    A = (p.?request → computation → p.!reply → A) + {p.?request,
p.!reply}.
    B = (p.?request → q.!request → q.?reply → p.!reply → B) +
{p.?request, p.!reply, q.!request, q.?reply}.
    ||C = (A || B) /{p/q}@{p}.
```

*Figure 4.* Behavioral specification example

ing of each component's role. The structural information are necessary but insufficient to improve software architecture understanding tasks. In this section, we define our architecture type extension that adds behavioral information on component types. These additional details are gathered in *behavioral contract.* It describes the messages scheduling of a component type with its environment.

The building of new formal languages to describe component external behavior is a specific part of software architecture research area. In SafArchie Studio, we integrate existing works. External component types behavior are specified with FSP language [18]. This language is already used in Darwin ADL[17]. It is well-adapted with hierarchical architecture model.

The external behavior of a component type is described in term of sequences of exchanged messages with its environment. The two kinds of interaction (Remote Procedure Call (RPC) and messages) are described by asynchronous messages. These messages can be sent or received by the component. Then, in a behavioral contract, one or two messages represents each operation.

A component type behavior is defined as finite state processes in FSP using action prefix "→", choice "|", and recursion. Let *?x* a received message and *!p* a sent message, $?x \rightarrow !p$ defines a process that initially waits the message x and then sends message *p*.

A composite type process is the parallel composition of their contained component behaviors. Communication is achieved through synchronization of shared actions. The FSP hiding operator @ captures the concept of delegated port in SafArchie. The behavior of every composite is computed from that of its subcomponents with reachability analysis. Messages that are not in one composite interface are hidden and the behavior is minimized with respect to observational equivalence[21].(see [19] and section 3.3 for more details).

Take the example of a replicated calculator described in section 1. The behavior of a component typed A is simple. When it receives a request, it computes the calculus and replies a result.

The behavior of a component typed B is a proxy behavior. When it receives a request, it forwards it to a component typed A and waits the reply to send it. The composition identifies a synchronization between the messages belonging to *accept* and the messages belonging to *forward* (see behavioral specification in Figure 4). The behavioral specification identifies the message with the name of its port (*P*, or *Q*) and the name of its operation (*accept*, *reply*). The composition result gives a simple external behavior of a composite typed C. It can receive a request and it can reply a result.

## 3.3 Towards a safe software architecture type

Each architecture type should be consistent in order to build safe software architecture. From three sources of information, which are architecture types, assertion contracts and behavioral contracts, we check the architecture type consistency.

**Structural reasoning about an architecture type**
From the architecture type, we link several checking mechanisms. The first step studies the architecture type without the contracts.

First, we check that software architecture type is being carried out in accordance with the software architecture type meta-model presented in Figure 1.

Second, we verify the assembly by checking the compatibility of two bound port types. Two port types are compatible if all the provided operations of one port type have a compatible required operation in the other port type. Moreover, the compatibility between operations consists in checking their signatures compatibility.

Finally we check the possible cardinality violation. Indeed each binding declared in a composite type specifies a possible link between two ports. The cardinality analysis compares the two couples of cardinality: *(component type child cardinality, port type cardinality).* A couple (1,1) could be safely bound only with a couple (1,1). All other bindings could create cardinality violation.

**Reasoning about assertion contracts**

The second step of analysis checks the assertion contracts defined in OCL (Object Constraint Language) [23] in an operation context (see example in section 3.2.1). First, we consider well-formed OCL expressions by verifying the syntax and the navigation expressions in accordance with the architecture type meta-model. For example, the post condition in Figure 3 will be valid if the component has an attribute named *accountValue* that can be compared to an integer value.

Second, OCL expression analyzer verifies compatibility between two operation assertion contracts belonging to two bound port types. Indeed assertion contracts can be viewed as subtype definition for parameters. OCL analyzer checks the covariance and contravariance respect for these sub-types. For example, in Figure 3, if the required operation defines a precondition with a withdraw lower than 4, the OCL expression is true on the first check step, but the second pass detects an incompatibility between these two assertion contracts.

**Reasoning about behavioral contracts**

Finally, we work on behavioral contracts. From an architecture type, there exists an infinity of valid software architectures instances. Therefore, we can not analyze all the possible behaviors. We only check the behavior consistency from only one software architecture behavior specification. This specification is defined from the architecture type with only one instantiation of each composite type, component type, and port type with its minimum cardinality. From each binding between two port types, we create a connection between two ports. We generate FSP specification relating to this generated software architecture behavior.

LTSA tool checks this specification [9] with Compositional Reachability Analysis (CRA). It performs an exhaustive search of the state space of the Label Transition System model. This LTS model corresponds to the behavior specification. More specifically, given the structural architecture of a system, and the behavioral contracts of the component types, the behavior of the system is computed for analysis in steps. The behavior of every composite type is computed from its sub-components FSP specification with reachability analysis. Actions without communication interface are hidden. The behavior is minimized with respect to *observational equivalence* [21].

Due to the automatic generation of only one behavioral specification, the behavioral analysis is incomplete. We could only conclude when the analysis detects a problem that the architecture type is invalid. However a non failure detection does not mean the behavioral safety of architecture type. New verifications should be done at the deployment perspective (see section 4). If a consistency mistake is detected during a checking step, architect can not define a logical model (see section 4.2) instance of this architecture type.

## 3.4 A new diagram in ArgoUML for building safe software architecture type

Building new plugin in ArgoUML [27] is easy and well-documented. Moreover ArgoUML environment is a free, well-known, multi-platforms software engineering tool. Finally ArgoUML add the concept of *design critics*[24] to assist the software designer. Therefore, we define our design perspective prototype of SafArchie Studio as a *plugin* in ArgoUML in accordance with our meta-model. This plugin provides graphical design of architecture types. By this way, architects have a global tree view of their architecture type. They can edit all their architecture type properties inside simple panels. They can load or save their architecture types through XML files defined with a public XML schema. SafArchie Studio type perspective checks architecture type consistency and creates a global report for an architecture type.

On the left side of the figure 5, a graphical tree represents the architecture type hierarchy. Architect uses it for browsing or editing an architecture type. For each element, contextual menu and drag and drop actions improve the tool ergonomy.

On the right side, the second frame provides a graphical tool to manipulate an architecture type. An architecture type is built from component types, composite types, port types and bindings between port types. We manage one graphical layer for each composite content. Only one layer can be edited at one moment. However we could have a reduced graphical view of the content of a composite type. The navigation between the graphical layers is automatic thanks to the

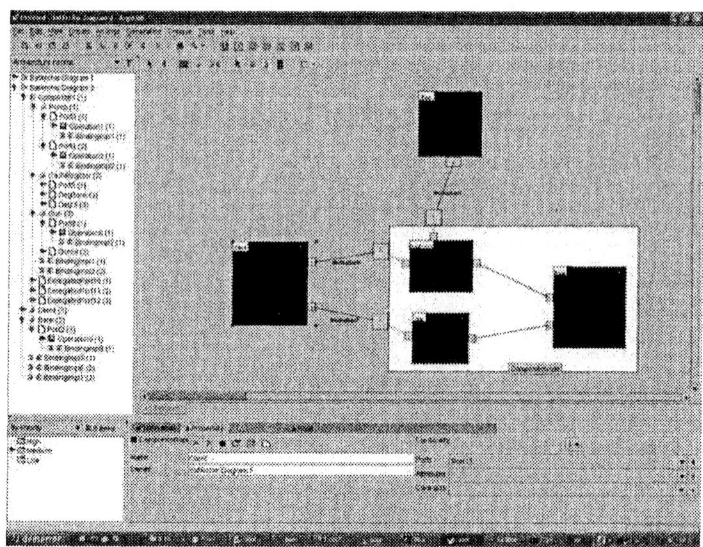

*Figure 5.* SafArchie Studio snapshot

graphical tree. When choosing an element in the tree, you immediately see its graphical layer.

The selection of an object in the tree panel or in the graphical panel activates the property panel (bottom right panel in Figure 5) of the target element. From it, architect can edit internal properties of each architecture type element.

The architecture type meta-model is described in UML (in Figure 1) but also with a XML schema. Architect can save an architecture type in a XML representation. XML schema corresponds to the grammar of the SafArchie Architecture Type Description Language.

An architect can automatically check an architecture type definition. SafArchie Studio checks the structure (described in section 3.3) but also assertion contracts validity and conformity (described in section 3.3) with two different tools. The first one, already used in ArgoUML, is an OCL library[14] for the checking of well-formed OCL navigation expression. We develop a facade pattern for our architecture type meta-model in order to use it. The second is an internal tool based on CIAO prolog[8]. It checks the covariance and contravariance principles between bound operations that are enriched with assertion contracts.

Finally, to verify the compatibility between behavioral contracts, SafArchie Studio generates global system behavior specification (as described in section 3.3), and starts the LTSA external model checker to verify the consistency of this specification.

# 4. Deployment of a typed software architecture on a distributed environment

In SafArchie, we decompose our approach in several points of view. In section 3, we presented the design perspective of our approach for building *architecture types*. They define a set of respected invariants in a design stage. In this section, a second perspective instantiates a typed software architecture and deploys it on a physical environment.

## 4.1 A three-step deployment step

An architecture type defines a set of possible values (i.e. infinity of possible architecture instances). An architecture instance is a connected graph of component instances through their ports. Each component instance and its relations should be conformed to its referenced architecture type. We call this instance model: *logical software architecture*.

Software architecture scope is larger than this model of interconnected component instances. This component based software architecture represents a static view of component instances deployed on a physical architecture at one moment. In SafArchie, the physical model is an abstract view of hosts configuration, hosts capacities and network topology. This abstract view of physical platforms called *Physical Architecture* is light. We only model distributed nodes, their interconnection and some information about their based software as middleware and network protocols. The last step of deployment perspective consists in mapping the logical software architecture on an abstract physical architecture.

## 4.2 Logical software architecture

Logical software architectures are represented by a graph of component instances connected through their ports. Each logical architecture instance must conform to its referenced architecture type. Therefore, ports, components, or composites are typed by an existing port type, component type, or composite type of architecture type. Besides, any relation between these elements should be declared in the architecture type. Finally all port connection must be defined in the binding description between these two port types.

**Example** Let's take the example described in section 1. A valid software architecture could be the following (see Figure 6). The replicated calculator has three replicas (a1, a2, a3). Each one is connected to a component Proxy (b1) through ports. Proxy can receive requests from the environment. It delegates the computation to a replica.

In SafArchie Studio, we add a second diagram for defining logical software architecture. As the first diagram, it is composed of four panels: A panel for global tree-view of software architecture, a panel for graphical software architecture building, a panel for adding critics on this specification and a set of property panels for each logical architecture element.

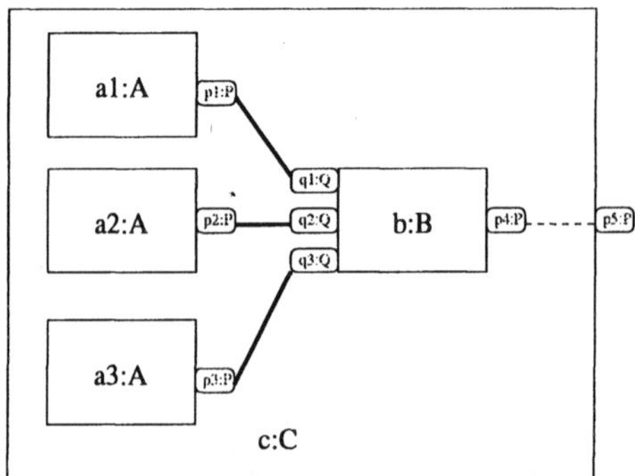


*Figure 6.* Replicated calculator architecture

From a logical software architecture definition, we could directly map its model to non distributed platform as ArchJava [2] or Julia, the implementation of Fractal Model [7]. SafArchie Studio transforms automatically its logical architecture XML representation and architecture type XML representation towards XML Fractal ADL. On the other hand, ArchJava projection is manual. SafArchie Studio creates an ArchJava file specification for each component specification.

## 4.3 Abstract physical architecture

For our model of physical architecture, we choose the highest abstraction level possible. The abstract physical architecture model contains five main elements: Computing node, communication node, communication interface, communication link, and route . They represent hosts configuration, hosts capacities and network topology.

A computing node communicates with its environment through communication interfaces. It can contain software components. By default, we consider that it has an appropriate middleware. A software component can be deployed, executed and managed on it. However, architects can specify the middleware properties.

A communication node also communicates with its environment through communication interfaces. It could not contain any software component. But an architect could declare route between two of its own communication interfaces. A route specifies that all messages that arrive into a communication interface are forwarded towards the "routed" communication interface.

Finally two communication interfaces could be bound. The communication link represents the ability of a communication interface to send or receive a message to or from an other communication interface. The communication link can only bind two communication interfaces.

Therefore, in SafArchie studio, we define a diagram for modelling the network topology.

## 4.4 Mapping a logical architecture to a physical architecture

Starting from a logical architecture, this step consists in mapping the component or composite instances onto the computing nodes of the physical architecture.

When architect finishes his/her mapping, he/she can check the accordance of the connection declared in the logical model architecture with the communication link declared in the physical architecture. For each connection, a route must exist between the computing nodes that contain the connected component instances.

## 4.5 Next features of SafArchie Studio: Supervision of a software architecture

The next step consists in building the run-time perspective. The goals of this perspective consist in following the software architecture evolution. This work is still in progress. The software architecture supervision could be synchronous or asynchronous. In synchronous mode, we follow the architecture evolution in *debug* mode. Each architecture evolution should be in accordance with the architecture type (creation of component instances or connection). A *watch dog* component will be in charge of this checking task. In asynchronous mode, we follow the architecture evolution in order to keep a global view of software architecture. But the architecture model is only notified of the evolution, it can not interfere with it.

In other hands, lots of work should be done to add the support of evolution in physical architectures. This feature is essential to use SafArchie in an ubiquitous computing context where the physical topology changes.

# 5. Related work

Nowadays, most of industrial projects use informal notations (boxes and arrows) for specifying software architecture. These notations are ambiguous, imprecise, unanalyzable. Due to the lack of tools, software architecture management is expensive and time consuming. On the other hand, software architecture research community focuses on building formal notations in order to define structure and behavior of software architecture. They are recognized in Architecture Description Languages (ADL) domain. An ideal architectural description language would provide[12]: A composition model that provides operators for composing existent libraries of components and connectors. An abstraction level for defining components and connectors with only useful details putting in evidence some properties. A potential reusability for existing components, connectors, and whole architectures in order to develop new components, connectors and system architectures. Finally a set of analysis for validate architectural descriptions.

Currently, no ADL or architecture software tool responds to all these goals. In this section, instead of a catalog of ADL characteristics, we focus on three significant directions for software architecture definitions. SafArchie Studio is highly inspired by the main characteristics of these works: the specification and the analysis of dynamic distributed software behavior for Darwin[17] or Wright[3], the strong link with the implementation for ArchJava[2] or Fractal [7], and the building of architecture-driven software development environment for ArchStudio[10].

Some ADLs, such as Wright[3] and Darwin[17], support the specification and analysis of relatively complex component communication protocols. They provide formal basis for architectural description. They can be used to provide a precise, abstract, meaning to an architectural specification and to analyze a component assembly.

ADLs as Fractal[7] or ArchJava[2] are implementation oriented. Lots of existing approaches decouple implementation code from architecture. ArchJava is an extension to Java that seamlessly unifies software architecture with implementation, using a type system to ensure that the implementation conforms to architectural constraints. Fractal is generic software composition framework. As ArchJava, it is based on a hierarchical component model. Components can be nested in composite components - hence the "Fractal" name. Besides, this model is reflexive, i.e. components have full introspection and intercession capabilities. Finally, the Fractal component model is language independent, and fully modular and extensible. Fractal provides an XML based Architecture Description Language. Contrary to Darwin or Wright, ArchJava and Fractal ADL provide no behavior specification. The composition analysis is only structural. However, the abstract Fractal's or ArchJava's component models are efficient and adapted for programming step. In SafArchie, we follow their models to keep a strong link between the specification and the component platform. Moreover, we add a physical platform specification with the deployment perspective.

On the fringes of ADLs, other projects aim at improving the use of software architecture concepts in software engineering. For example, ArchStudio[10] mainly developed by the Institute for Software Research at the University of California, Irvine, is an architecture-driven software development environment. Indeed, while most development environments, like Microsoft Visual Studio and IBM Eclipse are code-driven development environments, ArchStudio focuses on software development from the perspective of software architecture.

SafArchie Studio is higly inspired by these three aproaches. It provides a complete tool suite to build, analyse and deploy a software architecture and to transform ADLs in an effective vehicle for communication and analysis of a software system.

## 6. Conclusion

This paper highlights our research in architectural modelling, refinement, and consistency checking. As part of architectural modelling, we define a three-view approach. The first specifies the software architecture type. It defines invariant properties for a software architecture. From this structural and behavioral specification, we analyze the component assembly. The second perspective specifies a typed software architecture, i.e a component graph deployed on an abstract physical architecture. Finally, the run-time perspective gives administrator a global view of his/her system for the architectural supervision. For consistency among the different views, we use SafArchie's ability to provide a common component baseline to link those perspectives.

For the moment, we have tooled many of the concepts discussed in this paper and created a tool suite: SafArchie Studio. This tool is a set of new extensions for ArgoUML. It gives programmers, administrators, or designer an architectural view of software with different perspectives.

SafArchie approach is also the foundation for an other project: TranSAT[5] [6] (Transformation of Software ArchiTecture). Indeed, most of the time, the software architecture models are unsuitable for improving features of software systems. So, adding new concerns in software architecture is often a difficult and manual operation for architect. Moreover, the rules of integration are not described, saved, or analyzed. TranSAT focuses on these lacks of software architecture models. It proposes a framework for designing software architecture with step by step refinements: from an architecture which contains only business concern to a global architecture which contains business and technical concerns. The main idea of this project is inspired from Aspect Oriented Software Development (AOSD) [16] concepts.

TranSAT ensures three main features: It defines a mechanism to add new concerns in software architecture specification. It provides a description model for software architecture which saves the integration rules of a specific concern. It specifies rules which guarantee the correct integration of a technical concern inside a business model. Associated with TranSAT, SafArchie provides an architecture centric approach to build consistent software step by step.

## References

[1] J. Aldrich, C. Chambers, and D. Notkin. Architectural Reasoning in Archjava. In *Proceedings ECOOP 2002*, volume 2374 of *LNCS*, pages 334–367, Malaga, Spain, june 2002. Springer Verlag.

[2] J. Aldrich, C. Chambers, and D. Notkin. ArchJava: Connecting Software Architecture to Implementation. In *Proceedings of the 24th International Conference on Software Engineering (ICSE-02)*, pages 187–197, New York, May 19–25 2002. ACM Press.

[3] R. Allen. *A Formal Approach to Software Architecture*. PhD thesis, Carnegie Mellon, School of Computer Science, Janvier 1997. Issued as CMU Technical Report CMU-CS-97-144.

[4] R. Allen, R. Douence, and D. Garlan. Specifying Dynamism in Software Architectures. In *Proceedings of the First Workshop on the Foundations of Component-Based Systems*, Zurich, Switzerland, Septembre 1997.

[5] O. Barais and L. Duchien. SafArch : Maîtriser l'Evolution d'une Architecture Logicielle. In *Langages, Modèles, Objets - Journées Composants (LMO-JC'04)*, Lille, France, Mars 2004. Hermès Sciences.

[6] O. Barais, L. Duchien, and R. Pawlak. Separation of Concerns in Software Modeling: A Framework for Software Architecture Transformation. In *IASTED International Conference on Software Engineering Applications (SEA)*, pages 663–668, Los Angeles, USA, november 2003. ACTA Press. *ISBN 0-88986-394-6.*

*[7] E. Bruneton, T. Coupaye, and J.B. Stefani. The Fractal Component Model, version 2.0-3. Online documentation http://fractal.objectweb.org/specification/, February 2004.*

[8] *F. Bueno, D. Cabeza, M. Carro, M. Hermenegildo, P. López, and G. Puebla.* The Ciao Prolog System. *Technical University of Madrid, June 2002.*

[9] *S. C. Cheung, D. Giannakopoulou, and J. Kramer. Verification of Liveness Properties using Compositional Reachability Analysis. In* Proceedings of the 6th European conference held jointly with the 5th ACM SIGSOFT international symposium on Foundations of software engineering, *pages 227–243. Springer-Verlag New York, Inc., 1997.*

[10] *E.M. Dashofy, A. Van Der Hoek, and R.N. Taylor. An Infrastructure for the Rapid Development of XML-based Architecture Description Languages. In* Proceedings of the 24th International Conference on Software Engineering (ICSE2002), *Orlando, Florida, 2002.*

[11] *L.G. DeMichiel. Entreprise Javabeans Specification, version 2.1. Online documentation http://java.sun.com/products/ejb/docs.html, June 2002.*

[12] *D. Garlan and M. Shaw. An Introduction to Software Architecture. In V. Ambriola and G. Tortora, editors,* Advances in Software Engineering and Knowledge Engineering, *volume 1, pages 1–40. World Scientific Publishing Company, 1993.*

[13] *G. Heineman and W. Councill, editors.* Component-Based Software Engineering, Putting the Pieces Together. *Addison-Westley, 2001.* ISBN: 0-201-70485-4.

[14] *H. Hussmann, F. Finger, and R. Wiebicke. Using Previous Property Values in OCL Postconditions - An Implementation Perspective. In* International Workshop UML 2.0 - The Future of the UML Constraint Language OCL, *York, UK, October 2 2000. http://dresden-ocl.sourceforge.net/.*

[15] *J.M. Jezequel and B. Meyer. Object Technology: Design by Contract: The Lessons of Ariane.* Computer, *30(1):129–130, January 1997.*

[16] *G. Kiczales, J. Lamping, A. Menhdhekar, C. Maeda, C. Lopes, J-M. Loingtier, and J. Irwin. Aspect-Oriented Programming. In Mehmet Aksit and Satoshi Matsuoka, editors,* Proceedings ECOOP, *volume 1241, pages 220–242. Springer-Verlag, 1997.*

[17] *J. Magee. Behavioral Analysis of Software Architectures using LTSA. In* Proceedings of the 21st international conference on Software engineering, *pages 634–637. IEEE Computer Society Press, 1999.*

[18] *J. Magee and J. Kramer.* Concurrency. State Models and Java Programs. *wiley, 1999.*

[19] *J. Magee, J. Kramer, and D. Giannakopoulou. Behaviour Analysis of Software Architectures. In* 1st Working IFIP Conference on Software Architecture (WICSA1), *San Antonio, TX, USA, 22-24 February 1999.*

[20] *B. Meyer. Applying "Design by Contract".* Computer, *25(10):40–51, October 1992.*

[21] *R. Milner.* Communication and Concurrency. *Prentice-Hall, 1989.*

[22] *OMG. CORBA Component Model, v3.0. Online documentation http://www.omg.org, June 2002.*

[23] *OMG. OMG Object Constraint Language specification, version 2.0. http://www.omg.org/docs/ptc/03-10-14.pdf, October 2003.*

[24] *J.E. Robbins and D.M. Hilbert D.F. Redmiles. Using Critics to Analyze Evolving Architectures. In* Second International Software Architecture Workshop held at SigSoft'96, *1996.*

[25] *R. Soley. MDA, an introduction. Online documentation http://www.omg.org/mda/mda_files/Soley-MDA/MDA-Seminar-Soley.htm, 2002.*

[26] *C. Szyperski.* Component Software: Beyond Object-Oriented Programming. *ACM Press and Addison-Wesley, New York, NY, 1998.*

[27] *L. Tolke and M. Klink. Cookbook for Developers of ArgoUML, an Introduction to Developing ArgoUML, March 2004.*

# ENHANCING THE ROLE OF INTERFACES IN SOFTWARE ARCHITECTURE DESCRIPTION LANGUAGES (ADLS)

Seamus Galvin, J.J. Collins, Chris Exton and Finbar McGurren
*Software Architecture Evolution (SAE) Group, Dept. of Computer Science and Information Systems, University of Limerick, Limerick, Ireland*

**Abstract:** One of the key reasons why ADLs are yet to be adopted commercially on a large scale is due to shortcomings in their ability to describe adequate interface specifications. An interface specification that is vague, lacking in detail, too style focused or too language-specific results in an ADL description with a restricted scope of use. This paper demonstrates how an XML-based ADL (xADL 2.0) can be extended to model detailed, meaningful interface specifications, and is used as part of a simple prototype to demonstrate how they form an integral part of an architectural description, paying particular attention to interface-level constraints. The approach is based on the principle that an ADL's interface modeling features should provide sufficient flexibility to allow them to reflect stakeholder's interface concerns at all stages in the lifecycle.

**Key words:** Software Architecture; ADLs; interface specification; interface constraints.

## 1. INTRODUCTION

Architecture Description Languages (ADLs) provide a structured means of representing a system's architecture that is both human and machine-readable, and have been proposed as a modeling notation to provide support for some of the problems experienced in architecture-based development [1]. However, the diverse nature of existing ADLs indicates a lack of clarity with respect to the kind of language an ADL should be and how it should be used. Some ADLs have a narrow usage scope, providing highly specific support during the early stages of architectural analysis, while others perceive varying degrees of relationship between architectural description and the underlying implementation. Also, it is still unclear how ADLs and their associated descriptions might interrelate with other design and runtime artifacts, such as requirements and domain models, modeling tools, implementation platforms and execution engines. The lack of such relationships minimizes the ADL's potential.

While these realities present a broad range of problems, a fundamental requirement is the provision of adequate interface modeling capabilities. An accurate interface description is an essential part of an architectural specification, and a key requirement of architectural stakeholders at all stages in the project lifecycle [2]. It is pivotal to an ADL's malleability as constrained and monolithic interface support results in a limited ADL. Most importantly, it is required to establish an accurate relationship between architectural description and the underlying implementation, allowing the ADL to support maintainable and evolvable software.

The remainder of the paper is summarised as follows. Sections 2 and 3 provide a brief overview of ADLs, the latter paying attention to their diverse approaches to supporting interface description. Section 4 discusses interface modeling concerns in architectural documentation. Section 5 discusses two approaches to defining an ADL meta-language for interface description using the XML-Schema standard. Section 6 discusses the application of the second approach to a suitable ADL, section 7 demonstrates an example of its application and section 8 offers conclusions and discusses future work.

## 2. OVERVIEW OF PROMINENT ADLS

The goal of achieving architecture-driven development and architecture-centric evolution presents many diverse challenges, and this is reflected in the ADLs that have been developed throughout the research community, some of which are listed in Table 1. Despite the lack of a common, universally acceptable definition of software architecture [3], all adopt a relatively standard approach to modeling basic architectural structure. Most recognise an architecture as being a set of components (or modules) whose interactions are represented as connectors [1]. Relationships between components and connectors are represented as links (or attachments). Some ADLs allow components to be directly linked to one another; others require them to communicate via connectors, while some allow direct links between connectors. ADLs allow these basic architectural elements to be refined to various degrees, thus allowing the notion of a sub-architecture to be modelled. They also attempt to distinguish between template definitions of architectural elements and instances of those elements that are defined in actual instantiations of a particular architecture.

While there is a general conformance to this core set of architectural concepts, there is significant diversity in their detailed ADL features, e.g. naming conventions and keywords used, their scope of concern, and their associated technologies and tools. For example, Darwin, Wright and Rapide have focused on static and dynamic analysis of abstract architectural descriptions; Aesop has investigated the customisation of architectural design environments; Unicon has identified and implemented commonly occurring connector abstractions; ArchJava investigates communication integrity; SOFA highlights the relationship between architecture and component-based middleware; xADL aims to support rapid prototyping and tailoring to assist ADL research, and ACME and ADML strive for ADL standards and recognition. Some of these ADLs have a narrow scope of use, providing high-level, conceptual support during the early stages of architectural analysis. Others perceive a relationship between the architectural description and the underlying implementation. The nature of this relationship varies; some ADLs provide code generation facilities, while others aim to represent the architecture explicitly in the underlying system. Both conceptual and more concrete ADLs have yet to receive widespread acceptance. This indicates a difficulty in providing an architectural language that is sufficiently conceptual to support high-level abstractions, yet simultaneously capable of supporting and governing the code level in an acceptable manner. Important issues still remain largely unaddressed by ADL research – these include the lack of explicit support for the definition of architectural viewpoints [4] and the insufficient emphasis on the relationship between ADLs and other developmental and runtime artefacts such as requirements models, design models, domain models, modelling tools and languages, implementation platforms and execution engines.

# 3. ADL SUPPORT FOR MODELING INTERFACES

An overview of the interface modeling characteristics of a broad range of existing ADLs (including UML) is given in Table 1. Different keywords are used, e.g. ports, roles, players, interfaces. They are difficult to compare and categorise, as ADL interface modeling characteristics are often influenced by their primary intended use. For example, if the ADL is geared for formal analysis, then the interface modeling support is influenced by the formal methods used (e.g. Wright, Darwin, Rapide), or if an ADL is closely aligned to a particular architectural style or underlying platform, style or platform specific interface features are provided. This is sufficient to fulfill the ADL's primary intent, at the expense of constraining its capability in other respects. ADLs and modeling notations aiming for a broader usage scope allow detailed interface features to be represented as user-defined properties (e.g. ACME and UML). This allows any interface feature to be modeled, but the language's native tools cannot interpret them, leaving this task to the ADL user, and hindering the possibility of a more standardized representation. Also, as this approach does not provide specific syntax for the features within the core ADL, it is more difficult to clarify feature semantics.

*Table 1.* ADL support for modeling interfaces

| ADL | Type | Keyword | Key Features | Semantic Modeling |
|---|---|---|---|---|
| **Aesop [5]** | Implementation independent | Ports and Roles | Allows ports/roles to be associated with a style | Semantics associated with certain architectural styles |
| **ACME [6]** | Implementation independent | Ports and Roles | Allows ports/roles to be associated with a style | User-defined properties |
| **ADML [7]** | Implementation independent | Ports and Roles | XML version of ACME – same as above | Same as ACME |
| **Wright [8]** | Implementation independent | Ports and Roles | Uses CSP notation to capture interaction semantics | Port/Role behaviour can be modeled in CSP |
| **Darwin [9]** | Implementation independent | Interface | Interfaces can contain provides and requires services, focuses on bindings between interfaces specified in pi-calculus | Supports parameterization and subtyping, portal semantics added using tags |
| **Rapide [10]** | Implementation independent | Interface | Can model synchronous and asynchronous features, advanced parameterization and subtyping possible | Poset (event) patterns characterised using behaviour and constraint declarations |
| **xADL 2.0 [11]** | Implementation constraining | Interface | C2-specific features | C2-specific semantics |
| **Unicon [12]** | Implementation constraining | Players and Roles | Players/roles associated with specific component and connector types | Specific properties associated with port and role types |
| **ArchJava [13]** | Implementation constraining | Roles | Java-like syntax, ports can have provides, requires, broadcast features | Provides features can include a Java implementation |
| **C2SADL [14]** | Implementation constraining | Interface | Can model C2-specific provides/requires features | C2-specific semantics |
| **UML** | Implementation independent | Interface | "Lollipop" or rectangular notation can be used | Semantics modeled using properties and tagged values |

# 4. INTERFACE CONCERNS IN ARCHITECTURAL DOCUMENTATION

In order to develop adequate support for the high-level, platform independent modeling of interfaces during the early stages of the project lifecycle, one should take cognizance of the features found in the interface documentation of architectural specifications. Bachmann et al. suggest a standard organization for architecture-level interface documentation [2]:

1. Identity - This identification may include versioning information.
2. Resources provided - This includes syntactic (e.g. name, arguments etc.) and semantic information (i.e. the implications of using the resource).
3. Data types - user-defined data types declared on the interface.
4. Errors raised by interface resources.
5. Configuration information - This might involve the passing of parameters to the interface.
6. Quality attribute characteristics.
7. What the associated element requires from its environment.
8. Rationale and design issues - This may be a narrative description of the motivation/considerations behind the interface's design.
9. Usage guide - This allows stakeholders to gain a better view of the interface's overall role. This can be achieved by identifying and depicting resource usage scenarios that the architect expects to repeatedly occur.
10. Exceptions - These could be errors on the part of the actor invoking the resource, or errors that occur due to software or hardware events that result in a violation in the element's assumptions about its environment.

Like all aspects of architectural documentation, some of the discussed features are structured and should be carried through and directly reflected in design and implementation. Other information is prose based and is intended to enhance the understanding of the structured information. The structured architectural information would ultimately be much more useful and accurate if it was a part of the system, rather than being part of the associated documentation. Therefore, the ADL's language features should be sufficient to allow the modelling of the structured information by providing explicit syntax for relevant features, and should also support the formal or semi-formal specification of features where required (in order to support the latter, it should facilitate more than one formal notation if required). Also, ADL modelling tools should allow this structured information to be annotated with relevant prose-based information.

## 5. TOWARDS AN ADL META-LANGUAGE FOR INTERFACE DESCRIPTION

A suitable ADL interface meta-language should facilitate the definition of abstract, language-independent interfaces and should also support their transition into concrete, language-specific ones. Also, it should be extensible – this is required to support the diversity in existing ADLs, architectural documentation, development platforms, and the many different, and possibly unanticipated ADL usage contexts. Also, the approach should reflect the commonality that exists between interface modeling features of the different platforms. This will allow each platform's interface modeling requirements to be defined in terms of a common format and will ease the future addition of features related to other, possibly newer platforms. It will also facilitate the definition of structured mappings between language-independent and language-specific interfaces, a trait which is advocated by the Model Driven Architecture (MDA)[15]. This section discusses the potential of two possible approaches to providing a suitable interface meta-language for ADLs. The experimentation discussed in this section is applied to the interface features of Java, C# and OMG's IDL3, the latter a part of the CORBA Component Model (CCM). To ease the application and extension of the approaches, both have been defined using the XML-Schema standard.

## 5.1 First approach – generic language-independent schema and language-specific extensions

The first candidate approach is based on the premise that the common, or overlapping features of language-specific interface specifications provide a basis from which an ADL's language-independent interface features can be built. Their specific, differing features act as a basis for refinement in detailed design. For example, all of them exhibit notions of identity, resources provided and input/return parameters. Most of them allow properties or constants to be defined – these can be primitive or user-defined. However, while they allow syntax to be specified unambiguously, they generally do not support the specification of resource semantics [16], a void which could be addressed by an ADL.

To investigate the potential of this approach, the overlapping interface modeling features of Java, C# and IDL3 were identified and represented in an XML-Schema as complex types. This provided the basis for the language-independent interface description. Based on the language-independent schema in the study, their differing features were then modeled as separate schema complex types. Each of these types used the XML-Schema extension capabilities to extend the language-independent complex types. To demonstrate the potential for modeling semantics, the generic schema also contains features for specifying design-by-contract [17] constraints. The relationship between the language-independent and language-specific schemata for this experiment is shown in Figure 1. The language-independent schema contains three nested complex types that support the modeling of optional and mandatory features, including interface identity, references to extended interfaces, preconditions, postconditions, invariants, operation names, and input/return parameters. The three language-specific schemata contain specialist features outside this generic set. For example, the Java specific complex types (JavaInterfaceDefinition JavaInterfaceBody and JavaInputParam) contain the AccessType feature for optionally specifying the interface's accessibility (i.e. public, private, protected etc.) and features for constant declarations, references to exceptions, inner interface declarations and inner class declarations. In a similar fashion, C# interface specifics are represented in C_SharpInterfaceDefinition, C_SharpInterfaceBody and C_SharpInputParam, and IDL3 specifics in CCMInterfaceBody, and CCMInputParam. C# specific features include attributes, access types, properties, indexers, and events and support for specifying input parameters as being of type value, output, reference or array, while IDL3 specific features include events, constants, types, attributes and exceptions, and also support for specifying input parameters as 'in', 'out' or 'inout'.

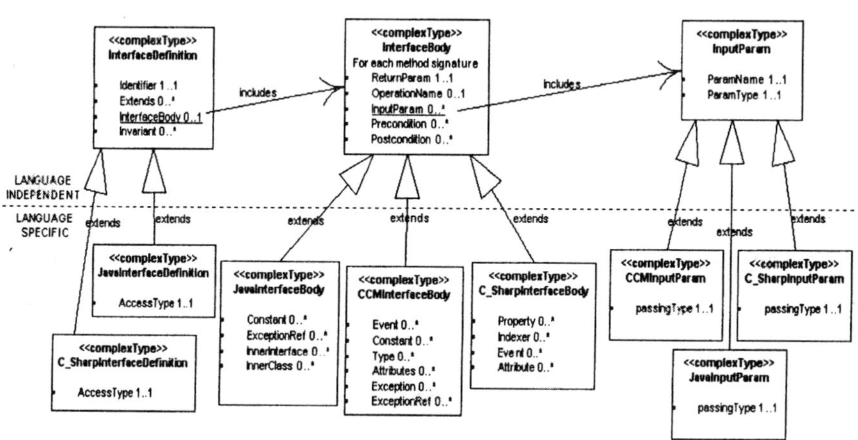


*Figure 1.* Conceptual overview of first approach - interface features of Java, C# and IDL3. Common features are represented in the language-independent schema, differing features are modeled in extension schemata.

The language-independent schema is a good representation of the main interface features in commonly used programming languages and middleware technologies, but it has shortcomings that hinder its potential to support all of the previously discussed guidelines. First, the approach does not support the establishment of a stable boundary between the sets of features contained in the language-independent and language-specific levels. Most notably, the set of language-independent features depicted in Figure 1 would become smaller if more interface examples from other programming languages and middleware technologies were factored into the approach. Also, as the features contained in the language-independent interface are directly based on those in language-specific interfaces, changing it in response to syntactic changes in platform-specific interface modeling features, or to accommodate new language-specific platforms would be cumbersome. The approach supports language-specific concerns well, but its ability to support language-independent concerns is restricted by its narrow feature set, which restricts its ability to extensively support the criteria for architectural documentation in Section 4. The narrow language-independent feature set would also restrict its ability to support the simulation and analysis of language-independent architectural models at an early stage in the lifecycle, like other ADLs such as Rapide. Also, the schema layout in the approach is rather unintuitive, making associated tool support more difficult to construct.

## 5.2 Second approach - core set of feature declarations

The second approach involves the definition of a broad set of individual feature declarations and their use as the basis for constructing the language-independent and language-specific schemata (Figure 2). It consists of three parts - the first being the core set of feature declarations, the second part being a language-independent schema that is defined using the core feature declarations, and the third part which facilitates the definition of language-specific interface schemata. A language-specific schema may use features from the core set as a basis for definition, and may additionally define exclusive features to represent interface features that are not supported by the core set.

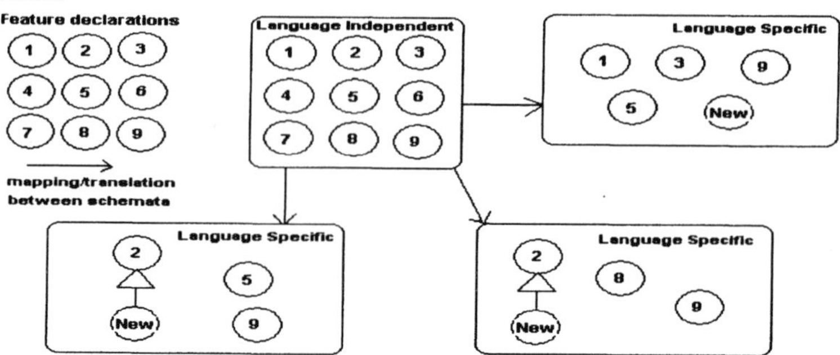


*Figure 2.* Conceptual view of interface model

As interface descriptions based on the schemata are defined in XML, XSL stylesheets could be used to transform language-independent interface descriptions into language-specific ones, and/or to generate code if required. Some of the defined language-independent features are also explicitly represented in corresponding language-specific schemata (e.g. InterfaceName, ExtendedInterface, ResourceDeclaration and ResourceName). Other language-independent features may be realised in the implementation of an element that implements the interface at a language-specific level, rather than being explicitly represented in the language-specific interface. For example, the language-independent schema in Figure 3 contains features for modeling the configuration parameters of an interface, but the Java specific interface schema does not contain this feature. Instead, a Java implementation might represent the configuration parameters in the constructor of a class that implements a corresponding Java interface. In this case, a translation could generate corresponding code outside the ADL's scope of description if a particular usage context required it.

*Table 2.* Core types in interface model

| Feature | Overview of Semantics |
|---|---|
| AccessType | Represents the accessibility scope of the interface. |
| Array | Represents a CORBA-like array declaration on an interface. |
| AttributeDeclaration | Represents a CORBA-like attribute declaration – attributes indicate the variables in an element that are accessible to clients. |
| ConfigParam | Facilitates the configuration of elements through configuration parameters (e.g. specification of size of data structure element that implements interface). |
| ConstantDeclaration | Represents the declaration of a CORBA-like constant declaration on an interface. |
| Enum | Represents a CORBA-like enumerated type declaration . |
| Event | Represents an event declaration. Elements that implement the interface will either publish the event or subscribe to it. |
| Exception | Represents the specification of any exceptions that can be raised by resources declared in the interface. |
| ExceptionRef | Represents any references to exceptions that may be made in an interface-level resource declaration. |
| ExtendedInterface | Represents a reference to an interface that is extended by this interface. ADLs and platforms generally allow an interface to extend multiple interfaces. |
| InOutParam | Represents an 'inout' parameter which combines value and return parameters, allowing a calling method to pass and receive a value. |
| InParam | Represents a value (or input) parameter. Parameter passed by method caller (actual parameter) is copied into the parameter used by the called method (formal parameter) when the method is invoked. |
| InterfaceName | Represents the identity of the interface – may also include versioning information. |
| Invariant | Represents specification of interface invariants, i.e. constraints enforced for all elements that implement the interface. |
| I_OptParam | Represents the optional specification of a formal parameter. Implicitly supported by some programming languages in the form of variable length arrays. However, in the context of documenting an architecture's interfaces, one may prefer to represent optional parameters explicitly. |
| I_RefParam | Represents a reference parameter – address of formal parameter is the same as actual parameter. Subtle difference between reference and result parameters is that any changes to the formal parameter immediately affect the actual parameter. |
| OutParam | Represents a result (or output) parameter. Value of formal parameter is |

| Feature | Overview of Semantics |
|---|---|
| | copied into the actual parameter when the procedure returns. |
| O_RetParam | Represents a return parameter returned as a function result. |
| PostCondition | Represents a postcondition of a resource, i.e. a description of the effects of that operation on its parameters and element state [18]. |
| PreCondition | Represents a precondition of a resource, i.e. a definition of the situations under which a postcondition will apply [18]. |
| ResourceDeclaration | Represents the amalgamation of information for an interface resource – ResourceName, various types of resource parameter, preconditions, postconditions, references to exceptions etc. |
| ResourceName | Identify of an interface resource. |
| String | Represents a CORBA-like string declaration. |
| Struct | Represents a CORBA-like struct declaration. |

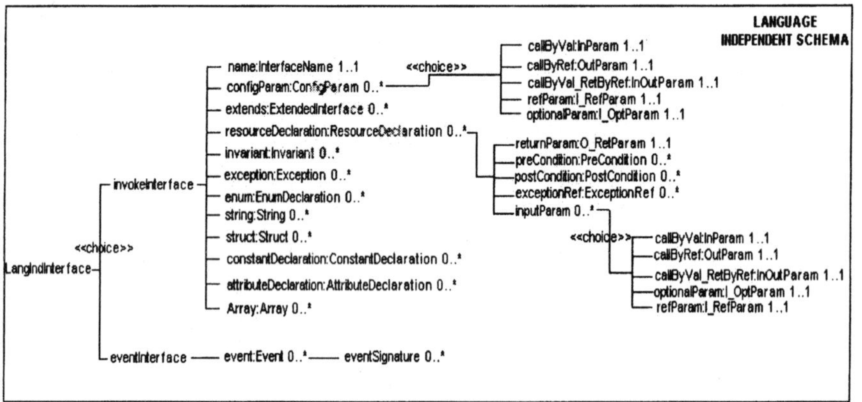


*Figure 3.* Language-independent interface schema

The selection of core interface feature types in Table 2 are influenced by a range of various sources, including the taxonomy in Section 4, Corba IDL, Java, C# and Visual Basic. Some of the features are a fundamental part of most linguistic approaches to modeling interfaces, for example, InterfaceName, ExtendedInterface, ResourceDeclaration, ResourceName and O_RetParam. CORBA IDL also has additional interface features that are intended to epitomize a broad set of language-specific features, and some of them are also suited for inclusion in the set. These are Event, Exception, ExceptionRef, Struct, AttributeDeclaration, ConstantDeclaration, Enum, String and Array. The classification in Section 4 identifies other important features that are not directly supported by Corba IDL, for example the explicit declaration of configuration parameters (ConfigParam) and accessibility (AccessType). The authors also mention resource semantics – while it may be more practical to document some of these concerns as prose, important resource semantics can be characterized as design-by-contract constraints using the PreCondition, PostCondition and Invariant types in the core set. The core set also includes six different types of resource parameters

- these are return (O_RetParam), input (InParam), output (OutParam), input-output (InOutParam), reference (I_RefParam) and optional parameters (I_OptParam). This broad set of core types is shown in Table 2, and is used as the basis for defining the language-independent interface schema in Figure 3.

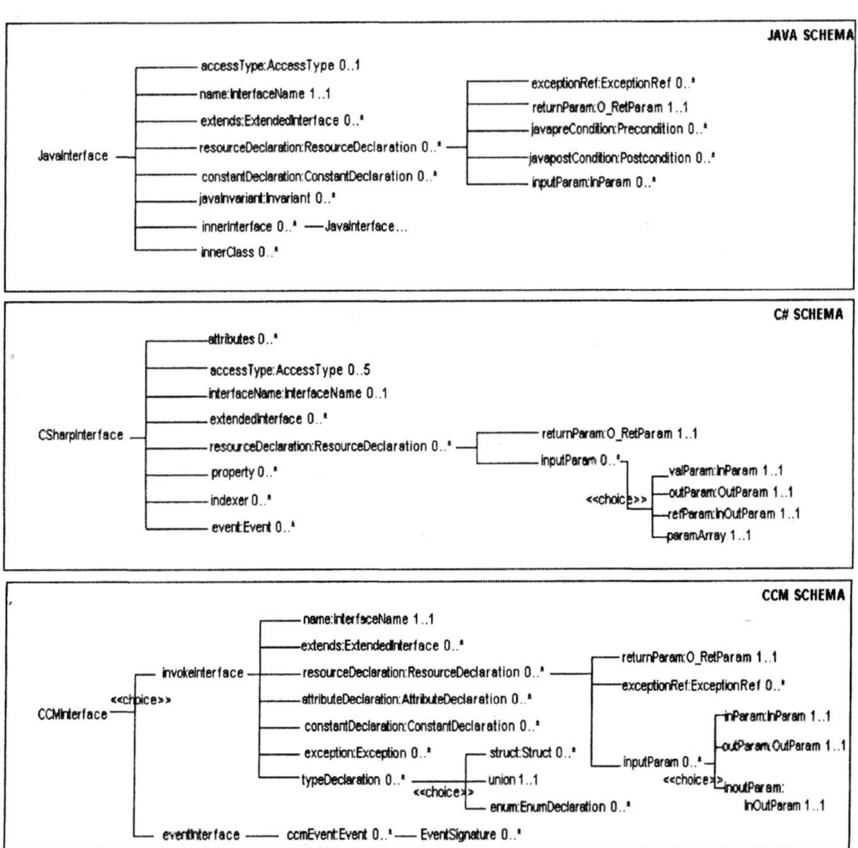


*Figure 4.* Language-specific schemata for Java, C# and IDL3 interfaces

The interface features of Java, C#, and CCM are depicted in Figure 4. While the official language-specifications of these platforms provide a detailed informal description of language semantics, rigourous formal descriptions are not provided. To show how the semantics of language-independent and language-specific interface features interrelate, input parameter features are used as an example. In the core types, five input parameter feature types are declared, each representing different parameter passing semantics – value or input parameters (InParam), output parameters (OutParam), value-result parameters (InOutParam), reference parameters

(I_RefParam), and optional parameters (I_OptParam). The language-independent schema allows a resource declaration to contain any of these features, whereas the three language-specific schemata have different sets of parameter passing semantics. Java only supports input parameters so it only uses InParam. IDL3 supports input, output and value-result parameters, so it uses InParam, OutParam and InOutParam. C# supports four types of input parameter, value, out, ref and param. Value and out use the InParam and OutParam core types respectively. However, despite its name, ref is semantically equivalent to InOutParam rather than I_RefParam. As param is not semantically equivalent to any of the core types, it is defined as a feature unique to the C# schema.

The second approach is influenced by some of the problems identified with the first approach and attempts to address them. In contrast to the first approach, overlapping features in the language-independent and language-specific schemata are defined in terms of the same set of core types, but the actual language-independent and language-specific schemata are independently defined. This means that the addition of new language-specific features do not force change upon the language-independent schema, and the number of features that can be included in the language-independent schema is no longer restricted, giving it the potential to provide broader support for language-independent interface modeling at an early stage in the lifecycle, while still providing adequate support for language-specific refinement at a later stage. Also, the schema layout is more intuitive and easier to apply in comparison to the first approach. Therefore, as the second approach is a more comprehensive solution, it is currently the basis of our future work, and is applied in the remaining sections of this paper.

## 6. APPLYING THE MODEL TO AN ADL

The most recent C2-based ADL (xADL 2.0) provides features for specifying architectural structure and supporting basic reconfiguration [11]. As it is based on XML-Schemas it is compatible with many existing tools. Also, xADL is designed to be extensible, allowing modifications to be made to it more easily than any of the other existing ADLs, and it is therefore used as the basis for experimentation. xADL 2.0's language structure is split across a number of interrelated schemata. The most important are the *Instance* and *Structure&Types* schemata. The *Instance* schema is designed to represent a completed, running architecture that is instantiated from a design-time *Structure&Types* architectural representation. The *Structure&Types* representation allows component, connector or interface elements to be represented as types. Design-time or run-time architectural topologies can be created using the *Structure&Types* or *Instance* schemata respectively by declaring one or more instances of a type and creating links between them. The interface meta-language is added by replacing xADL's style-specific interface modeling features with a new interface schema containing the core, language-independent and language-specific parts. This modification is made in the *Structure&Types* schema, where the existing construct used to model interface types is extended.

Alternatively, other ADLs such as ACME and Darwin provide support for extensibility in the form of properties or tagged values. Such ADLs can apply the presented interface meta-language by referencing XML interface descriptions that conform to the presented XML-Schemata.

# 7. APPLYING THE INTERFACE EXTENSIONS – STACK EXAMPLE

To demonstrate the approach in practice, the modified ADL is used to represent a stack component (StackImpl) and two interfaces that it implements (Stack and RemStack), using a Java-based design-by-contract framework. As StackImpl is a binary Java class, the Java-specific interface schema is used to provide a concrete definition of Stack and RemStack. These interface definitions also contain design-by-contract constraints (Figure 5). To demonstrate how the interface model can be used to broaden an ADL's set of support, a generator was written to process the ADL description, producing a series of files for each defined interface. Figure 5 depicts StackArch.xml and the files generated from it. First, a language-specific interface file is generated for each interface – in this case, Stack.java and RemStack.java. It also generates a proxy that intercepts all interface invocations and checks the relevant constraints specified in the ADL description. In the example, three files are generated - Stack_StackImpl.java and RemStack_StackImpl.java contain the constraint-checking code, while StackImplProxy.java carries out the runtime checks. The constraint checking mechanism is greatly influenced by DBCProxy, a Java-oriented design-by-contract framework [19]. DBCProxy uses Java's dynamic proxy mechanism and reflection to enforce constraints. However, as this approach is highly Java-specific, it has been used to develop a simpler, static solution that is clearer, more efficient and more applicable to other programming languages.

Instantiation and invocation of the proxy is shown in Figure 6. The proxy is used by calling the static getInstance() method. A variable of interface type Stack is declared and assigned to getInstance(). The proxy contains boolean switches that enable/disable the assertions for each interface that the component implements. If an interface's constraints are switched on, getInstance() returns a proxy instance, otherwise it returns an instance of the component. Once the client attempts to place an item on the stack, the call is rerouted through the proxy. In this example, StackImplProxy uses Stack_StackImpl to check the relevant assertions. In this case, it firstly checks any preconditions on put(), and then it invokes the actual operation on the component. It then checks any postconditions and finally any interface invariants to ensure that the component is in the correct state.

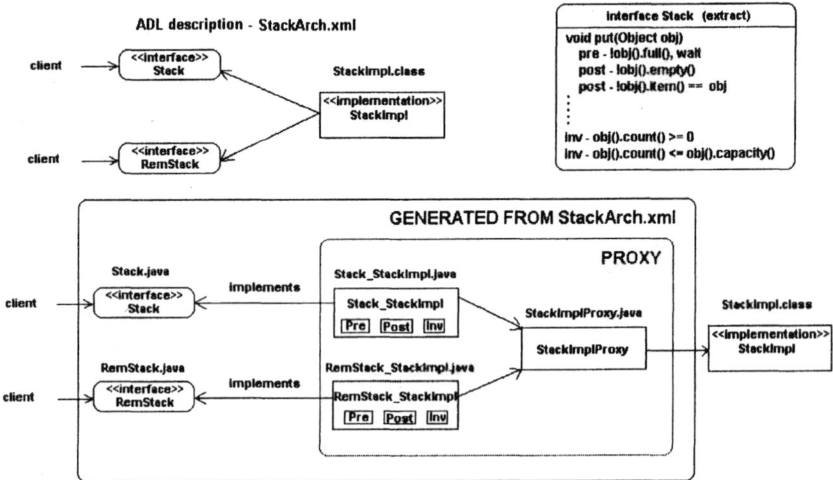


*Figure 5.* Stack Example - files generated from ADL description

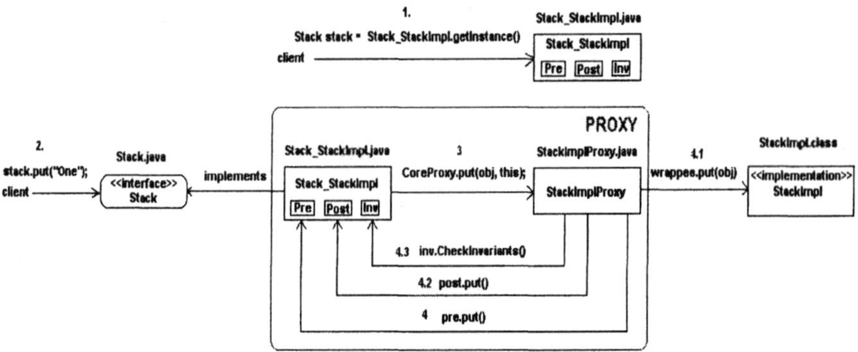


*Figure 6.* Example proxy instantiation and invocation

An ADL-based environment should be able to provide concrete support for exception handling. Beugnard et al. identify four approaches to dealing with constraint violations [20]. The generated proxy addresses some of these concerns for interface-level constraints:

1. Reject - Raise an exception and propagate it to the client.
2. Ignore - Proceed with the operation, ignoring any adverse effect.
3. Wait - If a precondition fails, this mode defaults to waiting until the precondition becomes true. This synchronization protocol is based on separate objects [21], first used in Eiffel. Obviously, this only applies in concurrent contexts.
4. Negotiate - This involves the renegotiation of the client-server contract, allowing the client to retry the operation, possibly with new values.

The proxy in this example defaults to the Reject mode. The Ignore mode can be applied to any constraint by appending an "ignore" parameter to it. Also, the proxy allows the Wait mode to be applied to a precondition by appending a "wait" parameter, inheriting this feature from the DBCProxy framework. At present, the proxy does not support the Negotiate mode, but future work will investigate the implications of doing so.

## 8. CONCLUSIONS AND FUTURE WORK

The approach discussed in this paper provides a foundation that allows ADLs to support concrete, practical interface descriptions, thereby broadening their scope of use. Its treatment of platform independent and platform specific concerns is pivotal to allowing the ADL description to be a permanent, meaningful artifact from high-level architectural analysis through to maintenance and evolution. It is compliant with the Model Driven Architecture (MDA) philosophy, providing a basis for the transformation of platform independent ADL interface descriptions into platform specific ones. This is a step towards allowing platform independent ADL descriptions to evolve into platform specific ones.

In order to provide precise mappings between language-independent and language-specific interfaces, future work will aim to add further clarification of informal feature semantics, and also to demonstrate how the approach can be used to support a typical component-based development process.

## ACKNOWLEDGEMENTS

This research has been funded by QAD Ireland Ltd and Enterprise Ireland Innovative Partnership grant IP-2003-154.

## REFERENCES


1. Medvidovic, N. and R.N. Taylor, *A Classification and Comparison Framework for Software Architecture Description Languages.* IEEE Transactions on Software Engineering, 2000. **26**(1).
2. Felix Bachmann, L.B., Paul Clements, David Garlan, James Ivers, Reed Little, Robert Nord, Judith Stafford, *Documenting Software Architecture: Documenting Interfaces.* 2002, Software Engineering Institute, Carnegie Mellon University, Pittsburgh.
3. SEI, *How Do You Define Software Architecture?* 2003, Software Engineering Institute (SEI), Carnegie Mellon University.
4. IEEE, *IEEE P1471/D 5.0 Information Technology - Draft Recommended Practice for Architectural Description.* 1999, IEEE Architecture Working Group.
5. Garlan, D., *An Introduction to the Aesop System.* 1995, Carnegie Mellon University, Pittsburgh.
6. David Garlan, R.T.M., David Wile, *Acme: Architectural Description of Component-Based Systems.* Foundations of Component-Based Systems, ed. G.T.L.a.M. Sitaraman. 2000: Cambridge University Press.
7. Unknown, *Architecture Description Markup Language (ADML) - The XML-based standard for IT architecture interoperability and re-use.* 2002.
8. Allen, R., R. Douence, and D. Garlan, *Specifying and Analyzing Dynamic Software Architectures.* Lecture Notes in Computer Science, 1998.
9. Jeff Magee, N.D., Susan Eisenbach, Jeff Kramer. *Specifying Distributed Software Architectures.* in *Proceedings 5th European Software Engineering Conference (ESEC 95).* 1995. Barcelona, Spain.
10. Luckham, D.C. *Rapide: A Language and Toolset for Simulation of Distributed Systems by Partial Orderings of Events.* in *Proceedings of the DIMACS Partial Order Methods Workshop IV.* 1996. Princeton University.
11. Eric M. Dashofy, A.v.d.H., Richard N. Taylor. *An Infrastructure for the Rapid Development of XML-based Architecture Description Languages.* in *Proceedings of the 24th International Conference on Software Engineering.* 2002. Orlando, Florida.
12. Mary Shaw, R.D., Gregory Zelesnik. *Abstractions and Implementations for Architectural Connections.* in *Third International Conference on Configurable Distributed Systems.* 1995. Annapolis, Maryland.
13. Aldrich, J., C. Chambers, and D. Notkin. *ArchJava: Connecting Software Architecture to Implementation.* in *ICSE 2002.* 2002. Orlando, USA.
14. Richard N Taylor, N.M., Kenneth M Anderson, James E Whitehead Jr, Jason E. Robbins, Kari A. Nies, Peyman Oreizy, Deborah L. Dubrow, *A Component- and Message-Based Architectural Style for {GUI} Software.* Software Engineering, 1996. **22**(6): p. 390-406.
15. OMG, *Model Driven Architecture Guide Version 1.0.* 2003, Object Management Group (OMG).
16. Clements, P., et al., *Documenting Software Architectures - Views and Beyond.* 2003: Addison Wesley.
17. Meyer, B., *Applying Design by Contract.* IEEE Software, 1992. **25**(10): p. 40-51.
18. Cheesman, J. and J. Daniels, *UML Components: A Simple Process for Specifying Component-based Software*, ed. A. Wesley. 2000.
19. Eliasson, A., *Implement Design by Contract for Java using Dynamic Proxies.* JavaWorld, 2002.
20. Beugnard, A., et al., *Making Components Contract Aware.* IEEE Computer, 1999: p. 38-45.
21. Katrib, M., et al., *Java Distributed Seperate Objects.* Journal of Object Technology, 2002. 1(2).

# HOW ADLS CAN HELP IN ADAPTING THE CORBA COMPONENT MODEL TO REAL-TIME EMBEDDED SOFTWARE DESIGN

Sylvain Robert[1], Ansgar Radermacher[1], Vincent Seignole[2], Sébastien Gérard[1], Virginie Watine[2], Stéphane Ménoret[2] and François Terrier[1]
*[1]CEA-LIST, CEA/SACLAY, 91191 Gif sur Yvette, France; [2]Thales/ALICE pilot program, Thales Communications, 91300 Massy, France*

Abstract: Coping with the increasing complexity of software in embedded and distributed real-time systems is becoming a major concern. Even if promising as far as this latter aspect is concerned, design techniques issued from the middleware components (or framework-based) approaches have until now fall short in achieving their breakthrough in the real-time and embedded community. They are usually perceived as complex, monolithic and resulting in oversized applications, and thus, as not adapted to RT/E software development constraints. In an attempt to bridge this gap, we[1] aim at contributing to the adaptation of the lightweight CCM [1] to real-time and embedded systems. The originality of our approach, mainly resides in the emphasis on high-level (or design-time) issues of the development process, on the contrary to the usual focus on low-level ones: we raise QoS issues from implementation level to analysis and design level. In such a process, we have found it would be worth integrating considerations from the software architecture/ADL field in middleware components approaches. We especially claim that interactions configurability at design time is a major requirement in the class of systems we target and that, on this latter aspect, middleware components approaches could benefit from a separation of concerns between computation and interactions, as in most ADLs.

Key words: Real-Time Embedded, CCM, ADL, Connectors, Components

[1] The work set out in this paper is performed in the context of the ICE (Interaction of Components during Execution) research project, lead jointly by CEA-LIST and Thales/ALICE pilot program. For further information, see http://www.carroll-research.org.

## 1. Introduction

Real-time embedded software is generally considered as a category of software in which resources are constrained: the application design has to take into account such aspects as power and memory consumption, on top of classical real-time constraints. Thus, common reasons why middleware components approaches are considered to be poorly adapted to real-time and embedded systems area is that the runtime platforms consume too much resources (e.g. memory footprint), that they result in "heavyweight" components, and eventually because they do not properly address real-time constraints.

But this stance needs to be moderated: the term "RT/E systems" refers to a large family, where the requirements are quite heterogeneous. In particular, if the assertion made above about resources constraints applies to certain members of this family -this is for instance the case of distributed command and control systems, where sensors/actuators are associated with small units of computation, usually provided with very limited resources-, it is not completely true for all: for instance, some embedded communication systems own larger hardware configurations (about 1-2 Mb of RAM/ROM and even larger, sometimes close to those of common workstations). Then, middleware components approaches have numerous inherent advantages from which RT/E systems could benefit: they provide applications with standard platforms comprising an extensive set of extra-functional services (e.g. distribution management, security); they come with well-defined component's abstract models; they specify architecture of execution frameworks; they natively address deployment and packaging issues, and they provide guidelines which structure the components development process. Moreover, efforts have already been made to cut down the size of middleware platforms, for instance the initiative Lightweight CCM [1] which proposes a "low-fat" version of CCM mostly dedicated to resources-constrained systems. Even real-time aspects have (somehow) been addressed, by extending the original platforms with dedicated mechanisms: we can quote the example of real-time CORBA [3].

However, this continuous upgrading towards "RT/E-compliant" middleware platforms by means of iterative functionalities addition / subtraction diverts attention from several of their initial cons: they are extremely complex to understand (and to use), and they lack design-time configurability. The usefulness of the large range of provided services is mitigated by the difficulty for the developer to appropriate these services in accordance with his specific requirements. Thus, our belief is that major issues for bridging the gap with RT/E reside not only in enhancing the platforms themselves, but also in simplifying their use and, in enabling the application designers to adapt the platforms to their specific needs. The objective is thus to identify key issues which would contribute to answer these two concerns. Researchers from middleware have obviously a bottom-up approach, which consists in a constant rising in abstraction -from, for instance, CORBA to CCM-. In order to have a complementary view, we have chosen to consider approaches which have had a top-down process, hence our focus on ADLs-based approaches. This paper presents the first step of our work, in which the focus is on *interactions between components* in CCM. It explains why we have chosen to introduce the concept of ADL *connector* concept in CCM, and gives some insights about how we intend to proceed. The structure of this paper is as follows: Section 2 is an introductive overview of CCM, with a focus on the aspects linked to our study. In Section 3, our focus on interactions is justified, and we describe the rationale which has lead us to the "CCM connector" choice. Section 4 describes the primitive set of connectors we have built for integration in CCM. Eventually, Section 5 gives some insights about the needed CCM extensions, before concluding.

## 2. Introducing CCM

This section presents some fundamentals of framework-based approaches and gives an overview of the CCM.

### General concepts of framework-based approaches

Frameworks have been recognized to capture best practices in some engineering domains: they provide templated implementations of patterns that were seen as leveraging issues in particular domains. A main characteristic of many frameworks is the inversion of the control flow: the application specific code is invoked by the framework to perform specific tasks and not vice versa (as opposed to a library).

Middleware components approaches use the abstraction of an encapsulated *component.* A key characteristic of a component is that it is loosely coupled, i.e. there are no dependencies to other components – only to certain interfaces. This is achieved by the separation of interface and implementation. A component *implements* a set of interfaces and it *requires* components implementing a set of other interfaces.

A component requiring an interface can be *bound* to another component offering a *compatible* interface (usually compatibility is defined via inheritance hierarchies or via a structural equivalence). The bindings are usually specified by a separate assembly descriptor.

Components are often embedded into *Containers* that mediate requests from and to the component. Containers are part of the *execution framework* for components that provides frequently used services such as persistency or security. It can be tailored towards the application needs. The bindings between components are enabled by means of a packaging format as well as a deployment infrastructure.

The CORBA Component Model

In the CORBA Component model, the external connection points of components are called *ports*. There are four different kinds of ports, called facets, receptacles, event sources and event sinks. Facets correspond to provided (implemented) interfaces, receptacles to required interfaces (containing method calls specified in IDL – Interface Definition Language). Event sources and sinks are the event based counterparts to receptacles and facets. Sources emit events of a certain type, event sinks are named connection points into which events can be pushed. Besides the facets, the component always implements a primary interface, called equivalent interface. Figure 1 shows a CCM component. Receptacles can be connected to facets, as depicted for the second receptacle on the right.

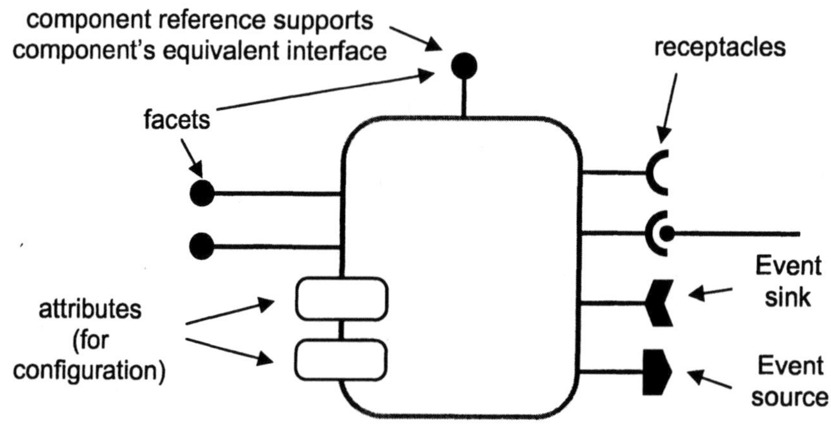


Figure 1: CORBA Component Model

Component instances are managed by a component home, which is in charge of instantiating and deleting components, i.e. the components life cycle (not shown).

We give below an example of a component description in IDL3, as well as the description of its associated interfaces, event types, and home:

```
interface intf1 {
  void do_something( in string s );
};
eventtype E {
```

```
  public string s;
};
component C {
  provides intf1 a_intf1;
  consumes E a_E;
};
home C_home manages C {
  attribute string foo;
};
```

The CCM introduces a so called *component implementation framework* (CIF) with the objective to separate concerns: the component should not be responsible for instance to manage connections or know how to emit an event via an underlying CORBA service.

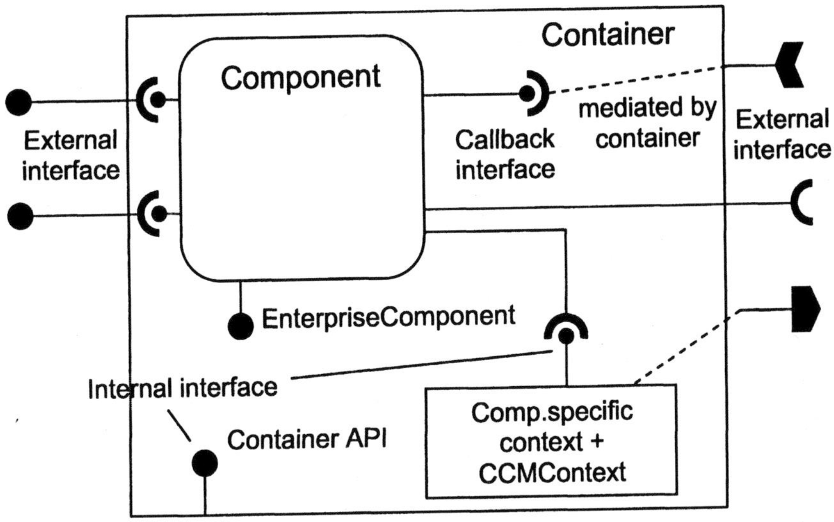


Figure 2: Components are embedded into a container

The *container* is the glue between a component and the underlying execution platform as shown in Figure 2. It provides a programming interface for the component, the internal interface. This interface consists of a standardized container API and a component specific context object. The code of the context object is completely generated from the IDL definition. It provides an interface that allows the component to retrieve references for used interfaces and operations related to the publishing of events (a reference to an implementation of the Context is passed by the container to the component). If the latter are invoked, the context object generates suitable events of the underlying event mechanism, usually the CORBA notification service. For incoming events, the component has to implement a callback interface and the container mediates the event by invoking a method provided on this interface. Please note that this form of event delivery does not allow the component to poll for new events, it is always "pushed" into the component. Since the container shields the component by intercepting its communication, it can implement some non-functional requirements such as logging or security.

The CCM provides an explicit deployment step within the development process. In this phase, component instances (including values of their attributes) as well as their interconnections are specified. This task might be supported by a suitable tool. The specification is done by means of different descriptors files in XML, in particular a component descriptor and component assembly descriptors.

We omit further details of the CCM, since they are not necessary in order to understand the rest of the paper.

## 3. Answering the need for a CCM interactions improvement

In [14], the author states that (static) configurability is a paramount concern in real-time embedded systems. This is particularly true when talking about components interactions: industrial practices tend to favor different architecture styles depending on the application domain considered. As examples, in the field of communication protocols, a layered approach together with a pipes and filters generalized pattern is commonly used. In the signal processing domain, a data-flow approach is considered most of the time. In some distributed systems like command and control-ones, a common practice is to use variations around publish-subscribe. The variety of practices thus highlights the necessity, to provide developers with means to properly configure the interaction mechanisms to be used in their applications and, to ensure the adherence to specified features (e.g. QoS ones) at execution. And yet, as most middleware components approaches, CCM offers rather poor means to express and configure components' interactions modalities at design time.

In order to bridge this gap, we have first considered various attempts to adapt CBSE to real-time embedded software design. In these latter, three issues are generally distinguished:

- Adaptation of the *component model*, which is an informal representation of what should be a component. It usually specifies the content (e.g. binary [12]) of components, the interaction points with the environment (e.g. event channels [13]), and often a set of non-functional features associated to the component. The originality of these approaches compared to classical ones usually lies in this latter point. For instance, many authors seem to agree on the integration of WCET in components.

However, in some cases, the list of features to integrate can be much larger, e.g., memory needs, deadline, power requirements.

- The *development process* of an application with components is often described as a complement of the component model. This issue often emphasizes the need to enable the reuse of components and the necessity to have a connection with off-the-shelf validation tools, for instance to assess the schedulability of the resulting system. The guidance provided for development process may also be a mean to introduce common real-time architecture patterns [11].
- The last aspect usually addressed is *architectural configuration*, i.e. representation of applications by connected graph of components. The approaches demonstrate the way components may be composed, or how the resulting system architecture may be validated, e.g. with regards to interfaces compatibility or exclusion constraints.

A common point arising from these approaches is the focus on the component model specification. Very little attention is paid to the interaction modalities, which are implicitly specified by the components' interfaces and the representation of the connections between these interfaces in the architectural configuration. This focus is also obvious in [9], where the authors list a set of industrial requirements for the CBSE approaches to be suitable for automotive real-time embedded systems: all the requirements regard either development process or component model issues.

The most relevant answer to our concern was actually found in approaches issuing from the Software Architecture / ADLs field. ADLs provide features for modeling software systems' conceptual architecture, independently from implementation concerns [16]. An ADL usually provides, on top of the *component* modeling concept, the notion of a *connector*, which represents an architectural building block used to model interactions among components and rules that govern those interactions. Connectors are considered as first-class model elements [6] in the sense that they have quite the same attached features as components, e.g. interfaces, semantics, constraints, non-functional properties. For instance, Unicon [4] proposes to specify a protocol for each connector which provides a connector type, and assertions constraining the interaction (e.g. roles). Each connector specification provides also an implementation which may be built-in. Non-functional attributes may also be attached, e.g. real-time ones to perform a schedulability analysis. In [5], a comprehensive framework is provided to perform a classification of all kinds of connectors. This approach chooses to classify connectors according to the service they provide, their types, and the dimensions along which these types may be refined. This work follows a bottom-up pattern: instead of designing connectors and implementing the corresponding mechanism, the authors have made an attempt to perform an exhaustive classification of existing interaction mechanisms in software. In [18], the author proposes a radically different view of connector. After having noticed that usual connectors address rather primitive interactions mechanisms, he proposes to consider connectors as "pattern-like transferable abstractions": connectors express only abstract interactions -mainly specified by roles and protocols- which have no direct mapping to the implementation of the application.

As noted in the introduction, one of the CCM drawbacks is that it does not provide an abstract view of many aspects relevant for RT/E systems (these are hidden in the implementation that may configure for instance a CORBA timeout for synchronous operations). Many facilities are provided by the communication layer, but they require a high level of expertise to be used properly. Introducing connectors would constitute an opportunity to provide a high-level translation of these mechanisms in a more understandable manner. Connectors are also likely to facilitate the integration, reuse and replacement of components, especially when building applications from off-the-shelf ones. These connectors should not, of course, result in a one-to-one representation of the underlying mechanisms. The aim is to provide the developer with easily configurable interaction facilities, shielding him the complexity of the platform. However, unlike [18], we believe that introducing connectors is bound to have an impact on the CCM component model and accompanying artifacts (e.g. IDL), and that connectors shall have an implementation counterpart. On top of that, the native architecture of CCM appears to be adapted to perform the introduction of connectors. For instance, with its intermediate positioning between the communication layer and the application, the components' container is a relevant place holder for an implementation of the connectors. Another important issue to consider is the integration in the development process: our opinion slightly differs from the "connectors as first-call elements" software architecture's leitmotiv. Since we do not intend to act on the communication layer, but only on the CCM level, the connectors to be built will be largely constrained by the native mechanisms of the underlying platform. In our view of the development process, connectors will not be *designed* in the same way components are designed, but a set of primitive connectors will be predefined and provided to the application developer, who will be able only to *configure* them in order to fill the application requirements. Following these high-level requirements, the points to deal with are thus: first to define these primitive connectors, then to ensure their configurability, and at last integrate them in CCM. In the next section, we explain how we have dealt with the first two points, based on both a bibliographical work in real-time platform and on the connector classification framework provided in [5].

## 4. Interactions reification: building the primitive connectors

Our aim was twofold: identifying main interaction mechanisms available in real-time platforms, finding means to express these mechanisms by means of configurable connectors. The first point has been addressed by trying to cover a large area in terms of technological trends in real-time systems in our bibliographical work. Thus, several standard platforms offering different levels of abstraction have been considered, from operating systems (e.g. OSEK [20]) to middleware layers (e.g. Fractal [21]). Furthermore, the main computation models in real-time systems have been studied (e.g. time-triggered [19] and event-triggered architecture). We have also benefit from the experience acquired in working on the Accord/UML platform [7], a complex real-time systems development facility designed at CEA-List. In order to deal with the second issue, we have chosen to use as a base the conceptual foundations of the connector classification framework provided by [5]. Our rationale is thus the following: defining basic connectors, refining them by attaching them sets of parameters/sub-parameters which may take different values, and assessing these connectors by expressing with them the mechanisms found in the various real-time platforms.

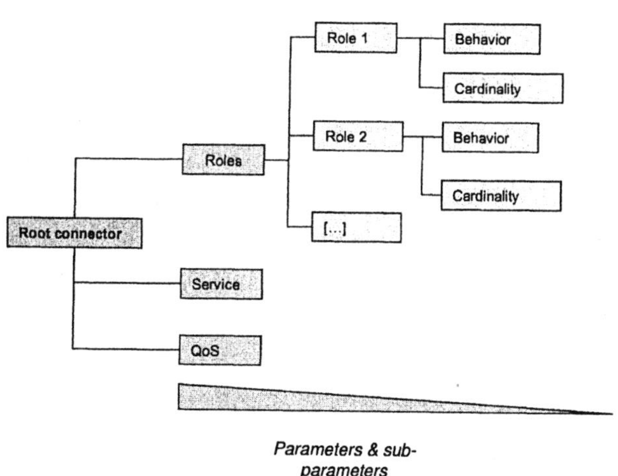


Figure 3: Root Connector

In order to set a starting point in the connectors design, we have tried to clarify the notion of interaction by introducing several basic characteristics: in our rationale, an interaction involves several *participants*, each acting in a given *role* (e.g. sender, subscriber); the *cardinality* of the interaction specifies the number of components instances associated to each role, and the *behavior* of a role precises the actions performed by a component playing this role. Interactions are also to be considered from the *service type* point of view: *communication* (i.e. data transmission) or *coordination* (i.e. synchronization). In RT/E applications, *Quality of Service* requirements (e.g. priority, deadline) may be associated to the interaction. These few characteristics specify a "root connector" (Figure 3) from which all our connectors derive.

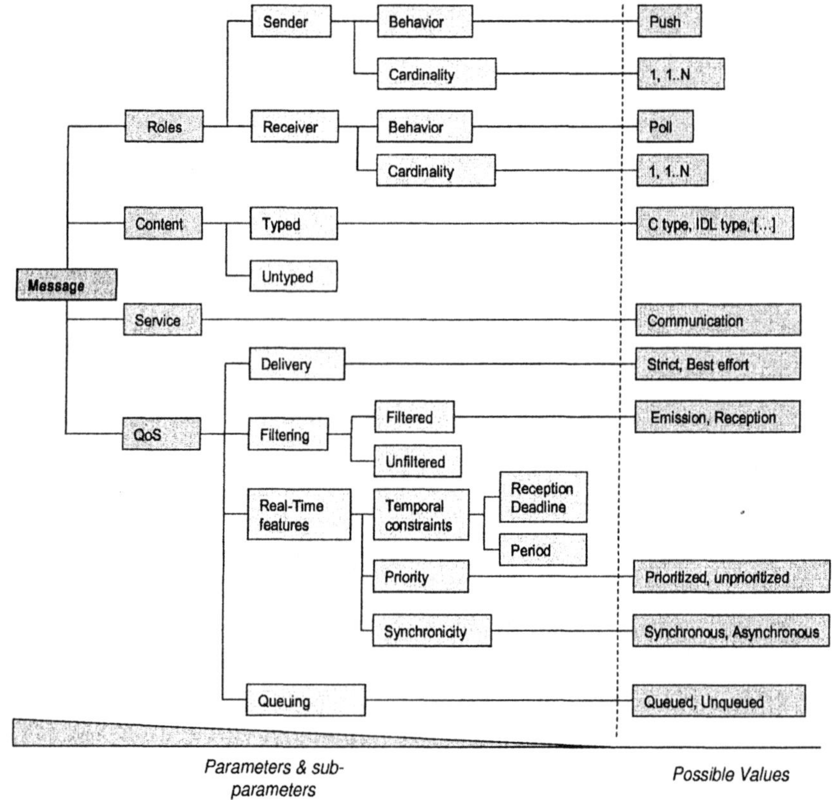


Figure 4: Message connector

From our bibliographical work, we have identified three main interaction mechanisms: message passing, event broadcasting and procedure call. These mechanisms have then been directly mapped to primitive connectors (message, event, and procedure call), and refined by adding parameters and sub-parameters, following the base pattern presented above. In the following, we detail an example of building such a primitive connector: the *Message* one. Message passing is a very common mechanism in real-time platform, which basically consists in a data exchange between tasks/components. To build the associated primitive connector "message", we have considered one by one its base parameters:

- Roles: In all platforms, message passing involves two roles: sender and receiver. Depending on the platform considered, cardinality may be 1 to 1, or n to m. The behavior is homogeneous among the different platform: the sender performs a *push* operation, and the receiver *polls* the incoming messages.
- Service: Message passing is a *communication* support.
- QoS: Depending on the safety requirements of the platform, the *delivery* of a message may be guaranteed (strict) or not (best-effort). Messages may be filtered (for instance, not accepting the same content multiple times) at reception or emission. Several Real-Time features may also be associated to a message connector: *temporal constraints* (period, deadline,...); *priority*: have all the message the same priority (prioritized)? Or can a priority be set for each message (prioritized)? *synchronicity*: asynchronous delivery, or synchronous.

The last aspect, not considered until now as not present in the root connector, is the *content*: depending on the approaches, this content may be typed (e.g. C type in OSEK) or untyped. Figure 4 shows the message connector type resulting from this analysis.

It is equally possible to describe the "event" connector, which is another common interaction mechanism in real-time systems. Briefly, let us precise that the majority of parameters identified in messages are applicable to events. However, roles behaviors are affected (for instance, the receiver will be invoked or will poll the received messages) and the focus is no more on the *content* since what matters is the *occurrence* of the event and not its format.

In the same way, we have built the *procedure call* connector. This set of three connectors has then been assessed with regards to its expressiveness, by using them to represent the interactions mechanisms offered by the studied real-time. Platform-specific mechanisms are expressed as subsets of the primitive connectors: depending on the platform considered, parameters/sub-parameters and values are removed. For instance, representing the POSIX message queues requires to remove from the message connectors the "filtering" QoS sub-parameter (and its associated values), as well as the "unprioritized" priority value, the "unqueued" queuing value, the "synchronous" synchronicity value, and the "strict" delivery value.

Once the primitive connectors built and assessed, we have looked for ways to integrate them in CCM. In the next sections, we list the issues which have to be dealt with, and give for several of them some elements of answer.

## 5. Lightweight CCM extension strategy

There are two extensions to the CCM model: the first is the introduction of connectors, the second an extension of port abilities.

A connector shares many properties with a component: it will offer ports as interaction points and provide attributes for its configuration. Therefore, its specification in IDL will "look like" a normal component specification in which the keyword component has been exchanged by the keyword connector. Of course, its implementation will be different to that of a component, as shown later. Unlike in the standard CCM, components will normally not be connected directly with each other, but use a connector in between. This means, that a component instance binds one of its ports to a suitable port of a connector instance which in turn will be bound via another port to the target component (in general, it should be possible that the interaction is mediated via additional connectors). QoS aspects can be configured either via the attributes of a connector or a specific, standardized interface.

The connection of components and connectors via ports motivates the second CCM extension: if a component interacts with a connector, it plays a certain *role*. For instance, it could be an event producer or an event consumer. In the CCM, ports always correspond to either implementing or using a certain interface. For general interactions, this is not sufficient, since a single role may imply using a certain interface and implementing another one. For instance, an event producer might want to receive a notification, if an event has been successfully delivered to all subscribed consumers (or if the delivery has failed). In this example, the producer role would imply implementing a delivery-status interface and using a push interface for the delivery at the same time. While it is possible to define this scenario via a pair of uses/provides specification in the IDL, we would not have the possibility to associate a single role-name with this interaction.

Therefore, we propose to extend the notion of a port in CCM into an element that consists of zero or more provided as well as zero or more required interfaces, i.e. closely resembling the UML2 [17] specification of a port – unlike in the current CCM. For the example, we would get the following definition:

```
Port PushWithNotification {
  provides IPush push;                  // provided interface
  uses IDeliveryStatus deliveryStatus; // required intf.
}
```

A component will have the ability to use or provide ports and supply a role name, using the syntax use_port <port-name> as <role-name> (analogous: provide_port <port-name> with <role-name>). The translation of this extended IDL code into the existing one is straight forward: the use (provision) of a port is replaced by the use (provision) of the interfaces provided by a port and the provision (use) of the interfaces required by it.

The role names are important during the assembly of components and connectors. If a component instance is bound to a connector instance, each use of a port of the component has to match the provision of a port of the connector and vice versa. Provided and used ports match only, if type and role name are identical. This implicit binding via a role name avoids an additional specification (implying a further complexity). We assume that it will not impose a restriction in practice, since the use of a different role-name will almost certainly be accompanied by a different semantics that would inhibit the (unchanged) reuse of a component or connector.

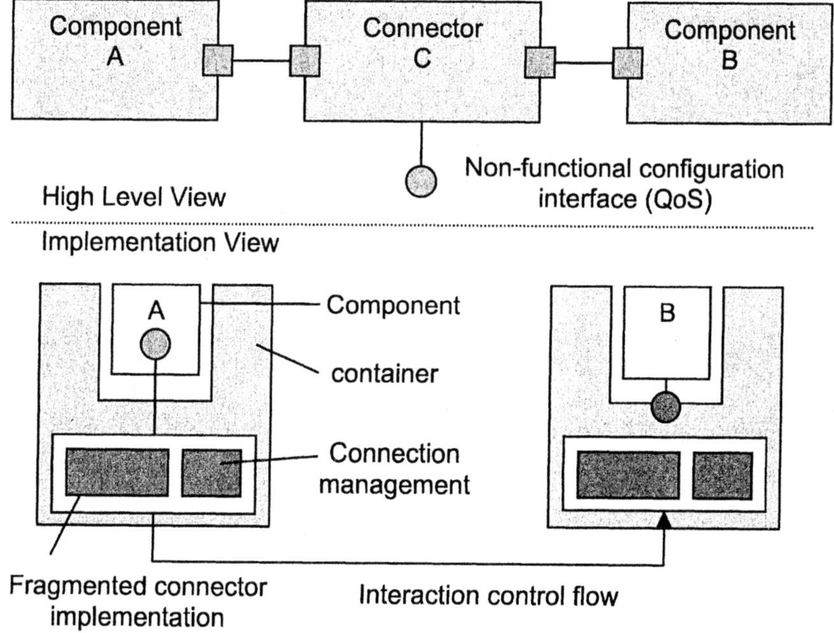


Figure 5: A first draft for architectural integration of connectors

However, the implementation of a connector – i.e. the connector's behaviour – is different to that of a normal component. It might behave almost like a normal component, e.g. in case of an event channel that is located on a specific node. However, in general, connectors can only be efficient, if their implementation consists of several parts, each co-located with a component that uses the connector in a specific role as shown in Figure 5. In addition, the connectors will be integrated in a different way with the container (it is not clear yet, whether the connectors should be considered as part of the container or not). Therefore, the CCM's code generation rules need to be adapted. It seems useful to support the fragmentation of a connector on the implementation level by different *executors* (compliant with CCM terminology; but different from component executors). Each of these executors would correspond to the use or provision of a port and would be co-located with the component bound to it.

The chosen component/connector model allows for the adaptation of invocations without modification: the connector would simply need to provide a port that assumes a certain style of usage and can internally transform and mediate requests to another port. An example is the transformation of a typed event at user level into an untyped event used by the underlying platform. It may be possible to generate the necessary adaptation code from a suitable description of the conversion.

There are two further aspects, connector packaging and assembly descriptors that need to be adapted as well. Since components are packaged into archives (containing descriptors, binary code for component), we propose to package connectors in archives, too. The rationale for this is to integrate the connector in the deployment procedure: it can be needed to instantiate part of the connector on a particular host (think about Event Channels). The component assembly descriptor format needs also to be adapted since, as shortly mentioned in the CCM description, the assembly descriptor format allows to describe direct binding between components (and matching port types), and hence does not allow to insert connectors between them.

## 6. Conclusions and Perspectives

We have described in this paper our ongoing work in the context of the ICE project, which aims at contributing to the adaptation of the CORBA component model to real-time software design domain. We have followed a process of real-time interaction mechanisms expression by means of connectors, supported and inspired by similar works from the ADLs area. We have laid the foundations for the next stage which will focus in concretely integrating these primitive connectors in CCM, and demonstrating the relevance of our approach through prototyping and application to use cases. The use cases selected have a close connection to "real" application domains and offer enough complexity to constitute an assessment of our conceptual and technical choices. For instance, we plan to deal with a simplified UMTS radio-protocol stack use case.

But CCM enhancement is of course still an open issue. Even if well-matured in some aspects, e.g., the extensive set of services provided with the middleware or the deployment issue, it still lacks major features. The main one regards what ADLs call *architectural configuration*, i.e. the ability to specify an application by means of a graphical representation, as well as addressing the associated issues (e.g. compositionality, refinement, scalability) [16]. Effectively, using CCM in its current state requires a sound knowledge of the underlying CORBA platform, and high skills in platforms implementation languages, which mitigate its usefulness for neophytes. Moreover, this absence of a high-level representation forbids the early validation of the developed application, an action commonly performed with ADLs.

Building this CCM architectural configuration requires in a first step to give an abstract view of the mechanisms provided by the CCM middleware platform. It sets also a need for an enhancement of the CCM component model. Our contribution regards these two issues, with a focus on interactions representation.

## 7. References


[1] Lightweight CORBA Component Model – OMG draft adopted specification, Object Management Group, 2003.

[2] CORBA Components, version 3.0, Object Management Group, 2002.

[3] RealTime – CORBA specification, version 2.0, Object Management Group, 2003.

[4] Abstractions for Software Architecture and Tools to support them, M. Shaw, Robert Deline et al., Software Engineering, vol. 21, number 4, 1995.

[5] Towards a Taxonomy of Software Connectors, N. R. Mehta, N. Medvidovic and S. Phadke, ICSE 2000.

[6] Software Connectors and their role in component development, D. Bálek & F. Plášil, DAIS'01.

[7] MDA Platform for Complex Embedded Systems Development, C. Mraidha, S. Robert et al., DIPES 2004.

[8] Specification for deployment and configuration of component based applications - draft adopted specification, OMG, 2003.

[9] Software Component Technologies for Real-Time Systems - An Industrial Perspective -, Anders Möller, Mikael Åkerholm et al., RTSS 2003.

[10] Towards Aspectual Component-Based Development of Real-Time Systems, Aleksandra Tešanovic, Dag Nyström et al, RTCSA 2003.

[11] Developing component-based software for Real-Time systems, Janusz Zalewski, 27th Euromicro conference, 2001.

[12] Components in Real-Time Systems, D. Isovic, C. Norström, RTCSA 2002.

[13] An Approach to Component-Based Software Engineering for Distributed Embedded Real-Time System, Uwe Rastofer, Frank Bellosa, WMSCI 2000.

[14] VEST: A toolset for constructing and analyzing component based operating systems for embedded and real-time systems, John A. Stankovic, Lecture Notes in Computer Science, vol. 2211, 2001.

[15] RNTL project ACCORD, http://www.infres.enst.fr/projets/accord.

[16] A Classification and Comparison Framework for Software Architecture Description Languages, N. Medvidovic, R. N. Taylor, IEEE transactions on software engineering, vol. 26, n. 1, 2000.
[17] UML 2.0 Superstructure (Final Adopted specification), Object Management Group, 2003, http://www.omg.org/cgi-bin/doc?ptc/03-08-02
[18] A Connector Model for Object-Oriented Component Integration, Stefan Tai, International Workshop on Component-Based Software Engineering, 1998.
[19] Time-Triggered Real-Time Computing, H. Kopetz, IFAC World Congress, Barcelona, July 2002, IFAC Press.
[20] OSEK/VDX Operating System version 2.2.1, OSEK/VDX, 2003.
[21] The Fractal project, ObjectWeb Consortium, http://fractal.objectweb.org/.

# UML 2 AS AN ADL HIERARCHICHAL HARDWARE MODELING

Arnaud Cuccuru
Arnaud.Cuccuru@lifl.fr

Philippe Marquet
Philippe.Marquet@lifl.fr

Jean-Luc Dekeyser
Jean-Luc.Dekeyser@lifl.fr

*Laboratoire d'informatique fondamentale de Lille*
*Université des sciences et technologies de Lille*
*France*

**Abstract** Taking into account the hardware architecture specificities is a crucial step in the development of an efficient application. This is particularly the case for embedded systems where constraints are strong (real-time) and resources limited (computing, power). This approach is called co-design, and it is found more or less explicitly in ADLs. Much work have been done around co-design and ADLs, but no standard notation and semantics have emerged. Concerning software engineering, UML has become a recognized standard language for modeling, proving the need of users for common syntax and vocabulary to specify their applications. We believe that it would useful to use the well achieved syntax and vocabulary of UML for both applications and hardware architectures, that is to say using UML as an ADL. Our approach consists in a clear specialization of an UML subset via a the proposition of a generic profile that allows the definition of precise semantic and syntaxic rules. The generic profile can then be extended to suit the need of the user. To illustrate our subject, we give a refinement example of the profile to get relevant informations for a simulation at the TLM level (Transaction Level Modeling). The modeling of the Texas Instrument OMAP2410 and OMAP2420 is provided as an example.

# 1. Hardware Modeling and UML

The usage of an ADL permits to represent static or dynamic characteristics of a system. This system is either a software or a hardware system. For embedded systems, both system are defined: you need to co-design your application and your hardware platform in the same time with respect to specific constraints.

Concerning software engineering, UML (Unified Modeling Language) [Object Management Group, Inc., 2003] has become a standard language for modeling. It does not present a particular methodology and it can be used to model different point of view of the same model. UML 2 introduces the component notion and structure diagrams that facilitate architecture modeling. With deployment diagrams, UML 2 also considers hardware descriptions and mapping. Unfortunately, the model for applications differs from the model for hardware. The same comment applies for the mapping of an application on a particular hardware, for example a System on Chip: we want to benefit from the component notion, the hierarchical constructs of the structural and behavioral diagrams for the hardware design as well as for the software design.

We define our hardware description metamodel based on the UML 2.0 component notion. The structural specification is sufficient to generate SystemC [Open SystemC Initiative, 2002] code to produce a TLM (Transaction Level Modeling) simulation once the mapping of an application on this hardware model is achieved.

## 1.1 Related Work

Several proposals, emerged from the OMG world or not, introduce hardware modeling techniques and/or concepts. Only a few ones are “sold” as ADLs.

**AADL** [Feiler et al., 2003] (Avionics Architecture Description Language) is the only proposal which clearly advocates the use of UML as an ADL. This language is based on MetaH. It is used to describe the structure of an embedded system as a gathering of software and hardware components. It can describe both functional (data inputs and outputs) and non functional (such as timing) aspects of components. A UML profile for AADL (based on UML 2) is under standardization, and will be soon submitted to the OMG. Concerning the hardware modeling part of this proposal, four concepts are introduced: ***memory***, ***processor***, ***bus*** and ***device***. We will see later in this paper that our proposal is not semantically far from this one. However, the goal of hardware modeling (called platform) in AADL is not the same as ours. The platform specification is more or less used to apply schedulability and fault tolerance analysis verification tools (that is to say to verify that a software associated to one platform meets the requirements that the system must satisfy), whereas the tools we plan to use are rather optimization tools (for mapping of computing, data, and communications). Moreover, we can't clearly see in the specifi cation of the language how the hardware concepts can be composed and/or assembled.

The **UML SPT Profile** [Object Management Group, Inc., 2002] (Scheduling, Performance, and Time analysis) is an UML 1.x OMG standard profi le for embedded systems modeling. It introduces various hardware (or more generally platform) modeling concepts and an interesting resource classifi cation according to three criteria: *purpose* (processor, communication and device), *activeness* (a resource is active when it is able to generate stimuli, and passive when it is only able to react when prompted by stimuli), and *protection* (a resource is protected when the access to services it offers is restricted according to some control access policy). However, the profi le gives no clear orientation and methodology on the way it can be used. Moreover, the underlying execution model (a resource is acquired and then released) is too restrictive and unfortunately does not suit our needs.

**HaSoC** [Green and Edwards, 2002a, Green and Edwards, 2002b] (Hardware and Software Objects on Chip) is a platform-based design methodology using UML to represent high-level structure and behaviour of the hardware architecture model of an application platform. The hardware architecture model of HASoC distinguishes general-purpose hardware (processors, memory), programmable logic (FPGAs), fi xed-function (custom) hardware, and interconnection elements. This model enables to generate SystemC code for simulation and particularly for hardware synthesis. For our purpose, distinction between programmable and non programmable units is not necessary [1], as hardware synthesis is not one of our goal. Moreover, this model doesn't seem to exploit hierarchical capabilities offered by UML 2.

The **SLOOP** [Zhu et al., 2002] (System Level design with Object-Oriented Process) design process integrates a methodology based on UML for both SoC modeling and performance evaluation at system level. The hardware model proposed is similar to those previously presented: it proposes hardware elements such as processors, memories, buses and hardware devices. However, the hardware architectures are modeled via deployment diagrams, with various stereotypes applied to "Nodes". This choice has the benefi t of being simple and relatively natural for people coming from the UML world. Indeed, deployment diagrams are used to coarsely describe execution platforms for applications. But we believe that deployment diagrams are too restrictive to model architectures (no hierarchy, no encapsulation via ports and interfaces, no behavior description...), and that the same model must be used for both hardware and software.

## 1.2 Proposal

Our approach consists in a clear specialization of an UML subset for which we can define precise syntactic and semantic rules. This prevents from all kind of ambiguities in the model[2].

The abstract syntax of our model is described by a MOF metamodel defined as an extension of the UML 2 metamodel. The metamodeling brings a set of tools which will enable us to specify our application and hardware architecture models using UML tools, to reuse functional and physical IPs, to ensure refinements between abstraction levels via mapping rules, to ensure interoperability between the different abstraction levels used in a same codesign, and to ensure the opening to other tools, like verification tools, thought the use of standards. The concrete syntax is defined by a profile for UML 2. This profile is, for the moment, only based on UML 2 class diagrams and internal structure diagrams[3]. In this paper, we focus on the description of the profile(there is almost a "one to one" equivalence between concepts introduced in the metamodel and stereotypes introduced in the profile). The generic rules and concepts are described in a generic part of the profile. This generic elements are then refined via an extension of the profile to fit to the needs of the user (documentation, simulation at various abstraction levels, optimization...).

The first part of the paper summaries the so-called "Y model approach" [Dumoulin et al., 2003], and describes the generic part of the profile, focusing on the set of "basic blocks" that define the syntax and semantics of our hardware architecture model. Therefore, we propose a classification, at the same time both functional and structural, in order to identify each kind of components[4] of our model. Then, we specify the construction rules which govern components assembling and composition.

The second part of this document shows how an extension of the profile can be used to refine the "basic blocks", in order to produce models suited to a particular use. For that, we give an extension of the used profile to gather relevant informations of a simulation at a TLM level in an environment such as SystemC. As a conclusion, we illustrate our subject with a case study: the TI OMAP2410 and OMAP2420 [Texas Instruments, 2004].

# 2. Y Model Approach

Our proposal is partially based upon the "Y-chart" concepts [Gajski and Kuhn, 1983]. A clear distincition is made between application and hardware, which are related via an explicit mapping.

The application and hardware architecture are described by different metamodels. Some concepts handle within these two metamodels are similar in order to unify and so simplify their understanding and use.

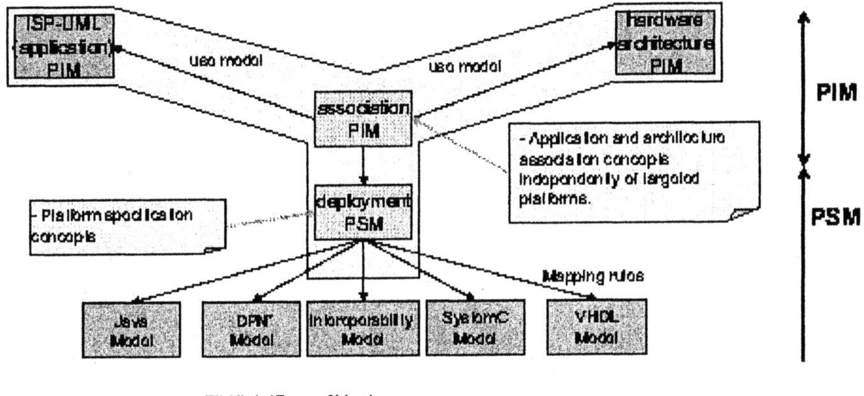


*Figure 1.* Y Model Approach

The proposed methodology is to separately design the two models for the application and the hardware architecture (maybe by two different people). At this point, it becomes possible to map the application model on the hardware architecture model. For this purpose we introduce a third metamodel, the so-called association metamodel, to express the associations between the functional components of the application model and the hardware components of the hardware model. This third metamodel imports the fi rst two metamodels.

## 3. Hierarchical Hardware Architecture Model

We present here the different hardware components that we introduce in our model, and we give the rules on the way to compose and assemble them with each other.

The hardware components represent abstractions of physical hardware architecture elements. A hardware component owns an interface materialized by its ports, and a structure defi ned by an assembly of components via an internal structure diagram.

### 3.1 Resource Classification

We propose to classify the resources according to two criteria: a functional criterion, and a structural criterion (Fig. 2). Each resource is characterized by a composition of these two criteria. In UML, it comes to apply two stereotypes to each component.

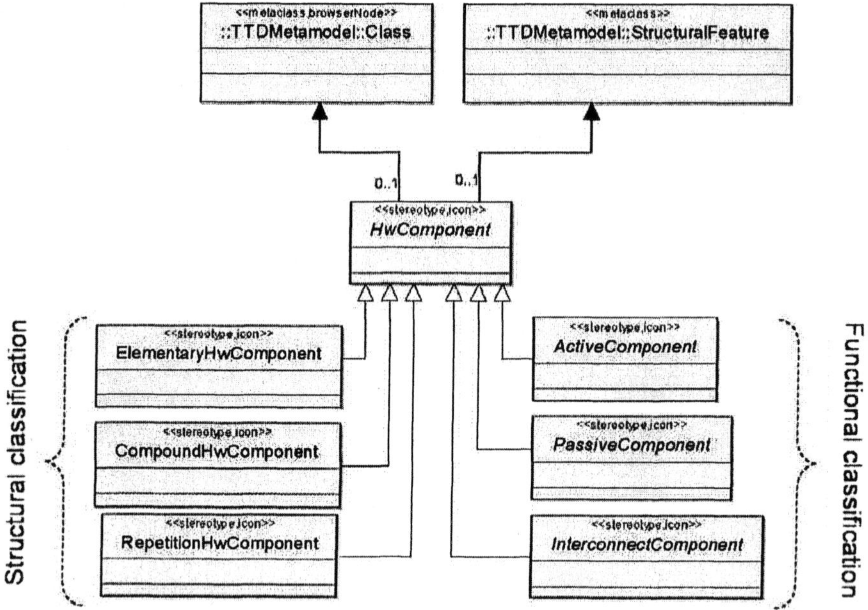


*Figure 2.* Resource classification

**Functional Classification.** We identify three kinds of function for a component (three stereotypes in UML): a component can be either passive, active, or for interconnection.

"`PassiveHwComponent`" A passive component symbolizes a resource which has the function of supporting data. Typically, we fi nd in this category elements such as RAMs, ROMs, sensors, or actuators.

"`ActiveHwComponent`" An active component symbolizes a resource which has the function or reading or writing into passive resources. It may modify, or not, the data. This category includes elements such as CPUs or DMAs. It also includes more coarse-grained elements, such as a SMP node inside a parallel machine.

"`InterconnectHwComponent`" An interconnection resource connects active and passive components, or active and active in the case of a distributed memory architecture. This category includes element as simple as a bus, or as complex as an omega interconnection network.

**Structural Classification.** The structural classifi cation is used ease introspection of models and, as a consequence, automatic or manual exploitation of gathered data (for example to optimize the mapping of an application on a hardware architecture). We identify three kinds of structure for a component (three stereotypes in UML): a component may be either elementary, passive, or for repetition.

**"`ElementaryHwComponent`"** An elementary component is a component without an internal structural description. For example, it could be used in the case where we have an hardware IP for this component, or in the case where we don't want to model the component more fi nely.

**"`CompoundHwComponent`"** A compound component is a component with an internal structure description. A compound component can represent an "executable architecture" (fully defi ned architecture) or a part of an architecture that will be reused in other contexts. A compound component may be defi ned with several hierarchy levels: a compound component may be described as the gathering of other "sub" compound components. The benefi ts of composition are numerous, and they are not specifi c to our model: encapsulation of structural details not needed at a given hierarchical level, reuse or repetition (in the case of a "`RepetitionHwComponent`") of predefi ned blocks to model other architectures...

**"`RepetitionHwComponent`"** A repetition component[5] is a particular case of the compound component. The repetition component structure contains a regular repetition of a single component. This kind of component is well suited to the modeling of massively parallel architectures and is motivated by the recent introduction of such architectures in the design of SoC such as the picoChip PC101 [picoChip, 2003].

## 3.2 Construction Rules

The construction rules (that is to say the composition and assembling rules) of our model are based on UML 2.0 rules. From generic UML rules, we defi ne coherent rules for the possible direction of ports ("required" or "provided") according to the function of each component ("active", "passive" or "interconnection"). Then, we propose rules for components assembling, based on rules given for ports direction. We also lightly modify the semantic of connection concept, but we remain coherent with defi nition given in UML 2 specifi cation. Finally, we give rules concerning component composition.

**Assembling Rules Defined in UML 2.** The components are linked together via connectors. The ports materialize the connection points. One or more required or provided interfaces are associated to each port. Two ports can be connected only if they have compatible interfaces, and if one port is "required"[6], and the other is "provided"[0].

The methods associated to each interface represent services. A component with a required port is able to emit services requests to its environment, whereas a component with a provided port provides a set of services to its environment.

**Ports "direction".** We use assembling rules defined in UML to restrict possible directions of ports (required or provided) associated to each kind of components of our architecture model.

A passive component only owns provided ports, as it can only propose services for data support (read/write) to active components. An active component typically owns required ports, as it can emit read or write services requests to passive components. It can also own provided ports to receive requests emitted by other active components, for example in the case of a distributed memory architecture. An interconnection component owns required and provided, as it has the function of linking active and passive components, or active and(Fig. 5) active components.

**Assembling Rules.** Respecting rules previously mentioned, two passive components can not be connected together (on both sides, there are only provided ports). We add the constraint that all connections between active and passive components or between active and active components must be done via an interconnection component. This constraint enables to ease and systematize the parsing of models. Moreover, a clear identification of the interconnection resources enables to associate properties to these resources (such as bandwidth, or latency).

**Connections Semantics.** Services associated to ports are implicit according to the function of the component and the definition we gave of these functions (the active components require read/write services to passive components via interconnection components). As a consequence, an incomplete model in the standard UML formalism (that is to say with no interfaces associated to ports) can be interpreted without ambiguities in the context of our profile. The user of the profile is free to add the interface suited to the case he is modeling.

Connections between ports are interpreted as potential data paths offered by architecture, more than paths for services exchanges. This semantics is close to the semantics of connections between modules in SystemC.

In our case, the association of interfaces to ports in a hardware architecture is a way to refine its specification according to application mapped on this architecture.

**Composition Rules.** A passive compound component may only contain other passive components. A active compound component can only contain other interconnection components. An active component can contain all kinds of component. The top level component in the hierarchy is necessarily a active compound (or repetition) component. By this way, the parsing of an architecture consists in a traversal of active compound or repetition components.

## 4. A Profile Refinement for TLM Level Simulation

In this section, we show a refi nement of the generic profi le designed to get relevant informations from a simulation at a TLM level, such as execution time, load of interconnection elements, load balancing of active elements... The profi le refi nement consists in extending stereotypes defi ned in the generic part by adding them properties. First of all, we describe data types associated to properties of various modeling elements. Then, we show successively a refi nement for active elements, for passive elements, and fi nally for interconnection elements.

### 4.1 Data Types

Data types described here are used to type properties added to various refi ned model elements:

`TimeExpression` is an expression representing a duration *("13ns")*

`FrequencyExpression` is an expression representing a clock frequency *("1.2MHz")*

`CapacityExpression` is an expression representing a capacity *("16Mo")*

`BandWidthExpression` is an expression representing a bandwidth *("3.5Go/s")*

### 4.2 Active Component Refinement

To refi ne the concept of active component, we introduce two kinds of components: "`CPU`" and "`DMA`" (Fig. 3). These components extend (in a UML point view, but particularly in a semantic point of view) the defi nition of the active component.

**"`CPU`" Component.** A CPU represents a resource able to read and write in passive resources, with or without data modifi cations. It also symbolizes a resource able to execute functions defi ned in the application model. It is potentially able to execute all functions, except if the list of functions is explicitly restricted[7]. CPU is a generic term gathering CPUs (strict meaning), DSPs, or even FPGAs (i.e. all kind of programmable or not programmable resource able to realize a computation on data). A CPU is characterized by four attributes:

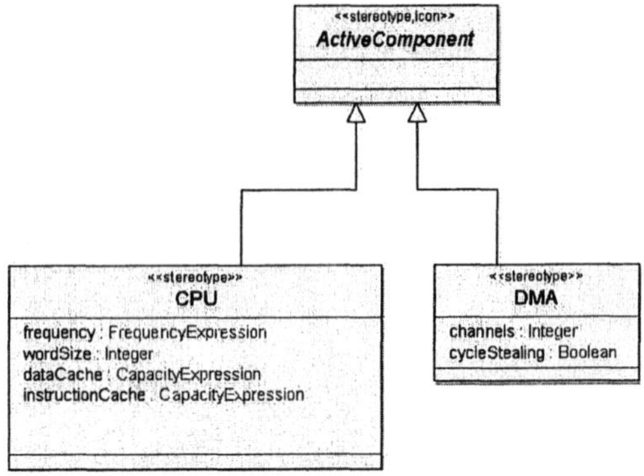


*Figure 3.* Active component refinement

`frequency: FrequencyExpression`. This property represents the clock frequency of the CPU. For example, it can be used to determin the execution duration of a function, in the case where the number of cycles necessary to execute this function on this CPU is known.

`wordSize: Integer`. This property represents the size of the words handled by the CPU. The size expression unit is the bit.

`dataCache: CapacityExpression`. This property represents the size of the data cache of the CPU.

`instructionCache: CapacityExpression`. This property represents the size of the instruction cache of the CPU.

**"`DMA`" Component.** A DMA is characterized by its number of channels and by the policy it uses: whether it is based on cycle-stealing or not.

## 4.3 Passive Component Refinement

To refine the concept of passive component, we introduce three kinds of component: "`Memory`", "`Sensor`" and "`Actuator`" (Fig. 4). These components extend (in a UML point view, but particularly in a semantic point of view) the definition of the passive component.

**"`Memory`" Component.** A memory has the function of supporting data. It is characterized by six attributes:

`capacity: CapacityExpression`. This property represents the size of the memory.

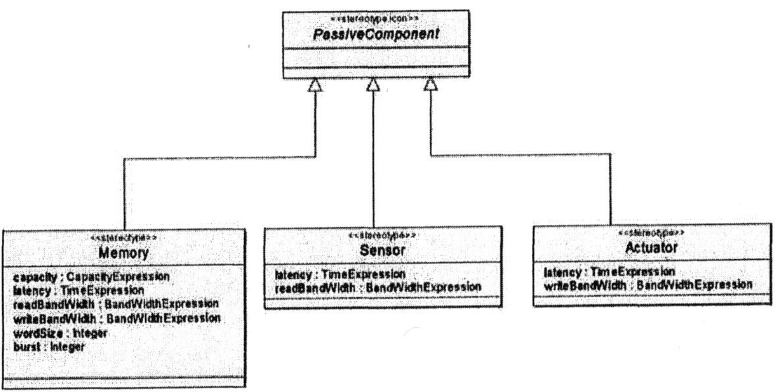


*Figure 4.* Passive component refinement

`latency: TimeExpression`. This property represents the latency related to a memory access. The value is expressed in time, and not in cycles, in order to make easier the reuse of memory component for several architecture modelings, or in the case of heterogeneous architectures (several kinds of CPU accessing the same memory component).

`readBandWidth: BandWidthExpression`. This property represents the read bandwidth of the memory.

`writeBandWidth: BandWidthExpression`. This property represents the write bandwidth of the memory.

`wordSize: CapacityExpression`. This property represents the size of a memory word.

`burst: Integer`. This property represents the number of memory word collected when an access in burst mode occurs.

**"`Sensor`" Component.** A sensor represents a resource able to periodically catch data from its environment, and put it at hardware architecture disposal. Sensors are classifi ed in the category of passive elements, in the way that they can be considered as read only memories. A active element can periodically get (read) data to compute or move from it. A sensor is characterized by two attributes:

`latency: TimeExpression`. This property represents the latency related to a read access.

`readBandWidth: BandWidthExpression`. This property represents the read bandwidth of the sensor.

**"Actuator" Component.** An actuator is the opposite of a sensor, that is to say a resource that provides data from the hardware architecture to its environment. Actuators are classifi ed in the category of passive elements, in the way that they can be considered as write only memories. An active component can periodically give (write) data to it. An actuator is characterized by two attributes:

`latency: TimeExpression`. This property represents the latency related to a write access.

`writeBandWidth: BandWidthExpression`. This property represents the write bandwidth of the actuator.

## 4.4 Interconnection Component Refinement

To refi ne the concept of interconnection component, we introduce one kind of component: "`Interconnect`" (Fig. 5). This component extends (in a UML point view, but particularly in a semantic point of view) the defi nition of the interconnection component.

**"Interconnect" Component.** The interconnect is not more precise semantically than the interconnection component defi ned in the generic part of the profi le. It's just an interconnection enriched with properties used for a simulation at a TLM level. It is characterized by two attributes:

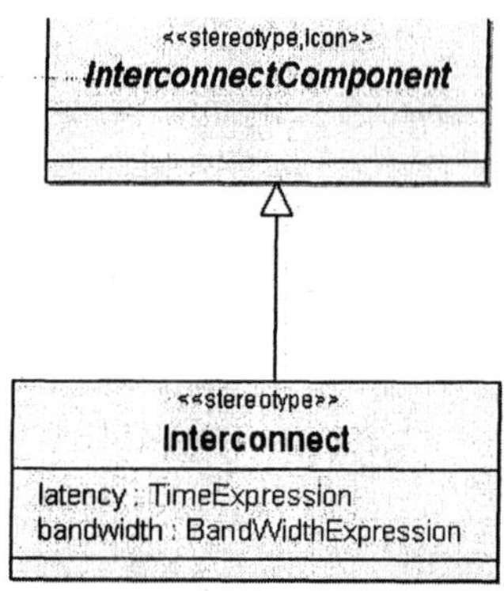


*Figure 5.* Interconnection component refinement

`latency: TimeExpression`. This property represents the latency related to an access to the interconnection component.

`bandWidth: BandWidthExpression`. This property represents the bandwidth of the interconnect.

# 5. Modeling examples: The TI OMAP2410 and OMAP2420

We present in this section two modeling examples. Specifi cations are deliberately not complete, and are just introduced for an illustration purpose. We illustrate the use of various modeling elements (refi ned or not) of our model,

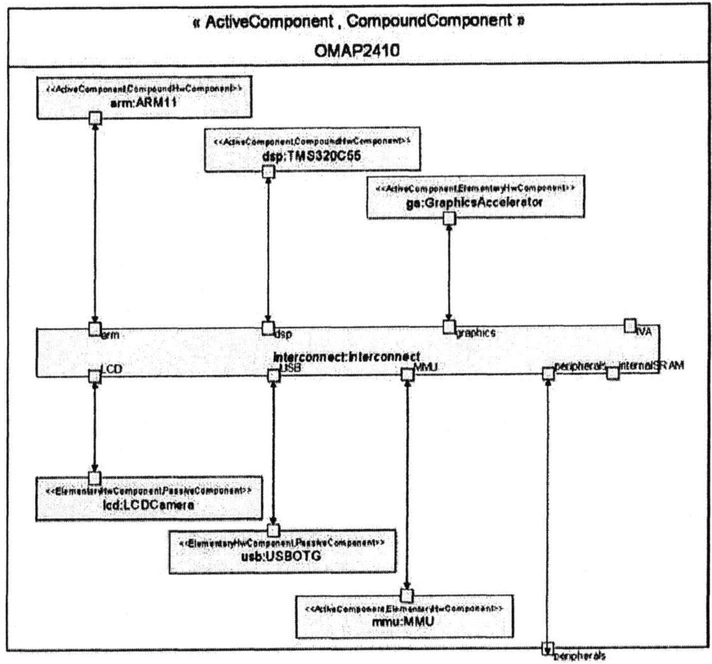


*Figure 6.* OMAP 2410 Structure

and the use of the inheritance mechanism of UML to define an hardware architecture by extension of another one.

The OMAP2410 and OMAP2420 processors are based on OMAP2 "All-in-One Entertainment" architecture [Texas Instruments, 2004]. They are designed to be used into smart-phones and portable media devices. They support high-end features such as multi-megapixel cameras, hifi music with 3D sound effects, high-speed wireless connectivity and more.

The OMAP2410 processor (Fig. 6) consists of an ARM11 that handles the operating system tasks and a TMS320C55 that works on the audio and video applications. It also contains additional features such as a hardware engine for three-dimensional images, a MMU (memory management unit), and interfaces to LCD/Camera, USB devices, and peripherals. Communications are made via a low-latency interconnection component.

The OMAP2420 processor (Fig. 8) is an extension of the OMAP2410. It extends the features of the 2410 with an IVA (Imaging Video Accelerator) and a 5 Mbit SRAM supporting a VGA display. As illustrated in Fig. 7, the OMAP2420 inherits the definition of the 2410.

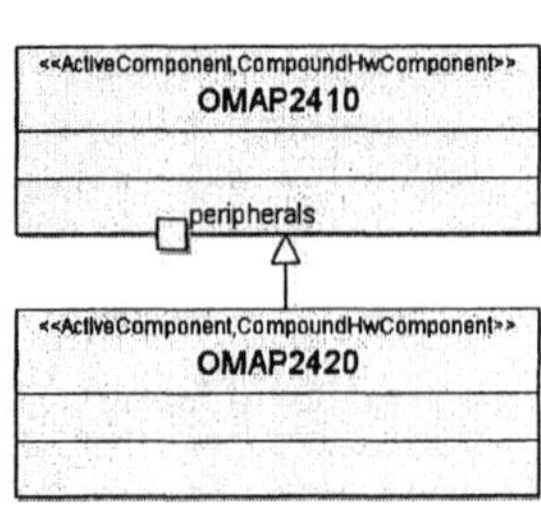


*Figure 7.* Inheritance link between OMAP 2410 and OMAP 2420

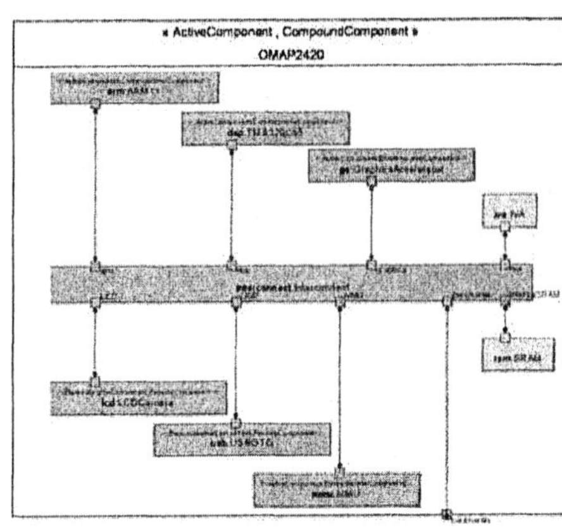


*Figure 8.* OMAP 2420 Structure

# 6. Conclusion

We have shown how we use UML 2 as an ADL, focusing on the hardware model of our approach. The model we have presented enables a description of hardware architectures at a high abstraction level. This model is implemented in a UML profile. This profile introduces generic concepts, with clear semantic and syntaxic basis, that can be refined for particular use. We gave an example of profile refinement to get relevant informations from a simulation at a TLM level, and we illustrated our subject with the modeling of the TI OMAP2410 and OMAP2420.

This is only the first step of our approach. We are currently working on mechanisms to express repetition of architectural elements. It enables for example to easily model regular hardware architectures such as hypercubes, or complex interconnection networks such as Omega networks. The repetitions are expressed in the context of the "`RepetitionHwComponent`", with mechanisms similar to ones used in the application model to express data parallelism via dependency expressions.

Moreover, we plan to soon introduce behavioral descriptions of hardware components. Typically, such informations would be taken into account in our simulation environment. For example, it would be useful the describe the behavior of a shared interconnect element (priority policy) to get informations about latency.

## Notes

1. As we'll see later, we just tell which functions can be executed by a processing unit

2. This restriction does not mean that the usage of the other UML elements are forbidden. It only means that all the elements added by a user in a model will not be taken into account by tools which exploit the profi le.

3. We are investigating the introduction of activity diagrams, and possibly state diagrams, to model hardware architecture behavior

4. In this document, the term "Component" refers to UML 2 "StructuredClass".

5. This kind of component is part of a work in progress and will not be detailed in this paper.

6. A "required port" refers to a port with a required interface , and a "provided port" refers to a port with a provided interface.

7. The way to restrict a list of executable functions is not described here. This problem is rather related to the association model.

## References

[Dumoulin et al., 2003] Dumoulin, Cédric, Boulet, Pierre, Dekeyser, Jean-Luc, and Marquet, Philippe (2003). UML 2.0 structure diagram for intensive signal processing application specification. Research Report RR-4766, INRIA.

[Feiler et al., 2003] Feiler, Peter H., Lewis, Bruce, and Vestal, Steve (2003). The SAE avionics architecture description language (AADL) standard : A basis for model-based architecture-driven embedded systems engineering. In *RTAS 2003 Workshop on Model-Driven Embedded Systems*.

[Gajski and Kuhn, 1983] Gajski, D. D. and Kuhn, R. (1983). Guest editor introduction: New VLSI-tools. *IEEE Computer*, 16(12):11–14.

[Green and Edwards, 2002a] Green, Peter and Edwards, Martyn (2002a). The modeling of embedded systems using hasoc. In *Design, Automation and Test in Europe Conference and Exhibition (DATE'02)*, Paris, France.

[Green and Edwards, 2002b] Green, Peter and Edwards, Martyn (2002b). Platform modeling with UML and systemc. In *Forum on specification and Design Languages (FDL'02)*.

[Object Management Group, Inc., 2002] Object Management Group, Inc., editor (2002). *(UML) Profile for Schedulability, Performance, and Time Specification*. `http://www.omg.org/cgi-bin/doc?ptc/2002-03-02/`.

[Object Management Group, Inc., 2003] Object Management Group, Inc., editor (2003). *(UML 2.0): Superstructure Draft Adopted Specification*. `http://www.omg.org/cgi-bin/doc?ptc/03-07-06/`.

[Open SystemC Initiative, 2002] Open SystemC Initiative (2002). SystemC. `http://www.systemc.org/`.

[picoChip, 2003] picoChip (2003). PC101 and PC102 datasheets. `http://www.picochip.com/technology/picoarray`.

[Texas Instruments, 2004] Texas Instruments (2004). OMAP 2 architecture. `http://focus.ti.com/docs/general/splashdsp.jhtml?&path=templatedata/cm/%splashdsp/data/omap2`.

[Zhu et al., 2002] Zhu, Qiang, Matsuda, Akio, Kuwamura, Shinya, Nakata, Tsuneo, and Shoji, Minoru (2002). An obect-oriented design process for system-on-chip using UML. In *Proceedings of the 15th international symposium on System Synthesis*, pages 249–259, Kyoto, Japan.

# SESSION 3: DOMAIN SPECIFIC ARCHITECTURE DESCRIPTION LANGUAGES

# SPECIFICATION OF INTEL IA-32 USING AN ARCHITECTURE DESCRIPTION LANGUAGE*

Jeff Bastian
*Texas Instruments*
*12500 TI Blvd, MS 8714*
*Dallas, TX 75243*

Soner Onder
*Department of Computer Science*
*Michigan Technological University*
*Houghton, MI 49931-1295*
soner@mtu.edu

**Abstract** Designing, testing, and producing a new computer processor is a complex and very expensive process. To reduce costly mistakes in hardware, the microarchitecture is usually designed and tested with the aid of a software simulator. The FAST System enables microarchitects to develop architecture simulators rapidly and is less error-prone than using a high level language such as C. In this paper, we describe how the FAST System's Architecture Description Language (ADL) has been extended to facilitate the description of complex instruction sets such as Intel's IA-32 instruction set architecture. In this respect, we demonstrate that the notion of inheritence, a key concept in object oriented programming languages can be extended for *selective inheritence* to enable the specification of complex instruction set architectures in architecture description languages.

**Keywords:** Architecture Description Language, IA32, automatic simulator generation, cycle-accurate simulators.

## 1. Introduction

Micro-architecture exploration is a difficult, error-prone and development intensive endevaour. Traditionally, there has been three distinct approaches to micro-architecture exploration; namely, hand-coding a custom simulator, generation through a hardware description language and automatic generation through an architecture description language.

Custom simulators for a specific architecture are hand-coded in a general-purpose high-level-language, e.g. C. This group includes SimpleScalar, SuperDLX, SPIM, and URM [2, 5, 3, 9] among others. The second group in-

*This work is supported in part by a grant from DARPA, PACC Award no. F29601-00-1-0183 to the Michigan Technological University and a CAREER award (CCR-0347592) from the National Science Foundation to Soner Onder.

cludes hardware description languages and simulators such as VHDL, VERILOG and ELLA [1, 12, 8, 4]. Most of these simulators are very specific to the architecture they simulate which makes it difficult to make modifications to the ISA or the microarchitecture to see how the changes affect performance. Ranging from several thousand to 30,000 lines of C code and taking 12-24 man months to develop, these are complicated software systems. Such simulators embody problems of all large scale software projects, despite the best efforts spent to increase maintainability. Trying to study such an existing simulator's source code and make changes without breaking anything can be problematic at best. Similarly, hardware description languages are not not suitable for micro-architecture exploration because they are designed to describe the hardware.

Architecture description languages on the other hand have the ability to specify the instruction set architecture (ISA), make automatic generation of support tools such as the assembler and the linker possible and hide the details of instructions from the programmer. As a result, they enable a clean model of the micro-architecture operation. More importantly, they can specify and model the operation of the micro-architecture without tying it to a particular hardware implementation and therefore seamlessly map the instruction set specification to the micro-architecture specification.

Flexible Architecture Simulation Tool (**FAST**) and its description language *Architecture Description Language* (**ADL**) [6] is one such system, which has been in use by a number of universities to describe and simulate micro architectures of varying complexity. Thus, FAST fills in a gap between high-level architecture-specific simulators, and low-level hardware simulators. Doing so, it allows automatic generation of the necessary system tools (assemblers, linkers, and so on) through the ADL description.

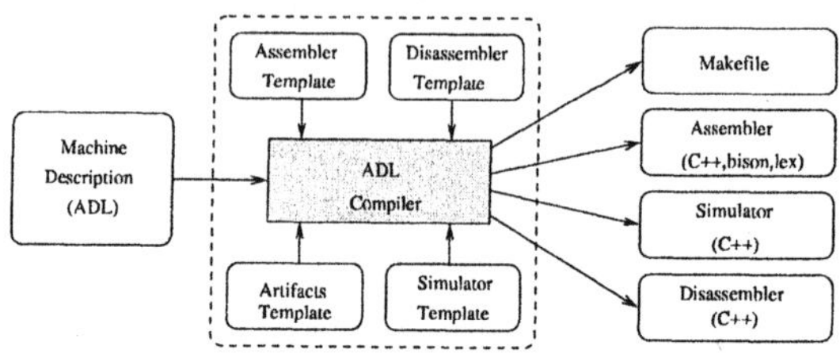


*Figure 1.* FAST System Components

The Flexible Architecture Simulation Tool (FAST) System shown in Figure 1 is a collection of four main components: (a) an ADL (Architecture Description Language) compiler; (b) support tools generated by the compiler (assembler, disassembler, linker, etc); (c) a cycle level simulator and debugger; (d) support tools for collecting and displaying statistics about the simulations.

The first step is to describe the architecture in question using ADL, the Architecture Description Language. An architecture described by ADL is made up of two distinct sections - one section describes the ISA, and the other section describes how the microarchitecture works (e.g., what are the pipeline stages and what happens during each stage). The instructions are described in a declarative form, while the microarchitecture is done in an imperative form similar to other high-level imperative languages, like C.

As an example of an instruction, consider the add instruction shown in Figure 2 from a MIPS description. The first line describes what will be seen in an assembly program - the add keyword followed by three registers. The emit line tells ADL how to translate the assembly instruction into its binary representation and consists of a series of assignments to instruction fields. This aspect of the specification is quite similar to SLED (Specification Language for Encoding and Decoding) [10, 11].

The **attributes** section serves as the glue between the instruction set specification and the micro-architecture specification and provides the necessary abstractions for independent specification of micro-architectures from ISAs. In particular, the micro-architecture specification makes references to instruction attributes and the ISA specification maps instruction fields as well as instruction particulars to these attributes. For example, the micro-architecture specification is concerned about what is the type of the current instruction, such as arithmetic, load, store, etc., to steer the instruction to the appropriate processing unit. Similarly, the micro-architecture specification is interested in knowing the values of source and destination register numbers so that instruction execution can be modeled, but not where these fields are located in an instruction. The ISA specification conveniently maps the destination and source register attributes to the appropriate fields.

Finally, the last section describes what the instruction does during a particular pipeline phase (such as s_EX): namely, the destination register gets the results of adding the left operand to the right operand. (The operands rs, rt, and rd are mapped to rop, lop, and dest during the decode stage of the pipeline. For an example of the microarchitecture description, let's look at a much simplified version of the instruction fetch stage of the MIPS pipeline shown in Figure 2.

During the prologue (the beginning of the clock tick), the instruction register (ir) reads an instruction from the instruction cache (icache) at the current program counter (pc), and then sets new_pc to be the next instruction, which is pc+4 since MIPS has fixed-length 32-bit instruction words. During the epilogue (the end of the clock tick), the current instruction and its context are delivered to the next pipeline stage and sets the new value of the program counter depending on whether or not the previous instruction was a branch instruction. ADL also includes many basic *artifacts* that are generic to most architectures, such as the memory and cache subsystems. Once the architecture has been

```
add rd rs rt
    emit opcode=_special rs rt rd shamt=0 funct=_add
    attributes ( exu       : integer_unit,
                 dest_type : integer_register,
                 lop_type  : integer_register,
                 rop_type  : integer_register,
                 i_type    : alu_type,
                 dest_reg  : rd )
begin
   exact s_EX
         dest=lop + rop;
   end;
end
```

```
procedure s_IF prologue | procedure s_IF epilogue
begin                   | begin
   ir = icache[pc];     |    send s_ID;
   new_pc = pc+4;       |
end s_IF;               |    if (branch_input) then
                        |        begin
                        |           branch_input=0;
                        |           pc=branch_target;
                        |        end
                        |     else
                        |        pc=new_pc;
                        |     new_context;
                        | end s_IF;
```

*Figure 2.* MIPS Instruction and Micro-architecture Specificiation in FAST/ADL

described in ADL, the file is processed by the ADL compiler. The compiler generates an assembler, a disassembler, and a simulator, as shown in Figure 1.

The FAST System was originally designed to be flexible enough to describe most modern architectures, including everything from as simple and clean-cut as a RISC processor to the most esoteric and exotic digital signal processors (DSPs). However, in early versions of the ADL compiler, certain assumptions were made and "shortcuts" taken to make it easier to implement FAST. Thus far, the MIPS architecture and a few variations on MIPS have been implemented and tested with FAST. The SPARC architecture ISA has also been specified and is in the process of being integrated with existing micro-architecture specifications. Similarly, some DSP Extensions to ADL for use with StarCore's SC-140 ISA have been described [7], but have not yet been implemented in the FAST ADL compiler. These extensions include regular expression support for addressing mode descriptions which are also useful for x86.

## 2. IA-32 Architecture

The latest incarnation of IA-32 as seen in the Pentium 4 processor has its roots in the 8086 and 8088 processors from 1978. The ISA embodies a variable length instruction set encoding and the processor supports many memory models including segmented memory. The architecture also include overlapping registers. There are very few, if any, wasted bits in a typical x86 instruction. All these properties make the Intel IA-32 architecture quite challenging for an ADL specification.

In this section, we will take a closer look at these properties of IA-32 and look at how we tackled these challenges.

**Variable Length Instructions:** Currently FAST uses a bit numbering scheme to identify instruction fields. Although this approach is particularly appropriate for fixed length instruction formats, it is not the best approach for handling varying length instruction formats. When referencing fields in ADL, the bits are numbered right-to-left (i.e., a 32 bit word is numbered 31 to 0, the most significant bit in position 31). With this positioning scheme, the fields can "move" in a variable length instruction set. For example, using the syntax [start_bit, length], an 8-bit opcode in a 32-bit instruction is bits [31,8], but in a 16-bit instruction, the opcode moves to [15,8]. Furthermore, there are no special fields in ADL, including the opcode. Rather, ADL automatically distinguishes one instruction from another. The ADL compiler looks through all of the defined instructions and tries to identify a unique constant valued field for each instruction. If a series of instructions have a constant valued field but share the same value for all the instructions, they are grouped together and a second field is searched for (e.g. extended opcodes). The compiler keeps looking until it finds a unique constant valued field (or set of fields) for each instruction. This field (or set of fields) becomes the "opcode". The compiler will have the same problems as the programmer, if the fields start moving around because of their variable lengths.

An x86 instruction can have up to four prefixes that modify the semantics (e.g. to use 16-bit or 32-bit registers), one or two bytes of opcode (a few reserved opcodes indicate to use the second opcode byte), a ModR/M byte for memory or register arguments, an SIB byte to help the ModR/M if necessary, and displacement and immediate fields. In other words, the fields making up the instruction format appear depending on the particular instruction format. The basic algorithm of discovering the opcode fields has to be modified so that a decoder for the architecture can automatically be synthesized.

**Many Memory Addressing Modes:** There are many addressing modes used in IA-32, which are, for the most part, independent of the instruction since they are encoded using the ModR/M byte (and an SIB byte if necessary).

| Displacement (or Absolute) | mov %ecx, 0xDEADBEEF |
|---|---|
| Base | mov %ecx, [%esp] |
| Base+Offset | mov %ecx, [%esp-4] |
| Base+Index+Offset | mov %ecx, [%esp+%edi-4] |
| Base+(Index*Scale)+Offset | mov %ecx, [%esp+%edi*2-4] |
| Base+Index | mov %ecx, [%esp+%edi*1] |
| Base+(Index*Scale) | mov %ecx, [%esp+%edi*2] |
| Index+Offset | mov %ecx, [%edi*1-4] |
| (Index*Scale)+Offset | mov %ecx, [%edi*2-4] |

*Figure 3.* Intel IA-32 addressing modes

IA-32 addressing modes are shown together with examples in Figure 3. The challenging aspect of the many addressing modes in IA-32 is trying to define them succinctly in ADL, since the fields are mostly independent of the opcode. That is, the opcode alone does not indicate all of the fields that follow the opcode. For example, the mov instruction shown in the above table has the opcode of 0x89, which indicates that the opcode byte will be followed by a ModR/M byte, with the Reg/Opcode field of the ModR/M byte selecting a general purpose register. What follows the ModR/M byte, if anything, is indicated by the ModR/M byte. Thus, each byte in the instruction provides a hint as to what comes next.

The simplest way to approach this problem is to enumerate every possible variation of an instruction as if it is a separate instruction, since ADL allows instructions to be overloaded, just like functions in C++. For example, the mov instruction overloaded for Displacement and Base addressing modes:

```
mov reg32 disp emit opcode=0x89 mod='00'b regop=reg32 rm='100'b disp ...
mov reg32 base emit opcode=0x89 mod='00'b regop=reg32 rm=base ...
```

However, this leads to the problem of having to overload the same instruction many times due to the many addressing modes. There are nine addressing modes listed above, however, three modes (Base + Displacement, Base + Index + Displacement, and Base + (Index*Scale) + Displacement) can use either an 8-bit or a 32-bit displacement, giving us 12 effective modes. Furthermore, there are restrictions on when %esp and %ebp can be used for base or index registers. Treating these restrictions as special addressing modes (which would be necessary in the current version of ADL) gives us 6 additional special case modes, for a total of 18 addressing modes!

Creating separate ADL instruction definitions for every combination of x86 opcode with addressing mode would generate thousands of ADL instructions. This is tedious and highly error-prone.

**Overlapping Registers:** The IA-32 architecture is 99.9% fully backwards compatible with the original x86 processor (the 0.1% difference is the addition of certain instructions that allow the processor to switch between operating operating modes, e.g., protected mode, system management mode, or real mode). One of the features of this backwards compatibility is a set of registers that have overlapping parts.

IA-32 includes eight 32-bit general purpose registers: EAX, ECX, EDX, EBX, ESP, EBP, ESI, and EDI. However, in order to maintain backwards compatibility, there are aliases for 8-bit and 16-bit parts of the registers. For example, AL, AH, and AX all describe different parts of the EAX register. AL and AH are two 8-bit registers that represent the lower and upper 8 bits of the 16-bit register AX, and AX is the low 16 bits of the 32-bit register EAX.

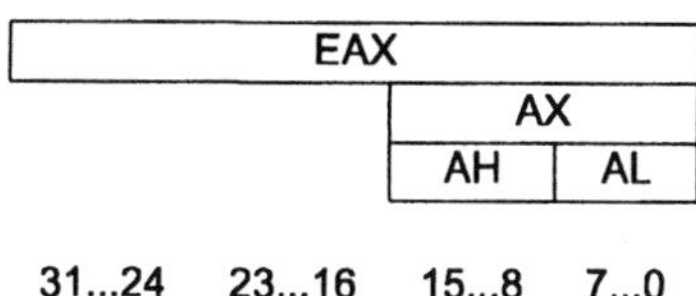


Registers ECX, EDX, and EBX are broken down in a similar fashion. Registers ESP, EBP, ESI, and EDI have aliases for the lower 16 bits SP, BP, SI, and DI respectively. As a side note, while the above eight registers are noted as general purpose, the registers occasionally have special uses, hence the seemingly obtuse names of the registers.

**Mixed Arguments:** Unlike RISC architectures, instructions in CISC machines can operate directly on memory. That is, RISC machines, or load-store architectures, only have two instructions that can operate on memory, load and store, while all other instructions must operate on registers. CISC instructions have no such restrictions. This leads to instructions that can have a variety of arguments. The mov instruction takes two arguments, a source and a destination, one of which must be a register, the other can be either a register or a memory address. The address can come in any one of the 18 modes listed above. In addition to creating a plethora of instructions (also described above), many instructions will need to access memory at some point during the execution which will result in a lot of replicated ADL code (i.e., every instruction description will contain the same copied-and-pasted ADL code to read from or write to memory).

Although some of these issues have been addressed within the context of *instruction set specification* with the SLED approach, as it can be seen, the approach taken by SLED is inadequate for automatic generation of simulators. Although one can describe x86 ISA in less than 500 lines of code in SLED, the language was only designed for encoding and decoding instructions (as the name implies). Many instructions in x86 are encoded/decoded the same way with the only difference being the opcode, so *patterns* are used to define many instructions in one line. On the other hand, in order to tie in the micro-architecture specification, one needs to be able to specify the semantics of each instruction. Since the semantics of each instruction are very different, attaching semantics to many opcodes cannot be done with one line, and an alternative technique must be sought.

## 3. Our Solutions

An IA-32 processor can run in many different modes. For the purposes of our work, we were able to simplify the model with a few assumptions and restrictions: (a) no segmented memory (i.e., flat address space); (b) 32-bit mode (16-bit instructions require 0x66 prefix); (c) no 36-bit Physical Address Extension (PAE) support; (d) no ISA extensions (MMX, SSE, SSE2).

We made these restrictions based on the way modern applications run on x86 platforms. Very few programs use segmented memory except the occasional device driver. 16-bit mode is only used when running old programs compiled for DOS or Windows 3.1 and earlier. 36-bit PAE mode is only used by programs with intense memory requirements on high end servers, such as large database systems that require more than 4GB of RAM. We chose to exclude MMX, SSE and SSE2 for now in order to get a framework in place; when this is done, the new instructions will be easily added with little or no changes to the framework necessary.

**Variable Length Instructions:** In the previous version of ADL, fields could be defined in any order since the start bit dictated where it would actually appear. This freedom is lost, but it was rarely (if ever) taken advantage of. Therefore, the problem of variable length instructions is addressed by removing the requirement that the start bit of individual fields need to be specified. Instead, the fields of an instruction now need to be specified in order and only the length of the field needs to be specified. With this scheme the compiler may look through every instruction and identify the longest instruction and use its length for a pseudo-fixed-length instruction (for x86, this will be 16-bytes, or 128-bits). Then the compiler can internally generate the start bits for each field based on this length (thus, for x86, the opcode will always be [127,8] (note that opcode prefixes are really just special opcodes)). Undefined fields will not generate pad bits in the encoded binary; i.e., a 16-bit instruction will only have bits 127 through 111 defined, but the binary encoding of the file will not have 111 padded bits following the instruction.

**Addressing Modes and Regular Expressions:** The DSP Extensions use a combination of flex-style regular expressions with register variables. We will use these extensions for x86 as well, with the addition of typesets. The syntax is fairly straightforward as shown in Figure 4.

The regular expressions in the addressing mode define the syntax of the addressing mode, but they do not define the semantics. For example, in base_index

```
# create groups of registers.
# Registers may exist in multiple sets.
typeset
  reg32 {%eax,%ecx,%edx,%ebx,%esp,%ebp,%esi,%edi},
  reg16 {%ax,%cx,%dx,%bx,%sp,%bp,%si,%di},
  reg8 {%al,%cl,%dl,%bl,%ah,%ch,%dh,%bh},
  reg32_noESP {%eax,%ecx,%edx,%ebx,%ebp,%esi,%edi},
  reg32_noESBP {%eax,%ecx,%edx,%ebx,%esi,%edi},
  reg32_noEBP {%eax,%ecx,%edx,%ebx,%esp,%esi,%edi},
  scaleVals { 1, 2, 4, 8 };

#- Instruction fields
#
type
    .....
    s8          signed integer   variable      8 bit,
    s16         signed integer   variable     16 bit,
    s32         signed integer   variable     32 bit;

addressing modes
  disp32            s32,
  base              "["  reg32_noESBP "]",
  base_index        "[" reg32_noEBP [-+] reg32_noESP "]",
  base_index_scale "[" reg32_noEBP [-+] reg32_noESP * scaleVals "]",
  index_disp32      "[" reg32_noESP * 1 [-+] s32 "]",index_scale_disp32
                    "[" reg32_noESP * scaleVals [-+] s32 "]",
  ... ;
```

*Figure 4.* Use of typesets to describe addressing modes

mode above, the assembler does not know if reg32_noEBP is the base or the index; it only knows to expect a 32-bit register excluding %ebp. Mapping the two registers to some meaningful value like base or index is handled by a user-defined procedure.

**Instruction Templates:** Most of the problems we encountered (overlapping registers, variable length instructions, etc.) were handled by a simple extension of ADL or modification of an existing syntax. The real problem with x86 was the combination of instructions with multiple addressing modes. With over 400 instructions and many of them using up to 18 modes for memory addressing, plus register-to-register arguments, we could easily end up with thousands of descriptions if we were to enumerate each permutation as a separate instruction.

We toyed with many ideas for reducing the number of enumerations. Although it is possible to write a wrapper program to enumerate the instructions and generate the ADL code, such a solution is specific to the instruction set at hand and defeats the purpose of using an architecture description language in the first place. What is needed is to increase the power of the ADL so that these instructions can also be specified seamlessly and naturally. Furthermore, to a lesser extend similar problems make RISC instruction set descriptions in ADL also somewhat longer than necessary. Therefore these language extensions can be generic enough to be useful for other architectures (e.g., making the existing MIPS implementation shorter and more concise with our new language extensions).

Our careful study of the SLED encoding scheme where patterns are extensively used lead us to believe that it may be possible to define an encoding pattern for the addressing modes and let each instruction inherit the right pattern? This turned out to be the key idea for the x86 extensions to ADL: treat instructions as objects and use multiple inheritance with a twist!

The encoding patterns would be defined by a series of templates, and the real instructions would inherit the properties from these patterns. The *objects* in ADL are the instruction templates and the instructions themselves. Templates differ from normal instructions in two ways.

Fields in instruction templates can be grouped or made optional with the use of regular-expression like syntax. Parentheses group fields together, (*field1 field2* ...), to indicate that all of the fields in the group must appear together. That is, *field1* cannot exist without *field2* , and vice-versa. This is useful for larger fields like the ModR/M byte in IA-32, which consists of three smaller fields: the 2 bit mod field, the 3 bit reg/op field, and the 3 bit r/m field, used to describe how memory and/or registers will be addressed. A '?' following a field indicates the field is optional. For example, the SIB byte is optional depending on the ModR/M byte, thus, it appears as (scale index base)? . A '?' is really just shorthand for { *n,m* } syntax (where n=0 and m=1) which says the previous item must appear at least *n* times but no more than *m* times. Finally, a | indicates logical-or, useful for fields that vary in size. Some instructions have 8-bit immediates, others 16-bit, and others 32-bit, and others none at all, so, putting it all together: (imm8 | imm16 | imm32)?

Templates do not exist in the actual instruction set. That is, when the generated assembler is assembling code, it will never try to match a template with a real assembly instruction.

Templates can inherit properties from other instruction templates and override fields or sections from the parent. This allows creation of a *master template.* A master template is really just another template (i.e., it is not a special type of template), but it helps the programmer avoid syntactical errors. In IA-32, there is one general instruction format:

| Prefixes | Opcode | ModR/M | SIB | Disp | Immediate |
|---|---|---|---|---|---|

In this format there may be up to 4 prefixes, where each prefix is 1 byte long. The opcode field can be 1 or 2 bytes long and is followed by the optional ModR/M and SIB bytes. Displacement and the Immediate fields can be anywhere from 0 to 4 bytes. templates and instructions inherit the properties illustrated in Figure 5.

```
instruction template
begin
   intel          # no arguments given
     emit prefix1? prefix2? prefix3? prefix4?
          opcode{1,2}
         (mod reg_op rm)?
         (scale index base)?
         (disp8 | disp16 | disp32)?
         (imm8  | imm16  | imm32)?
     attributes
         (i_class : intel_class,
          op_type : intel_ops )
     begin
        exact s_MEM_LD
           # read from memory, if necessary
        end;
        exact s_EX
           # execute stage
        end;
        exact s_MEM_ST
           # write back to memory, if necessary
        end;
     end, ....

intel_r8_bis rd8 base_index_scale inherits intel
      emit opcode=0xF1 mod=00 reg_op=rd8 rm=100
      scale=<base_index_scale.scale>
      index=<base_index_scale.index>
      base=<base_index_scale.base>
begin
   exact s_MEM
        # calculate address = base + (index * scale)
        # load from memory: temp = dcache[address]
   end;
end,
```

*Figure 5.* Instruction templates and Using inheritance

The first item to notice is on the 3rd line, no arguments are given to the generic instruction name intel. The non-existent arguments will be overridden by the following templates. The emit line, on the other hand, defines every possible field that might be emitted by a descendant and uses the ? and {n,m} modifiers to indicate optional fields. Only two attributes are defined at this time; more will probably be needed when the microarchitecture is implemented. Finally, there are three pipeline stages used to execute the instruction, an execute stage and a memory access before and after the execute stage for those instructions that need it (more on this below). Again, the pipeline stages may change with implementation of the microarchitecture.

An instruction that inherits from this intel master template is free to override the arguments, any of the emit fields, any of the attributes, or any pipeline stage. (Note that if a pipeline stage is overridden, the entire stage must be overridden, even if only one line is changed.) Inheritance is indicated by the inherits keyword following the instruction's arguments as shown in Figure 5.

The template intel_r8_bis has two arguments, an 8-bit destination register, rd8, and a memory location addressed by base_index_scale mode. It inherits from the intel master template and then defines exactly which fields will be emitted for this type of instruction. The scale, index, and base functions are built-in to the ADL language and, with the help of the regular expressions for the addressing modes, return the respective values for scale, index, and base. Finally, the s_MEM pipeline stage is used to load a byte into a temporary pipeline register which will be used by the s_EX stage in instructions that inherit from this template. (The code to actually load from memory will be specific to how the microarchitecture is implemented, so for now we describe what has to be done in comments.)

**Memory Addressing and Conditional Inheritance:** Once all the templates are defined as shown above, the final step is to create *conditional inheritance.* This borrows from the idea of multiple inheritance, except instead of inheriting all of the features from the parents, it only inherits from the one parent with the best fit. The best fit is determined by the arguments to the instruction. (Note that this implies the inherited arguments must be unambiguous.)

This allows us to create one template for each addressing mode. Each template will have the emit fields defined and other common properties. The child that inherits from the template then overrides the emitted opcode field and defines in the pipeline stage what exactly the instruction does (i.e., the semantics that make languages like SLED unfeasible for our work). The common addressing modes are then combined using the conditional inheritance feature into one template which the real instructions will inherit from. To reinforce the idea that this is not traditional multiple inheritance, the | operator (logical or) is used to split parents. For example, instructions that have a 32-bit register for a source and a 32-bit word in memory for a destination would inherit from the intel_r32_rm32 template that is shown in Figure 6.

Each of the 18 templates intel_r32_rm32 inherits from define an addressing mode (there are 12 modes plus 6 special modes for using %esp or %ebp as a base register). A real instruction then inherits from intel_r32_rm32 as shown in Figure 6. To see this in action, consider the following x86 instructions:

```
mov %eax, DWORD PTR [%esp - 4]
mov %eax, DWORD PTR [%esp + %ebp*4 - 4]
mov %ax, WORD PTR [%esp - 4]
```

The instruction is the same in both cases, movl, but the arguments differ. However, they differ in a unique and unambiguous way which allow the com-

```
intel_r32_rm32 inherits
(
intel_r32_d32    | intel_r32_b      | intel_r32_bi         | intel_r32_bis        |
intel_r32_id32   | intel_r32_isd32  | intel_r32_bd8        | intel_r32_bid8       |
intel_r32_bisd8  | intel_r32_bd32   | intel_r32_bid32      | intel_r32_bisd32     |
intel_r32_b_esp  | intel_r32_b_ebp  | intel_r32_b_bd8_esp  | intel_r32_bd32_esp   |
intel_r32_bi_ebp | intel_r32_bis_ebp
)
mov inherits intel_r32_rm32  emit opcode=0x8B
begin
   exact s_EX
         rd32 = temp;
   end;
end,
```

*Figure 6.* Conditional Inheritance and example instruction using inheritance

piler to match it against only one parent. The first instruction matches intel_r32_rm32 and its parent intel_r32_bd8 (base + 8-bit-displacement) (technically it also matches intel_r32_bd32, but the compiler will be smart enough to choose an 8-bit-displacement if it can via a *pragma*). Likewise, the second instruction matches intel_r32_rm32 but with a different parent, intel_r32_bisd8. The third instruction matches none of the parents in intel_r32_rm32, so the compiler looks for another instruction to match against (which, in this case, will be mov inherits intel_r16_rm16 and its parent intel_r16_bd8).

**Overlapping Registers:** C style unions and typesets were introduced to deal with overlapping registers. First, the physical registers are defined as generic 32-bit registers, then a union is used to define the symbolic registers and which parts of the physical register are used in [start_bit, length] notation and finally, a typeset is used to group the registers together into logical sets.

```
register file
    gpr [8, 32]  # 8 registers, 32 bits each
    %reg0  0, %reg1  1,  %reg2  2,   %reg3  3,
    %reg4  4, %reg5  5,  %reg6  6,   %reg7  7;

union
      %eax %reg0[31, 32], %ecx %reg1[31, 32], .... # 32 bit registers
      %ax  %reg0[15, 16], %cx  %reg1[15, 16], .... # 16 bit registers
      %al  %reg0[7, 8],   %cl  %reg1[7, 8],   .... # 8 bit low registers
      %ah  %reg0[15, 8],  %ch  %reg1[15, 8],
      %dh  %reg2[15, 8],  %bh  %reg3[15, 8];       # 8 bit high registers

typeset
  reg32 {%eax,%ecx,%edx,%ebx,%esp,%ebp,%esi,%edi},
  reg16 {%ax,%cx,%dx,%bx,%sp,%bp,%si,%di},
  reg8  {%al,%cl,%dl,%bl,%ah,%ch,%dh,%bh};
```

Typesets are also used to place registers into special groups. For example, the %esp and %ebp registers cannot be used as a base register in base addressing mode, so a special group is created minus those registers.

```
typeset reg_noESBP { %eax, %ecx, %edx, %ebx, %esi, %edi };
```

**Typesets** can be used to group more than just registers. The opcode prefixes are defined as **bitconstants** and are split into four groups and only one prefix from each group can be used in an instruction. The typeset is used to define the groups.

```
typeset
  prefix_lock_repeat {_lock,_repne,_repnz,_rep,
                      _repe, _repz },
  prefix_segment_branch {_cs_seg,_ss_seg,_ds_seg,
                         _es_seg,_fs_seg, _gs_seg,
                         _b_not_taken, _b_taken },
  prefix_operand { _operand_size },
  prefix_address { _address_size };
```

**Mixed arguments:** The mixed argument problem is also solved through inheritance. The microarchitecture pipeline has not been defined in this paper, but at least three stages will be needed: two memory access stages with an execute stage in the middle. This can be implemented as one major cycle with 3 minor cycles: s_MEM_LD to load from memory, s_EX to execute the instruction, and s_MEM_ST to store the results back to memory.

The instruction templates have code in the load and store minor-cycles that either load from memory into an internal temp register or store the data in temp back to memory. The execute stage uses the temp register instead of the second argument. Thanks to inheritance, this is mostly masked from the final instruction's description. The only concern an instruction has is whether it's working on register-to-register operands or a combination of registers and memory. It can tell which type it is by checking the inherited **op_type** attribute:

```
mov inherits intel_rm32_r32
    emit opcode=0x89
    begin
       exact s_EX  if op_type == reg_to_reg then
                      rd32 = rs32;
                    else
                      rd32 = temp;
       end;
    end,
```

In the above figure, a pipeline with three stages is shown. Real implementations of x86 are typically not pipelined due to the difficulties as seen above (instructions operating directly on memory). In order to pipeline x86 processors, such as the Pentium, the processor converts the x86 instruction into a series of micro-operations, and these RISC-like micro-ops are pipelined.

**Multiple Choice:** An interesting feature of the x86 instruction set is how there is often more than one way to encode an instruction. This is usually due to the shortcut opcodes for tasks instructions used often enough to warrant a shortcut. For example, push %eax, could be encoded two different ways such as [opcode=0xFF mod=11 regop=110 rm=000] as well as [opcode=0x50].

The push %eax instruction is used often enough that a special opcode was created just for it. The upside is that it saves a byte of memory. The downside is it presents the assembler with a dilemma on encoding the instruction. Fortunately, the dilemma is resolved easily enough – chose the instruction with the shortest encoding.

## 4. Conclusions and Future Work

The x86 is a powerful and compact ISA, but it's this same compactness that makes it so difficult to work with (in compilers, in simulators, and more). We have shown that by introducing the notion of conditional multiple inheritance we have tackled the most difficult challenges of x86 within the realm of an architecture description language.

Our future work on IA-32 on FAST can be broken into two broad areas, namely the implementation of the language constructs in the ADL compiler and the completion of the micro-architecture specification. Once running simulators are successfully generated from the ADL specification, we are planning to remove the restrictions and add the MMX and SSE/SSE2 instructions to the ISA.

## References

[1] J.R. Armstrong and F.G. Gray. *Structured Logic Design with VHDL*. New Jersey: Prentice Hall, 1993.

[2] D.C. Burger and T.M. Austin. The SimpleScalar Tool Set, V. 2.0. Technical Report 97-1342, Computer Sci. Dept., Univ. of Wisconsin Madison, 1997.

[3] J.R. Larus. SPIM S20: A MIPS R2000 Simulator. Technical Report 90-966, Computer Sci. Dept., Univ. of Wisconsin Madison, 1990.

[4] J.D. Morison and A.S. Clarke. *ELLA2000 A language for Electronic System Design*. McGraw-Hill, 1993.

[5] C. Moura. SuperDLX a generic superscalar simulator. Technical Report 64, School of Computer Science, McGill University, 1993.

[6] Soner Önder and Rajiv Gupta. Automatic generation of microarchitecture simulators. In *IEEE International Conference on Computer Languages*, pages 80–89, Chicago, May 1998.

[7] Robert Pastel. Describing vliw architectures using a domain specific language. Master's thesis, Michigan Technological University, 2001.

[8] D.L. Perry. *VHDL*. McGraw-Hill, 1991.

[9] David Poplawski. The unlimited resource machine (urm). Technical report, Michigan Technological University, 1995.

[10] Norman Ramsey and Mary F. Fernandez. The new jersey machine-code toolkit. In *Proceedings of the 1995 USENIX Technical Conference, New Orleans, LA*, pages 289–302, January 1995.

[11] Norman Ramsey and Mary F. Fernandez. Specifying representations of machine instructions. *ACM Transactions on Programming Languages and Systems*, 19(3):492–524, May 1997.

[12] D.E. Thomas and P.R. Moorby. *The Verilog Hardware Description Language*. Kluwer Academic Publishers, 1991.

# COTRE AS AN AADL PROFILE

Patrick Farail, Pierre Gaufillet
*Airbus France, 316 route de Bayonne, 31060 Toulouse Cedex 03, France*

Abstract: The COTRE Architecture Description Language, developed during the COTRE project, allows software designers to describe hierarchically static and real time architectures, their behavior and their functional or non-functional requirements. Due to different needs at the user and at the verification levels, the COTRE language has been split early in the project into 2 specialized sub-languages named respectively UCOTRE (User-COTRE) and VCOTRE (Verification-COTRE). As the UCOTRE concepts are very close to the AADL ones, and to avoid defining 2 concurrent languages, UCOTRE has become an AADL dialect, using its extension mechanisms. This paper focuses on the UCOTRE description as a set of extensions and restrictions to AADL.

Key words: Architecture Description Language, Real Time, Software engineering, model checking, modeling, COTRE, AADL

## 1. INTRODUCTION

With the increasing size and complexity of embedded systems, it is more and more important to have development methods allowing to keep the products mastery and to ensure working order and safety. This is all the more true for equipment like some avionics computers, and more generally for critical systems (flight commands, engine controller, nuclear domain, etc.). For this kind of product, we have to deal not only with functional requirements, but also with non-functional aspects like time, reliability and performance constraints.

By aiming to provide a design methodology and tools based on dynamic (aka threads, semaphores, buffers, ...) and static (modules, objects, classes, ...) software architecture modeling, the COTRE research project addresses this problem[1,2].

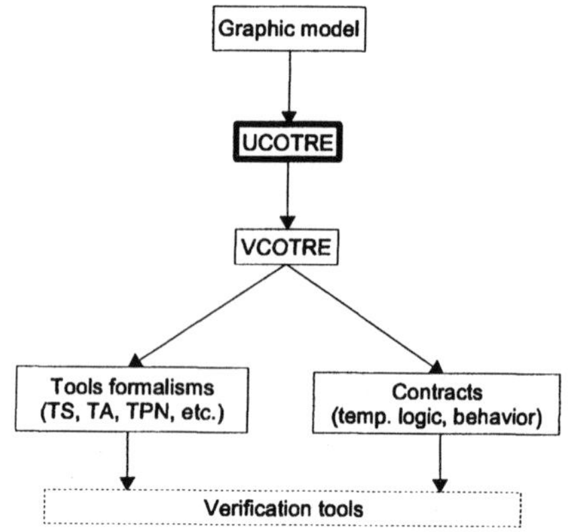


*Figure 1.* The COTRE transformations

Started at the beginning of 2002, the COTRE project has been funded by the French Ministry of Research & Education through the RNTL (Réseau National des Technologies Logicielles – Software Technologies National Network) for 2 years. This project gathers an end user, AIRBUS France[3], a software tool editor, TNI-Valiosys[4], FeRIA[5] – CNRS LAAS[6], UPS IRIT[7] and ONERA-DTIM[8] – and ENSTB[9] as academic partners specialized in formal languages and verification techniques.

As the ADL (Architecture Description Languages) are used to describe structural decomposition of systems and interactions between their components, it seems natural to express the COTRE models in a such language. The COTRE language, in addition to the common features of ADL, must :

- allow to describe formally the constraints the system must comply with,
- allow to describe formally its behavior,
- and have an associated graphic expression to make easier the system designer job.

To allow to work more easily on the user level modeling and on the verification layers, the abstract COTRE language is divided into two languages : the UCOTRE language, standing for User COTRE, and the VCOTRE language, for Verification COTRE. VCOTRE can be seen as an intermediate language between UCOTRE and the specific formalisms used by the verification tools (see Illustration 1). UCOTRE and VCOTRE should ultimately merge into an unique COTRE language.

The proximity of the UCOTRE needs and the AADL (Architecture Analysis & Design Language, formerly known as Avionics Architecture Description Language) ones leads us to open technical discussions with the AS-2C SAE subcommittee[10] in charge of its development.

In the description of the VCOTRE language[11], translations in the chosen verification formalisms (Time Petri Net, Timed Automata, Temporal/Timed Logics) and an application example are presented. Verification techniques which we are implementing in the COTRE platform, are based on formula satisfaction (temporal logic model checking) or on model comparison (behavioral equivalencies). Expressing and checking these properties may require different models, methods and tools, each kind of model typically comes with its tool suite. In the context of COTRE, the following tools have been investigated : UPPAAL[12], SMV[13], TINA[14], LPV[15].

In this paper, we will focus on the UCOTRE language, and its building based on the AADL. The section 2 deals with the AADL extension mechanisms, and the section 3 exposes, around a complete example already studied at the VCOTRE level[1], the main aspects of the UCOTRE language.

## 2. THE AADL EXTENSION MECHANISMS

The AADL core, in its version 0.96, offers 2 main extension mechanisms :

- Property sets : each architecture element can be associated statically with named values. The names, as their allowed values and the element types they can be associated to are described thanks to the property set statement.

```
PROPERTY SET my_ext IS
 int      : TYPE INTEGER -32767..32768;
 duration : TYPE UNITS (s, j => s * 86400,
                h => s * 3600,
                min => s * 60,
                ms => s * 0.001,
                us => s * 0.000001);

 rate : float => 0.0 APPLIES TO (SUBPROGRAM);
END my_ext;
```

In this example, `my_ext::int` and `my_ext::duration` are 2 new property types, and `my_ext::rate` is a new property of type `float`, with a default value of `0.0`, only usable for subprograms.

- Annexes : specific sections called annexes can be added to every AADL component. The content of the these annexes is entirely defined by the user. If a software tool does not know an annex, it just has to ignore it. In this way, a minimum compatibility level is ensured.

```
SYSTEM IMPLEMENTATION ex.default
 ANNEX <name> IS
  <free syntax>
 END ANNEX <name>;
END ex.default;
```

## 3. THE UCOTRE LANGUAGE

The UCOTRE meta-model was initially derived from the HOOD one (both HOOD 4 and HRT-HOOD[16]) and from real time objects used in the AIRBUS development process. When the UCOTRE language started to get closer to AADL[17], some new concepts had to be added, as the AADL types / implementations / instances features for example.

At this moment, some features are not supported in UCOTRE. The most important limitation is the lack of ports : as in the HOOD model, and because UCOTRE currently is not intended to handle multi-applications architectures, components communicate only thanks to subprogram calls. Nevertheless, ports should be used in a later version of UCOTRE to model communications between applications.

The software architecture presented here is called deadlock_verification. This example has already been used to illustrate the VCOTRE language[18]. In this system, as represented in Illustration 2, two periodic processes t_1 and t_2 use 2 semaphores sem1 and sem2 in the same or in the inverted order. The verification problem consists in the analysis of the deadlock possibility.

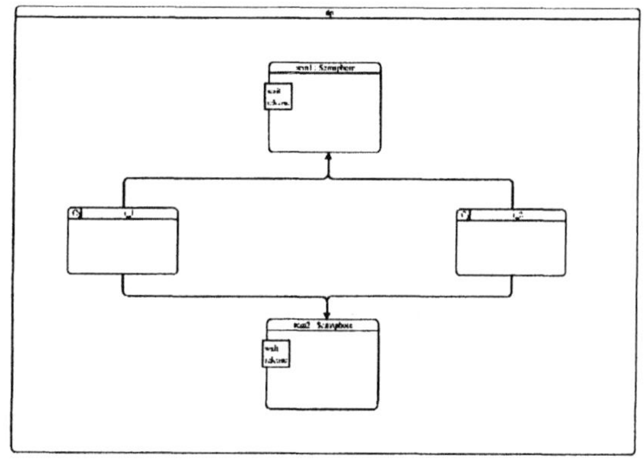

*Figure 2.* deadlock_verification HOOD view

The architectural description of this system with UCOTRE is :

```
SYSTEM deadlock_verification
END deadlock_verification;

SYSTEM IMPLEMENTATION deadlock_verification.default
  SUBCOMPONENTS
    dp : PROCESS Partition.A;
  ANNEX cotre.guarantees IS
    IS ALIVE;
  END ANNEX cotre.guarantees;
END deadlock_verification.default;

sys_deadlock_instance: SYSTEM ex_deadlock.default { };

PROCESS Partition
END Partition;

PROCESS IMPLEMENTATION Partition.A
SUBCOMPONENTS
  t_1 : THREAD t.t1(sem1 => sem_1, sem2 => sem_2);
  t_2 : THREAD t.t2(sem1 => sem_2, sem2 => sem_1);
  sem_1 : DATA semaphore.default;
  sem_2 : DATA semaphore.default;
END Partition.A;
```

This system only consists of the application dp, which contains the 2 threads t_1 and t_2 and the 2 semaphores sem_1 and sem_2. Inside this fragment, you can notice :

- first, the definition of the type of system deadlock_verification,
- then, the definition of the implementation of this type,
- and finally the instantiation of the system. This instance corresponds to the HOOD system_configuration concept.

At this level, the only COTRE specific construction is the contract `IS ALIVE` inside the `cotre.guarantees` annex, ensuring the system can not reach a deadlock. The UCOTRE contracts have been almost directly re-used from the VCOTRE layer[1]. They can express assumptions about component environment by the mean of the *cotre.assumes* annexes, and guarantees about component behavior in the *cotre.guarantees* annexes. It can be done using high level assertions or behavioral equivalences (based on automata).

**ANNEX** cotre.guarantees | cotre.assumes **IS**
((<assertion> | <behavioral equivalence>);)$^+$
**END ANNEX** cotre.guarantees | cotre.assumes;

The following assertions are defined :

*Table 1.* Assertions

| Assertion | Formal description | Comments |
|---|---|---|
| **potentially reset** | AG EF *init* | From any state, the component may go back to its initial state. |
| **unavoidably reset** | AG AF *init* | From any state, the component must go back to its initial state. |
| **is alive** | AG EF $EX_c$true | Some actions have always to be possible in the future. Applied to a root component, this assertion implies that there is no deadlock. |
| **no livelock** | AG AF $EX_c$true | The component must not stay forever idle. |
| **invariant**<exp> | AG <exp> | <exp>has always to be true. |
| <exp1> **leads to** <exp2> [**within** <exp3>] | AG(e1=>$AF_{<=d}$ e2) | The occurrence of <exp1> always implies the occurrence of <exp2> in less time than <exp3>. |

| **Assertion** | **Formal description** | **Comments** |
|---|---|---|
| **reachable**<exp1> **[from** <exp2>] **[within** <exp3>] | $AG(e1 => EF_{<=d}\ e2)$ | The occurrence of `<exp1>` may imply the occurrence of `<exp2>` in less time than `<exp3>`. |
| <exp1> **after** <exp2> | $AG(\neg EU(\neg e2, e1))$ | `<exp2>`always occurs after `<exp1>`. |

Using the syntax below, 3 equivalencies, with an increasing discrimination power, can be used :

- language equivalence : ensures that the observable executions of the abstract and real behaviors are the same. It takes into account neither the possibility of locking (states without any observable action) nor the possibility of divergence (infinite execution implying only non observable actions).
- observational equivalence : in addition to language equivalence, it takes into account locking states and the conservation of non determinism. Divergent executions are ignored.
- branching equivalence : in addition to observational equivalence, it takes into account divergent executions.

```
...
BEHAVIOR(<convention> equivalence)
 STATES
  <state name>(, <state name>)* : STATE;
  <state name> : INITIAL STATE;

 TRANSITIONS
  <transition 1>;
  <transition 2>;
  ...
  <transition n>;
END;
...
```

Let see now how the threads are modeled :

```
THREAD t
 REQUIRES
  sem1 : DATA ACCESS semaphore;
  sem2 : DATA ACCESS semaphore;
```

```
END t;

-- definition of the thread family
THREAD IMPLEMENTATION t.t1
 PROPERTIES
  Period => 13.96ms;
  cotre::Priority => 1;
  cotre::Phase => 0.0ms;
  Dispatch_Protocol => Periodic;

 ANNEX cotre.behavior IS
  STATES
   s0, s1, s2, s3, s4, s5, s6, s7, s8 : STATE;
   s0 : INITIAL STATE;
  TRANSITIONS
   s0 -[ ]-> s1 { periodic_wait };
   s1 -[ ]-> s2 { COMPUTATION(1.9ms, 1.9ms) };
   s2 -[ sem1.wait ! (-1.0ms) ]-> s3;
   s3 -[ ]-> s4 { COMPUTATION(0.1ms, 0.1ms) };
   s4 -[ sem2.wait ! (-1.0ms) ]-> s5;
   s5 -[ ]-> s6 { COMPUTATION(2.5ms, 2.5ms) };
   s6 -[ sem2.release ! ]-> s7;
   s7 -[ ]-> s8 { COMPUTATION(1.5ms, 1.5ms) };
   s8 -[ sem1.release !]-> s0;
 END ANNEX cotre.behavior;
END t.t1;
```

First, the thread type declares to need 2 semaphores in the core AADL syntax. The implementation t.t1 then shows an use of the COTRE properties `cotre::Priority` and `cotre::Phase`. The properties below, absent from the AADL core, are required for COTRE and defined explicitly in its property set :

*Table 2.* The COTRE property set

| Name | Type | Applies to | Default value | Notes |
|---|---|---|---|---|
| cotre::Description | string | every component / sub-component | - | Informal comments. |
| cotre::Min_Time | time | THREAD | - | Minimum time between 2 execution of a sporadic thread. |

| Name | Type | Applies to | Default value | Notes |
|---|---|---|---|---|
| cotre::Phase | time | THREAD | 0.0s | Phase of the beginning of execution for periodic threads. |
| cotre::Priority | integer | THREAD | - | Base priority of the thread (the precise semantic depends on the scheduling policy). |
| cotre::Protected | boolean | SUBPROGRAM | false | `true` if the subprograms calls are exclusive, `false` if they are concurrent. |
| cotre::Reentrant | boolean | SUBPROGRAM | false | `true` if the subprogram is reentrant, and `false` if not. |
| cotre::Requirements | string | every component / sub-component | | Requirements tracability informations. |

The definition of the t.t2 implementation is identical excepted for the `period` property, which is 17.26ms.

Finally, here is the semaphore model :

```
DATA semaphore
 PROVIDES
  wait: SUBPROGRAM;
  release: SUBPROGRAM;
 PROPERTIES
  cotre::Protected => TRUE; -- wait and release are exclusive
ENDsemaphore;

DATA IMPLEMENTATION semaphore.default
 PROPERTIES
  sem_p::Max_tokens => 1;

 -- Ensures the number of tokens remains in the authorized range
```

```
ANNEX cotre.guarantees IS
 INVARIANT tokens < Max_tokens;
 INVARIANT tokens >= 0;
END ANNEX cotre.guarantees;

ANNEX cotre.behavior IS
 VARS
  tokens : INTEGER 0..+infinity;
 INITS
  tokens := sem_p::Max_tokens;

 SUBPROGRAM wait
  STATES
   s0, s1 : STATE;
   s0 : INITIAL STATE;
  TRANSITIONS
   s0 -[ WHEN tokens > 0 => CALLED ? ]-> s1 { tokens := tokens -
1 };
   s1 -[ RESUME ]-> s0;

 SUBPROGRAM release
  STATES
   s0, s1 : STATE;
   s0 : INITIAL STATE;
  TRANSITIONS
   s0 -[ WHEN tokens < capacity => CALLED ? ]-> s1 { tokens :=
tokens + 1 };
   s1 -[ RESUME ]-> s0;
END ANNEXcotre.behavior;
END semaphore.default;
```

For any component, behavior is described thanks to Mealy machines. In the thread case, an automaton is globally linked to the object, when one is required for each provided subprogram for data components. Internal variables and their initial values have to be defined at the beginning of the annex. The states have then to be declared, and transitions are defined in this way :

(<label>:)* <origin state> **-[**<clearing condition>**]->** <arrival state> **{**<actions>**};**

The clearing conditions are expressed as follow :

**WHEN** <boolean condition> **=>** <synchronization event>

And the synchronization events known are :

*Table 3.* Synchronization events

| **Events** | **Comments** |
|---|---|
| <subprogram name> **!** [(<parameters>)] | Calls the named subprogram with the required parameters. The subprogram is identified by using the dotted notation `<object>.<subprogram>`. Parameters are separated by commas. |
| **CALLED** ? | The subprogram being described is called. |
| **RESUME** [ (<parameters>) ] | Give back the control to the caller (but the subprogram being described can go on running). |

Finally, actions can be :

*Table 4.* Actions

| **Actions** | **Comments** |
|---|---|
| **COMPUTATION(**<max_duration or range>**)** | Consumes a CPU time smaller then `<max_duration>` or bounded by `<range>`. |
| **DELAY(**<max_duration or range >**)** | The execution is deferred for a time smaller than `<max_duration>` or bounded by `<range>`. |
| **PERIODIC_WAIT** | Delays the execution of a periodic thread until the beginning of its next period. For an aperiodic thread, it is equivalent to **`SKIP`**. |
| SKIP | Does nothing. |
| <l_exp> := <exp> | Modifies the value of the variable `<l_exp>`. |

## 4. CONCLUSION

The COTRE project goal is to provide method and tools for real time software architecture design & verification. The approach adopted is based on formal languages and verification methods. The UCOTRE language is the user view of architectures, when VCOTRE is closer to verification methods requirements. The proximity of the needs covered by AADL and UCOTRE allows to use the AADL core as a base language. The extension mechanisms defined in AADL are sufficiently powerful to take into account the COTRE specific concepts, such as behaviors and contracts. These COTRE developments are identified as possible annexes for future AADL versions. Currently, the UCOTRE language is quite clearly defined, even if some points are still under construction. But the semantic coherency is not completely established between UCOTRE and AADL on one hand, and between UCOTRE and VCOTRE on the other hand. These precise mappings are being studied, as well as between the HOOD graphical representation and UCOTRE. A demonstration toolkit, able to assist designers from the graphical modeling until the formal verification is also in progress.

## 5. REFERENCES


1. P. Farail, P. Gaufillet, J.M. Farines, J.L. Lambert, P. Dissaux, H. Hafidi, P. Michel, M. Filali, J.P. Bodeveix, F. Vernadat, B. Berthomieu, P.O. Ribet, The COTRE project : how to model an verify real time architecture ?, 2004
2. http://www.laas.fr/COTRE
3. http://www.airbus.com
4. http://www.tni-valiosys.com, http://www.tni-world.com
5. http://www.feria.cnrs.fr
6. http://www.laas.fr
7. http://www.irit.fr
8. http://www.cert.fr/fr/dtim
9. http://www.enst-bretagne.fr
10. http://forums.sae.org/access/dispatch.cgi/TEAASD_pf/folderFrame/100144/0/def/aac9
11. J.M. Farines, B. Berthomieu, J.P. Bodeveix, P. Farail, M. Filali, P. Gaufillet, H. Hafidi, J.L. Lambert, P. Michel, F. Vernadat, The COTRE project : rigorous software development for real time systems in avionics, 27th IFAC/IFIP/IEEE Workshop on Real Time Programming - Zielona Gora (Poland), 2003
12. Paul Peterson and Kim G. Larsen, Uppaal2k, European Association for Theoritical Computer Science, 70, 2000
13. K. L. McMillan, Symbolic Model Checking, Kluwer Academic, 1993

14.B. Berthomieu, P.O. Ribet, F. Vernadat, The tool TINA - Construction of abstract state spaces for Petri nets and time Petri nets, Int. Journal of Production Research (to appear)
15.S. Dellacherie, Samuel Devulder, Jean Luc Lambert, Software Verification Based on Linear Programming, World Congress on Formal Methods, 1999
16.http://www.hood-method.org
17.SAE AS-2C, Aerospace Information Report, Architecture Analysis and Design Language, version 0.96, 2004
18.B. Berthomieu, P.O. Ribet, F. Vernadat, J.L. Bernartt, J.M. Farines, J.P. Bodeveix, M. Filali, G. Padiou, P. Michel, P. Farail, P. Gaufillet, P. Dissaux, J.L. Lambert, Towards the verification of real time systems in avionics : the COTRE approach, Electronic notes in Theorical Computer Sciences ENTCS - Volume 80, 2003

# EAST-ADL – AN ARCHITECTURE DESCRIPTION LANGUAGE

*Validation and Verification Aspects*

Vincent Debruyne[1], Françoise Simonot-Lion[2] and Yvon Trinquet[3]
*[1]PSA Peugeot-Citroën, 92000 La Garenne Colombe - France; [2]LORIA (UMR 7503) - INPL, Campus Scientifique - BP 239 - 54506 Vandoeuvre-lès-Nancy cedex - France; [3]IRCCyN (UMR 6597) Ecole Centrale de Nantes, BP 92101 – 44321 – Nantes cedex 3 – France.*

Abstract: The part of embedded electronic systems in vehicles is nowadays growing. The European EAST-EEA project aims to bring efficient methods and tools for mastering the complexity of these systems. We present EAST-ADL, an Architecture Description Language developed in this project et show how the verification and validation activities are linked to this language.

Keywords: ADL, Verification, Validation, Requirements, Real-Time Systems.

## 1. INTRODUCTION

For economical and technological reasons, the part of electronic and software is increasing significantly in automotive systems. The main characteristics of these systems are their distributed nature and the fact that they have to provide a level of quality of service fixed by the market, the safety requirements and the cost requirements. Furthermore, their development process is shared between different partners. Therefore their development and their production have to be based on a suitable methodology including modelling, validation, optimisation and test. Obviously, any error detected during the integration step leads to a costly feedback on the specification or design activities, and it must be avoided. So, in order to improve the quality of the design process, new methodologies are emerging. In particular, the actors implicated in the development of a system apply more and more methods and techniques ensuring the correctness of subsystems as early as possible in the design stages and a new trend is to consider the integration of subsystems at a virtual level [1]. This means that each partner involved in the development process will be able to design, prove and validate the models of each subsystem with respects to the requirements. Then the challenge is the validation of the whole system in a cooperative way. This paper demonstrates how the EAST-EEA project [2] brings some solutions to this challenge.

Specifically, the section 2 describes some approach related to this problem. A brief presentation of the context, the objectives and main results of EAST-EEA project is given in section 3. In section 4 we present how the validation and verification activities can be modeled in a consistent way all along the development process while section 5 focuses on performance properties and specifies how the model of an embedded system has to be completed in order to allow the verification process of this kind of properties. Section 6 brings some conclusions on this proposal.

## 2. RELATED WORKS

The way to improve the quality and the flexibility of an embedded electronic system while decreasing the development and production cost is to design and validate it at a virtual level. The development of complex systems requires frameworks that support functional and extra-functional specification at different steps of the development and methods for ensuring the system correctness. Therefore, the problem is, on the one hand, to identify the abstraction level at which the components and the whole system should be described. And on the other hand, in order to ensure the system correctness, we have to identify the validation / verification activities or the automatic generation techniques to apply. Consequently, we have to identify the formalisms supporting the identified models. Some main keywords are related to this problem: 1- *architectures*, referring to the Architecture Description Language concept (ADL), well known in computer science; 2- *components*, leading to modularity principles and object approach and 3- *Model Driven Architecture* [3], well-suited to generation of correct implementations.

An Architecture Description Language is an approach for software and system architecture specification [4]. In the avionic context, MetaH [5] developed at Honeywell, has been chosen, in 2001, as the basis for the definition of an Avionics Architecture Description Language (AADL) standard under the SAE authority [6]. The core AADL supports system modeling and execution platforms. It provides a way for describing control, data flow, some non functional aspects (timing requirements, fault and error behaviors, time and space partitioning, safety and certification properties). Efficient tools are provided with AADL for verification purpose as schedulability analysis.

The Cotre Project [7] targets the same objective. It provides a methodology for the development of real-time avionic systems by specifying in a formal way the links between the description of such a system expressed thanks to an Architecture Description Language and the formal techniques relying to verification activities. The formalisms used for verification activities are Transition Systems, Time Automata and Time Petri Nets (tools Uppaal, Tina or Aldebaran).

In automotive industry, recent efforts brought a solution for mastering the design, modeling and validation of embedded systems. A first result was obtained by the French project AEE (Embedded Electronic Architecture) [8]. A result of this project is a language named AIL_Transport (Architecture Implementation Language for Transport). It allows the specification in the same framework of embedded architectures at several abstraction levels. The highest one captures the requirements and give a functional view. The lowest level models an implementation [9], [10]. Two tools were developed in order to automate scaling and verification activities. They take, as input data, the system description in AIL_Transport. The first one is devoted to optimal distributed code generation realized by Syndex tool [11]. The second one is dedicated to performance property verification by using Opnet simulator (www.opnet.com.). A similar work is proposed in CAROSSE [12] through a language for implementation description (tasks exchanging messages over a communication architecture) and a timing property verification tool hiding the complexity of the required models.

The CLARA[13] ADL is a general purpose language developed for the design of asynchronous reactive real-time systems. Special attention was paid to the control flows. Indeed CLARA allows to express complex synchronization and activation laws, and timing requirements. Tools based on Time Petri Nets can be used for verification activity at the operational level.

Face with these works, the ITEA European project EAST-EEA, (July 2001 - June 2004), involving carmakers, suppliers and research institutes, investigates automotive embedded architectures and development aspects. It involves and aims to unify the concepts for automotive software development and moves towards a common notation, the whole approach being supported by suitable verification and validation (V&V) tools. Among the addressed, we focus in the next sections on the Architecture Description Language, named EAST-ADL, that was specified and on its use for the validation and verification activities. GME2000 tool[14] supports the meta model describing EAST-ADL.

# 3. EAST-ADL

The purpose of EAST-ADL is to provide a support for the non-ambiguous description of in-car embedded electronic systems at each level of their development. It provides a framework for the modeling of such systems through 7 views as shown in Figure 1 [15]. Each view, except the first one, capture an "architecture" this term being used with the sense of an entity organization. Each view is the result of a specific analysis among the development process: in EAST-ADL terminology it is called an artifact.

## 3.1 Abstraction layers supported by EAST-ADL

The EAST-ADL abstraction layers are quickly described hereafter.

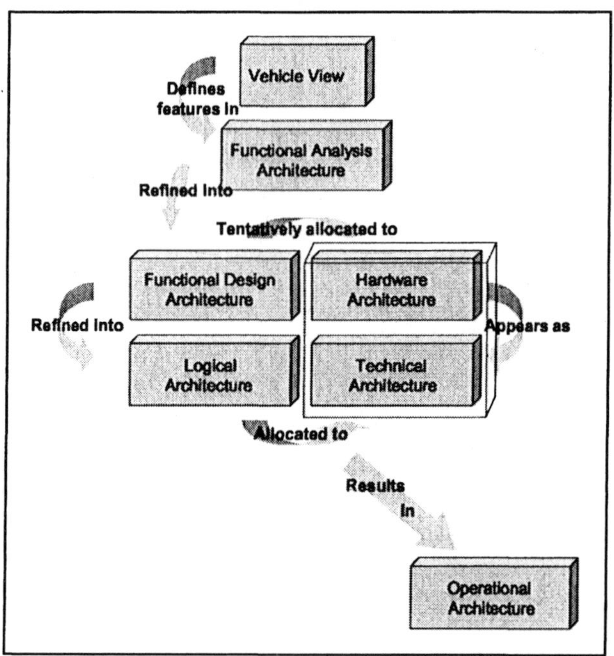


*Figure 1.* The abstraction layers of the EAST ADL.

- *Vehicle View* is the level where user visible features are described. Examples of such features are anti-lock braking or windscreen wipers;
- *Functional Analysis Architecture* level represents the functions realizing the features, their behavior and their cooperation. There is an n-to-n mapping between Vehicle View entities and Functional Analysis Architecture entities, i.e. one or several functions may realize one or several features;

- *Functional Design Architecture* level models a decomposition or refinement of functions described at *Functional Analysis Architecture* level in order to meet constraints regarding allocation, efficiency, re-use, supplier concerns, etc. Again, there is an n-to-n mapping between entities at Functional Design Architecture level and the corresponding ones at Functional Analysis Architecture level;
- *Logical Architecture* is a flat software structure where the Functional Design Architecture entities have been instantiated. This level provides an abstraction of the software components to implement on the Technical Architecture. The logical architecture contains the leaf functions of the Functional Design Architecture. From the Logical Architecture point of view, the code could be automatically generated in many cases.

In order to model the implementation of a system, EAST-ADL furnishes, on the one hand, a way for the description of the hardware platforms and their available services (operating system, protocols, middleware) and, on the other hand, a support for the specification of how a logical architecture is distributed onto a platform. For this purpose, three additional views are necessary:

- The *Hardware Architecture* level includes the description of the ECUs (Electronic Component Unit) and more precisely those of the used micro-controller, sensors and actuators, the communication links (serial links, networks) and their connections.
- At *Technical Architecture* level the model of the operating system and/or Middleware API and the services provided (schedulers, frame packing, memory management, I/O drivers, diagnosis software, download software etc.) are given. So programmer's view of the Hardware Architecture is given by the Technical Architecture.
- The *Operational Architecture* models the tasks, managed by the operating systems and frames, managed by the protocols. It is the result of the mapping of the Logical Architecture entities onto the Technical Architecture. At this lowest abstraction level, all implementation details are captured.

A system described at the Functional Analysis level may be loosely coupled to hardware. Indeed it may be based on intuition, various known constraints or as a back annotation from more detailed analysis on lower levels. Furthermore, the structure of the Functional Design architecture and of the Logical Architecture is aware of the Technical architecture. Finally, this EAST-ADL provides the consistency within and between artifacts belonging to the different levels, at a syntactic and semantic point of view.

This leads to make an EAST-ADL based model a strong and non-ambiguous support for building automatically models suited to formal validation and verification activities.

The compliance to UML2 was a constraint for the definition of the EAST-ADL language. A prototype, based on GME2000 tool [14], was realized. It provides, at present, an editor for each view previously described and a checker verifying the consistency of a model, according to EAST-ADL semantic. A complete model of a system is stored in an XML database.

The description of the language elements was divided into six parts corresponding to different language domains, as "structure domain" for the language elements describing the structural relation, or "behavior domain" for the language elements describing the behavioral models. In the next parts of the paper we give some information on the "requirement domain" and the "V&V domain".

## 3.2 Requirements modeling

As EAST-ADL supports all the activities done along the development process of an automotive embedded system, it provides a way for expressing the requirements that guide the building of a solution at each step of this development. So EAST-ADL defines the different requirements types that can be used. It allows to link them on the one hand to components defined at one or several architectural views and on the other hand to analysis models, design models and implementation models[16]. Finally the tracing activities between different requirements or between different versions of requirements can be expressed in this language.

Five types of requirements were identified. Each of them is characterized by a textual description possibly completed by a formal description, information supporting the tracing activities and a status which is to be set to specific values according to the result of particular design, validation or verification activities. The requirement types are:

- *EFeatures*: an EFeature object (EFeature) describes the required functionalities of an embedded system; this kind of object is used, mainly, for specifying the system at Vehicle and Functional Analysis Architecture levels. EFeatures may be decomposed into sub-features or variant features ("variant" stands here for the various type of equipments for a car);
- *Interactions*: this type is used to specify the cooperation modes between EFeatures through textual description, semi formal one (as use-cases) and possibly formal one (for example, Message Sequence Charts);
- *Functional Requirements*: this type aims to specify the behavior of EFeatures by means of a set of required properties; once more, a formal

description (state-transition diagrams, Messages Sequence Charts, ...) can complete the textual one;

- *Design Constraints*: this is a kind of requirement that constraint the research field for a solution; for example, such a constraints can impose a communication standard, a legacy tool for designing the system or a criteria to optimize (cost, power consumption, network bandwidth, ...);
- *Quality Requirements*: they are used to express extra-functional properties; among these Quality Requirements, we can cite performance properties, reliability properties, safety properties, ...

In this paper, we will focus on the Quality Requirements and on their links to formal validation and verification activities. For this purpose, we recall, in the following section, the main classes of validation and verification techniques that are used in automotive industry and how the validation and verification process can be modeled.

# 4. VALIDATION AND VERIFICATION ACTIVITIES

## 4.1 Main Validation and Verification techniques used in automotive industry

From an industrial point of view, two main objectives for validation and verification can be identified:

- Validation and verification of all or parts of a system at a functional level without taking into account the implementation characteristics. These activities ensure the consistency of the system mainly with respect to the EFeatures, Interactions and Functional Requirements. At this level, simulation or formal analysis techniques can be used;
- Verification of properties of all or part of a system at operational level. These activities take into account the performances of both the hardware and Technical Architectures and also the load that is due to a particular allocation of the Logical Architecture on the Technical Architecture. This objective can also be reached through simulation and formal analysis techniques. Note that, in this context the formal approach for the verification of the feasibility of a set of tasks and frames is done through a timing analysis method.

For these purposes, a model suited to the concerned techniques and to the associated tool has to be built. The way used to generate such a model will be explained in section 5. Some tools are of course of general interest in this context as, for example Matlab / Simulink or Stateflow as well as Statemate. In some cases, an interface encapsulates these tools in order to adapt the tool to the automotive context.

Moreover, these techniques that work on virtual platforms are completed by test techniques in order to verify that a realisation is correct. We can cite the test of software components, the test of logical architectures and the test of an implemented embedded system. Note that the testing activities as well as the simulation ones consist in providing a scenario of events and/or data that stimulate the system under test or stimulate an executable model of the system; then, in both techniques we have to look which events and/or data are produced by the system. The input scenario can be manually built or formally generated. In this last case the test or simulation activity is closely linked to a formal analysis technique.

## 4.2 Validation and Verification Process

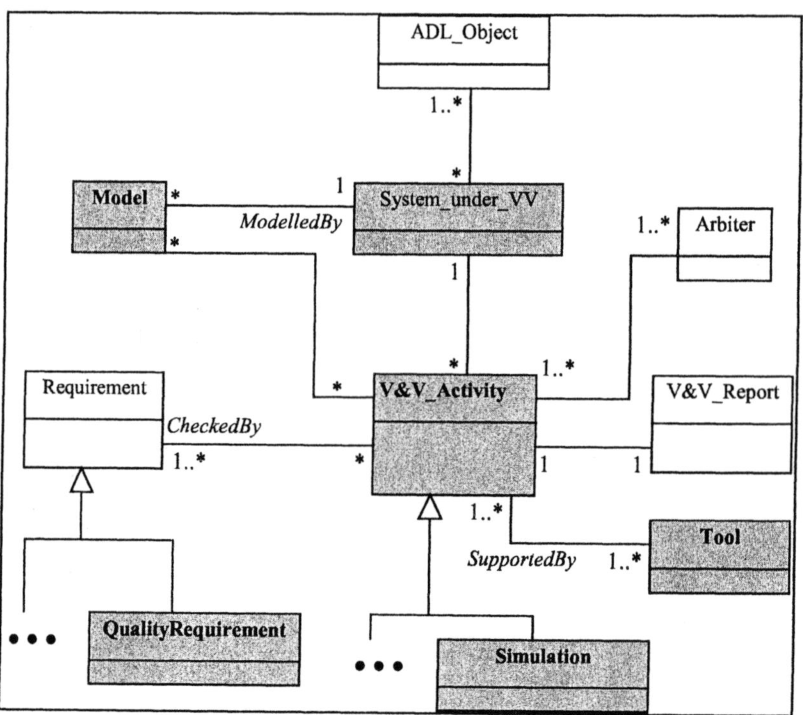


*Figure 2.* Validation and Verification process model

The EAST ADL language provides a way for supporting the Validation and Verification activities along the development process.

A main purpose is to formalize the relations between V&V activities and the other items supported by EAST ADL. These relations are illustrated by the figure 2. This description is largely inspired by the testing profile defined in UML2. In this figure, the classes that will be used in the case study are highlighted (*V&V_Activity*, *System_under_VV*, *Model*, *Tool*, *QualityRequirement*).

In particular, two links should be outlined:

- a first one with Requirement objects: the specified association establishes that one V&V activity can contribute to the checking of several requirements, while one requirement can be checked thanks to several V&V activities;
- a second one with embedded architecture objects: obviously, as the purpose is to validate or verify properties of all or part of an embedded system, a *V&V_Activity* object is associated to a set of objects related to an architecture layer. For example, a timing analysis applied to one Electronic Control Unit (one micro-controller) is concerned by the set of tasks (objects *TaskOS*) that are local to this ECU and by the scheduling policy used on this ECU and described by an *OperatingSystem* object. This set of ADL objects is named *System_under_VV*.

Furthermore, as introduced in the previous section, a V&V activity is a generic class that can be refined in several subclasses, modelling formal analysis or scenario-based techniques (simulation or test).

Because the way to conduct V&V activity depends on the techniques, several entities and associated attributes have been identified. Formal analysis is mainly based on a formalism, a property to verify and a verdict concerning the verification of the property. Test (or simulation) is based on a scenario, acceptable results corresponding to this scenario and a verdict which is elaborated thanks to actual results of the test (or simulation). *VV_Report* and *Arbiter* model the final verdict of a V&V activity.

# 5. CASE STUDY: PERFORMANCE PROPERTY VERIFICATION

EAST-ADL supports the consistency between architectural objects, requirements and validation or verification activities. We illustrate this by studying how can be applied the schedulability analysis of frames over CAN under error pattern assumption. In fact, we show two main characteristics of EAST-ADL. On the one hand, we identify how EAST-ADL supports the consistency between requirements specified at different steps of the development process and the verification activities used to ensure that these requirements are checked. On the other hand, as for any verification activity a model of all or part of the system has to be built, we demonstrate how this building process can be automated by exploiting the semantic of objects and interactions expressed in EAST-ADL.

Let us consider, as an example, two quality requirements specified during the development of an embedded system.

- QR1: "the system has to be tolerant to EMI perturbation following a profile due to a given type of radar"; this requirement can be given in the earliest steps of the development process.

- QR2: "a freshness constraint (2 milliseconds) is imposed to the signal <VehicleSpeed>; the average of respected freshness constraint has to be more than 80%"; this is required at functional level; let us assume that this signal <VehicleSpeed> is produced by a function and consumed by another one, so this requirement can be translated in "the percentage of missed deadlines (2ms.) for the exchange of signal <VehicleSpeed> has to be less than 20%".

These two requirements impose to the designer the verification of just one property at operational architecture level: the probability that the frame containing the signal <VehicleSpeed> misses its deadline (2 ms.) has to be less than 20% (we suppose here that producer and consumer of <VehicleSpeed> signal are deployed on two different nodes).

A way to check these two quality requirements for a system is to apply an analytical method for performance evaluation of the network that supports the exchange of the concerned signal as illustrated in figure 4. A tool, named VACANS, is available for this performance evaluation. It is based on a recurrent algorithm whose principle was given first by Tindell et al.[17] and that was extended for taking into account a more realistic error model by Navet[18] as needed in this verification requirement. It takes as entry, on the one hand, some characteristics of the CAN network and the specification of the frames that it supports and, on the other hand, some parameters for modelling the error occurrences due to a given EMI perturbation pattern. VACANS evaluates the worst-case deadline failure probability for each frame. The term worst-case is justified by two assumptions: each error is detected on the last bit of the frame and the time needed by each frame to gain the bus is the maximum possible. More precisions about this technique can be found in [18].

So, for checking the requirements QR1 and QR2, a verification activity named EMI_Tolerance, can be done by running VACANS tool. The result of this activity (worst case deadline failure probability for each frame) can then be analysed and a report that establishes the verdict about the property is produced. Note that several other results can be obtained as for example, the percentage of missed deadlines for each other frame, the mean bandwidth of the network, ... So, we consider in EAST-ADL that all these results contribute to a general evaluation report which can be linked to several verification activities, in particular, in this example, to EMI_Tolerance object.

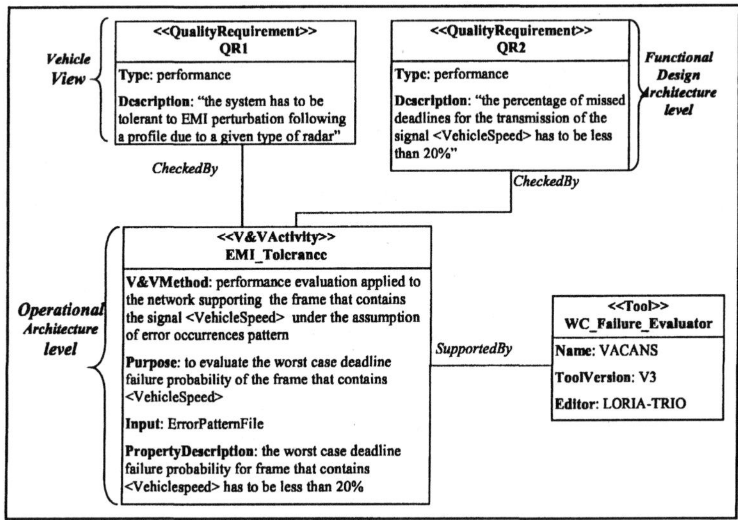


*Figure 3.* How quality requirements QR1 and QR2 are checked through a V&V activity

As shown previously, EMI_Tolerance realised thanks to VACANS tool, is applied to a set of related objects described in EAST-ADL. We illustrate in the following how these objects can be "*extracted*" from the EAST-ADL compliant repository.

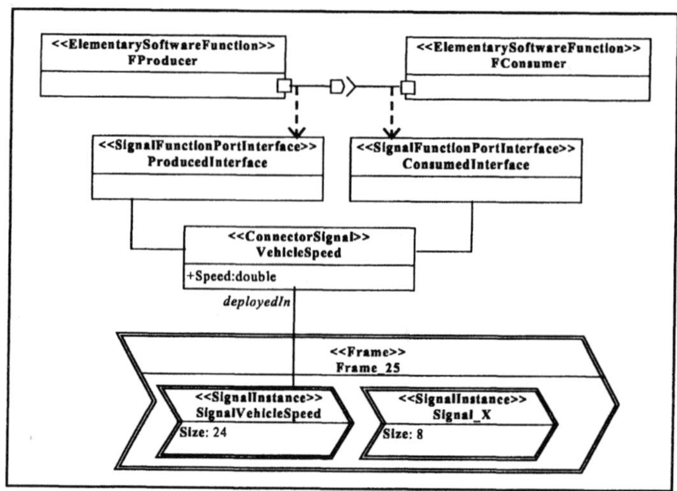


*Figure 4.* From the VehicleSpeed to the object Frame that contains its realization

***From functional level (a signal) to operational level (a frame).***

The entry point for this extraction is the object *ConnectorSignal* whose name is *<VehicleSpeed>*. This signal, its producer and consumers were identified at a functional level (see figure 4). In a following step, producer (*<FProducer>*) and consumer (*<FConsumer>*) of the signal were deployed in OSTasks allocated to different ECUs (Electronic Control Unit). Therefore, the *ConnectorSignal <VehicleSpeed>* is transformed in a *SignalInstance* object, named *<SignalVehicleSpeed>*, whose size is 24 bits and is deployed in an object *Frame* named *<Frame_25>*. The object under verification is this frame.

***From one frame at operational level to the network supporting this frame.***

The VACANS tool obliges us to gather all the frames that share the same network. For this purpose, from the object Frame_25, we obtain the object network supporting this frame.

***From a network to all the frames sharing it.***

Then, this object, named here *CAN_Chassis*, allow us to obtain the set of frames that we have to take into account for the verification activity (see figure 5).

Each Frame in EAST-ADL is characterised by several global attributes:

- Period: the trigger period (in ms.); it represents the nominal period for time triggered frames and the minimum inter-arrival time for event triggered ones;

- Offset: (in ms.); it gives the offset from the starting time; this attribute is only applied for time triggered frames;
- FrameSize: (in bits) the total length of the frame;
- DataSize: (in bits) the sum of the size of each object SignalInstance deployed in this frame.

These attributes can be extracted automatically from the repository describing the embedded system in EAST-ADL. Nevertheless, some other characteristics have to be completed before using VACANS. In particular, due to the object CAN_Chassis - whose protocol is CAN - we have to complete the characteristics of each frame by the attribute *Priority*. Furthermore, for establishing the verdict, a deadline characteristic is added to the Frame_25 (2ms. as explicitly given in the requirement QR2); as nothing is given for the other frames, we consider that their deadlines are equal to their periods.

The object CAN_Chassis has to be completed by several attributes:

- Throughput: in bits/s;
- Length: in m.

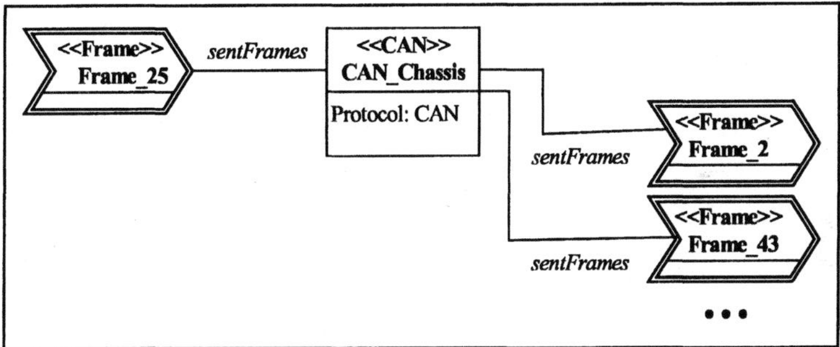


*Figure 5.* From Frame_25 to all the frames sharing the same network

Finally, the use of Vacans requires to fix the parameters used for specifying the errors occurrences according to a generalized Poisson Process[18]. These parameters are $<\lambda, u, \alpha>$ where the inter-arrival between two perturbations is given by $exp(\lambda)$; the length of a burst is given by the number of errors $u$ and, when an error occurs, $\alpha$ is the probability that it is a burst of errors and $1-\alpha$ is the probability that it is a single error (these parameters are illustrated in figure 6). The algorithm computes then the worst-case deadline failure probability for each collected frames.

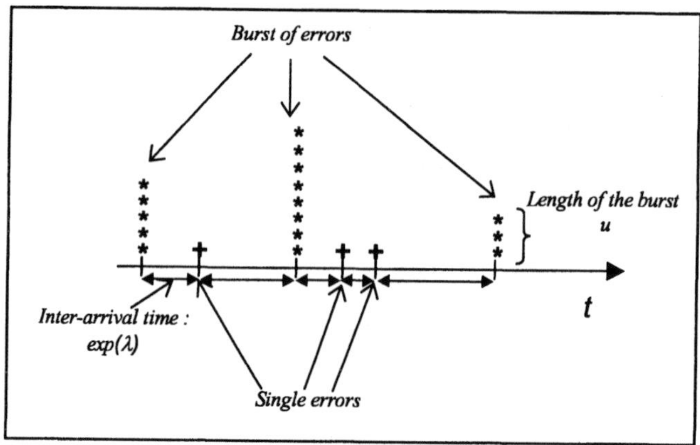


*Figure 6.* Parameters of error distribution

The complexity of the automatic generation of formal model used, in this case, as an entry of VACANS tool depends on the structure of the XML database. In the present prototype, the organization of the XML database is such that it needs for this case study:

- to browse a first time the XML file in order to find the object VehicleSpeed (ConnectorSignal object); the object SignalVehicleSpeed (SignalInstance object) is directly referenced;
- to browse a second time the XML file in order to find, among the objects Frame, the one that is connected to SignalVehicleSpeed; the object CAN_Chassis (CAN object) is directly referenced;
- to browse a third time the XML file, among the objects Frame, in order to find all the objects that are connected to CAN_Chassis object.

This example demonstrates that thanks to the semantic of the objects described according to EAST-ADL, some activities can be automated and that formal links connect objects at different levels. So EAST-ADL is not only a support for the non-ambiguous modeling of an electronic embedded system but also for its development process.

# 6. CONCLUSIONS

In this paper we have presented a few concepts of the EAST ADL common modeling language for automotive software development. Currently a major version of the language has been defined and used in demonstrators in the course of EAST-EEA project. This will probably give good expertise for language evolutions. The paper has focused on requirements and V&V aspects through an example at the operational architecture level. This example shows how some V&V activities can be automated and that formal links connect objects at different levels. Ongoing works are on the specification of the needed language attributes for various V&V methods as timing analysis, or model-checking.

## REFERENCES


1 P. Giusto, J.-Y. Brunel, A. Ferrari, E. Fourgeau, L. Lavagno and A. Sangiovanni-Vincentelli, Automotive Virtual Integration Platforms: Why's, What's, and How's, *Proceedings of the International Conference of Comp. Desc.* , July 2002.

2 ITEA – EAST EEA Project, www.east-eea.net/docs.

3 Object Management Group, Model Driven Architecture, http://www.omg.org/mda/

4 R.N. Taylor, N. Medvidovic, A Framework for Classifying and Comparing Architecture Description Languages, Tech. Report, University of California, Irvine, 1997.

5 S. Vestal, MetaH Reference Manual, Tech. Report, Honeywell Technology Center, 1995.

6 P. H. Feiler, B. Lewis, S. Vestal, The SAE Avionics Architecture Description Language (AADL) Standard, RTAS 2003, Washington, 2003.

7 B. Berthomieu, PO. Ribet,F.Vernadat, JL. Bernatt, JM. Farines, JP. Bodeveix, M. Filali, G. Padiou,P.Michel, P. Farail, P. Gaufillet, P. Dissaux, J.-L. Lambert, Towards the verification of RT systems in avionics: the Cotre approach, *El. Notes in Th. Comp. Science* 80, 2003.

8. AEE, Architecture Electronique Embarquée, http://aee.inria.fr, 1999.

9. J.P. Elloy, F. Simonot-Lion, An Architecture Description Language for In-Vehicle Embedded System development, 15th IFAC World Congress, Barcelona, Spain, 2002.

10. J. Migge, J.P. Elloy, Embedded electronic architecture, Proceedings of 3rd International Workshop on Open Systems in Automotive Networks, Bad Homburg, Germany, 2000.

11 R.Kocik, Y. Sorel, A methodology to design and prototype optimized embedded robotic systems, 2nd IMACS International Multiconference CESA'98, Hammamet, Tunisia, 1998

12 P. Castelpietra, YQ. Song, F. Simonot-Lion, Analysis and simulation methods for evaluation of a networked embedded architecture, *IEEE Trans. on Industrial Electronics*, 49-6, 2002.

13 Durand E., Description et vérification d'architectures d'application temps réel : CLARA et les réseaux de Petri Temporels. PhD thesis, Ecole Cdentrale de Nantes, 1998 (report in French).

14 A. Ledeczi, M. Maroti, A. Bakay, G. Nordstrom, J. Garrett, C. Thomason, J. Sprinkle, P. Volgyesi, GME 2000 Users Manual (v2.0), technical report, Vanderbilt University, 2001.

15 U. Freund, O. Gurrieri, J. Küster, H. Lönn, J. Migge, M.-O. Reiser, T. Wierczoch and M. Weber, An Architecture Description Language for Developing Automotive ECU-Software, INCOSE 2004, International Conference On Systems Engineering, Toulouse, France, june 2004.

16 M.Weber, J.Weisbrod, Requirements Engineering in Automotive Development – Experiences and Challenges. IEEE Software, vol. 20, no. 1, pp 16-24, 2003.

17 K. Tindell and A. Burns, Guaranteeeing message latencies on Controller Area network (CAN), 1st International CAN Conference, ICC'94.

18 N. Navet, Y.-Q. Song, F. Simonot, Worst-case deadline failure probability in real time applications distributed over CAN, in Journal of System Architecture, 46(7), 607-618.

# BUILDING TOOL SUITE FOR AADL

Jean-François Tilman
*Axlog ingénierie*
*19-21 rue du 8 mai 1945*
*94110 Arcueil, France*
*(+33) 1 41 24 31 33*
Jean-Francois.Tilman@axlog.fr

**Abstract** Architecture description languages (ADLs) are more and more considered in system engineering to model real-time applications (avionics, transportation, critical industrial systems, etc.). They provide means to formally specify architectures and support their design from the capture of the needs to the final validation. ASSERT, a european integrated project (IP) tackling improvement of system engineering process, is an illustration of this consideration.

Among all the existing ADLs, a few must be attentively considered because they should spread in the future. This is the case for AADL, an ADL initially dedicated to avionics applications, and now designed to support any domain critical application.

AADL may play a great role in industry to improve software and system development process. To achieve this objective, we need to strongly combine the description capabilities of AADL with tool suites used to develop, generate or test the system. This means that such tool suites have to explicitely support AADL.

AADL is based on MetaH, which is both an ADL and a tool set supporting it. In this paper, we will consider how an equivalent AADL tool suite could be built, possibly based on MetaH tools. We will also consider the industrial domains where it could be adopted and the role it could play.

## 1. Introduction

Architecture description languages (ADLs) are more and more popular in industry. After their development and use in laboratories, a lot of research is currently led by industry to transfer and integrate them into actual system engineering process. ADLs provide a means to formally describe system architectures. Many activities require such descriptions, and the introduction of such a formalism can help in their improvement.

The use of a description language in an industrial process requires its full support by the tools involved in this process. If not so, this language will not be adopted by users because its manipulation is unpracticable. Among all the existing ADLs, a few have the vocation to cover large parts of the industry needs. AADL [aadl] is one of them. For this ADL also, the support by tools is an issue to be considered.

In this article we will first consider the possible roles of ADLs in system engineering process and we will compare approaches of several domains, mainly automotive and avionics. Secondly, we will talk about the tool aspect of this subject: why is it important to support an ADL with tools, what are the existing bases to build such tools for AADL, what can these tools look like.

## 2. Interest of ADLs

### Role

When developing computer-based systems, we must avoid inconsistencies in each phase of the development: the capture of the needs must be complete and consistent, the specification must cover all the needs, the design must fulfil the specifications, and so on, until the last phases of the development cycle and the validation.

What is difficult here is to ensure that (1) each piece of information in a given phase is completely taken into account in the next phase during the refinement and (2) that the contents of each phase are consistent. This problem deals with the management of information. It is more accurate during the first phases, typically where we often use natural languages to describe the needs and the specifications.

The best way to solve this problem is to use formalism, and particularly use a formal means to describe the system architecture and the related requirements. This is the role of architecture description languages (ADLs).

"ADL" is a very generic acronym, and many ADLs exist to describe architectures of various domains : mechanics, electronics, software, etc. We will only consider those dealing with computer-based systems, that is, systems containing computers embedding software. Among them, some are specialized for a particular application domain (avionics, automotive, etc.), or for particular aspects (synchronous approach, distribution problems). For our purpose, we are interested by ADLs supporting the whole system, not only a subset, and during all the development cycle.

### Avionics domain

Avionics is a domain where industry has early considered the possible interest of formal descriptions in development process. These considerations are motivated by the high quality level required in this domain. The following examples show activity of avionics industry in these questions.

In 1990, MetaH [metah] has been initiated by Amcom (US army) and Honeywell. MetaH is both an architecture description language and a tool set. It enables the description of avionics software architectures in a bottom-up approach and the automatic generation of what is needed to agregate the user components and execute them in a given target.

MetaH has demonstrated the interest of this technique in terms of cost and duration of developments. Some operations like retargeting a source code for a new hardware can be significantly improved (up to 70 %). However MetaH has never been largely deployed in industry.

In 2000, Amcom and Honeywell decided to create an international standard for an architecture description language based on MetaH. This new language is AADL (originally meaning Avionics Architecture Description Language), and its standardization process is led under the authority of the Society of Automotive Engineers (SAE), aerospace division. The standardization committee includes American and European partners, many of them come from avionics industry. Now, AADL is no more specific for avionics and the meaning of its acronym has changed into "Architecture Analysis and Design Language" to avoid confusion.

In Europe, the ASSERT project is considering the same problems, but is more innovative and ambitious. Using a common architecture description language for the whole development cycle, it aims at improving the engineering process by using formal methods and proofs, and go towards the ***proof-based system engineering*** (PBSE). ASSERT is an integrated project (IP) for the 6$^{th}$ framework program for research and develoment of the European commission. Many of the large avionics and space European compagnies are involved in this project, like other ones coming from other industrial domains. At the end of this project, the results will have been applied and validated on real industrial systems.

## Automotive domain

The car industry has the same considerations as the avionics one. They also have projects based on architecture description language approaches. The French AEE project [aee] has defined some specifications of what is useful for the automotive industry. In particular it has designed a specialised ADL, ***AIL-transport*** [ES2002], which is more dedicated to this domaine.

Unlike more generic ADLs, AIL-transport details many categories of automotive components. So this ADL is strongly linked with the automotive architecture and cannot be adapted to other purposes. This choice may be explained by the fact that the development process of a car is shorter than the one of an aircraft.

AIL-transport and the results of this project are internally used by some ot its automotive partners. However, the lack of tools supporting them is a weakness and stresses the need for tools to promote new system engineering practices.

The European project EAST-EEA [east] is in a certain way the follow up of the AEE project. It demonstrates the interest of the automotive industry, at the European scale, for the formal description of architectures and the ADLs.

## AADL emergence

Among all the ADLs, AADL is currently emerging and could play a major role in industry in the future. This is illustrated by projects like ASSERT, which has chosen this language to support its system development lifecycle. Several explanations can be advanced:

- AADL is generic enough to cover all the real-time systems, in any domain;
- AADL is currently standardized by an international committee, what favours its adoption by a large community of users and its support by tool vendors;
- AADL is based on MetaH, which has experimented and validated for ten years the underlying concepts;
- a graphical version of AADL, based on UML 2, is currently under specification.

As seen previously, some other domains such as automotive have chosen more dedicated ADLs. It should be possible to map the concepts of these special ADLs on those of AADL. Such an approach could combine the advantages of AADL with specificities of a given domain. This idea is worth studying.

# 3. Tool support for AADL

## Needs

Whatever the quality of a method is, it will not be adopted by users if it is not supported by tools. This is especially the case for development methods in industrial domains, where training and process constraints are important. It is not thinkable to ask the users to write by hand formal descriptions of their systems, and manually translate them into other formats to communicate with their development tools.

This is also the case for AADL. This language provides a strong structure and a well-defined semantics for the description of system architectures. It is possible to build a good development process with it. But all this will only be done if tools help the users during the development. At the same time, tools will also ensure the correct use of AADL by avoiding mistakes, syntax errors and so on.

## Existing basis to build a tool suite

A tool suite supporting AADL does not need to be developed from scratch. Indeed, many tools exist and can be used as a basis to lead such development. Even if some of these tools can not be easily adapted, they demonstrate the feasibility of these concepts.

**MetaH.** As said before, MetaH is both an architecture description language and a toolset supporting it. The language has been used as a basis to define the AADL standard. Even if differences between them are sometimes important (MetaH has more restrictions for multi-processor systems, scheduling policies, etc.), the common part is large and ensures a strong basis for AADL. When considering the development of tools supporting the new AADL standard, it is natural to imagine the reuse of some MetaH tool technologies.

MetaH provides a graphical user interface called Dome. This interface enables the design of the architecture and its properties, and the generation of the description file. Dome has meta facilities which enable its easy adaptation to support the new AADL concepts. Moreover Dome has not the same restrictions as MetaH for exportation.

MetaH also contains some verification tools for architectures described in MetaH ADL. For example, it is possible to check the schedulability of the real-time tasks. It seems interesting to reuse such a tool with AADL. The schedulability problem is relatively simple with MetaH because the scheduling policy is imposed and all the related theories exist. AADL allows many different scheduling or communication policies. The theories that we need to prove the schedulability of a whole architecture are now more complex, when existing, and the reuse of the MetaH tools is perhaps not so easy.

The MetaH toolset contains code generators. This is due to its general principle, where the user components are agregated and linked by the generated code. In this approach, many constraints can be imposed to the user, since the expected result is the production of some embedded software. The principle of AADL is more a descriptive approach, that is, the capability to describe a possibly already existing system. In this case it is not possible to impose many technical solutions to the user. The MetaH code generator may be reused with AADL but it needs to be adapted to the new context and become more flexible.

Thus, MetaH can be used as a basis for several tools supporting AADL, but adaptations will be required in all the cases because of the differences between these two languages. The main risk is related to the current export restrictions imposed to MetaH by the US government.

**ADeS.** ADeS [ades] is a simulator of the behaviour of system architectures described with AADL. We developed it during a study with the European space agency (ESA) to evaluate the first draft versions of the AADL standard and to test the capability of this language to be supported by tools.

ADeS can be used during the development of an architecture to assess its behaviour. At each step of the lifecycle, the AADL description of the architecture is refined. ADeS parses this description and simulates the behaviour of all the components to show the global behaviour of the architecture. The accuracy of the result will depend on the accuracy of the description. On the one hand, during the first phases of the development we just get an overview of the global behaviour. On the other hand, at the end of the development, it is possible to plug user models in the simulator to have precise results. This capability of ADeS to accept user behaviour models is used to bypass current limitations of AADL in the description of architecture behaviours. We expect improvements of this point in the future.

Other tools can be used for similar simulation purposes (e.g., ObjectGeode [objectgeode], Matlab/Simulink [simulink], Scilab [scilab]). What is different with ADeS is the will to share a common architecture description language as a support for the whole information related to the manipulated architecture, including the simulation needs, and not to use a specific language for simulation aspects or particular subsystems. However, we have succeeded in the connection of ObjectGeode and Scilab with ADeS to take advantage of their specific capabilities.

However, ADeS can provide several interesting modules for the development of an AADL tool suite. Firstly, ADeS contains a full AADL parser, able to understand AADL descriptions, to provide a data structure representing the architecture in memory, to detect the syntactic and semantic errors, and to send an explicit error message to the user. This parser needs to be updated to take into account the last evolutions of the standard, but it is already very close to the AADL specification. As foreseen for the ASSERT project, this AADL parser can also be used to experiment changes in AADL to support additional informations.

Secondly, ADeS provides a graphical user interface (see figure 1) to visualize the structure of the system architecture, and not only the structure of the description. In other words, it recursively shows contents of all the component *instances*, whereas many common modelling tools show more the component types (or classes).

Lastly, ADeS has a simulation kernel where simulation elements are created to represent the system architecture elements. The simulation provides a good

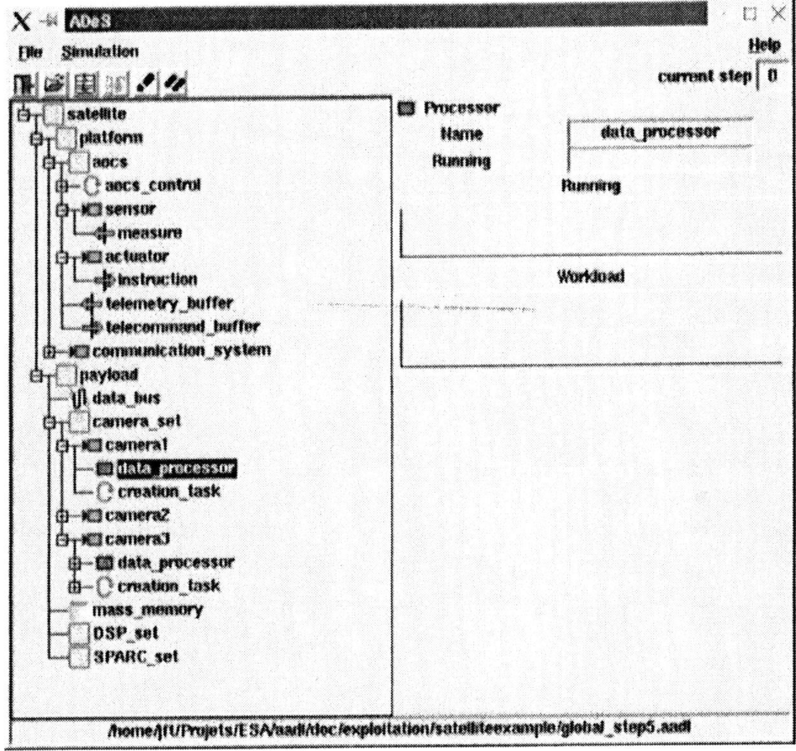


*Figure 1.* Snapshot of the man-machine interface of ADeS

means to evaluate the behaviour of the system under development. This tool can be extended to support many specific needs of the user.

A possible extension of ADeS is the addition of a capability to modify the manipulated AADL descriptions in order to easily prototype, dimension and assess solutions, and then reexport these changes into the AADL description.

## Possible services

Many services can be provided by a tool suite based on AADL, in several categories: modelling tools, verification, automatic generation, etc. These tools will share some common functions, such as the AADL parser. Figure 2 shows a possible organization of an AADL tool suite. Let us consider these possible tools.

**AADL manipulation.** AADL parsing is the first action for any tool using an AADL description as input. Thus, AADL parser is a typical example of a module which can be shared by all the tools supporting AADL.

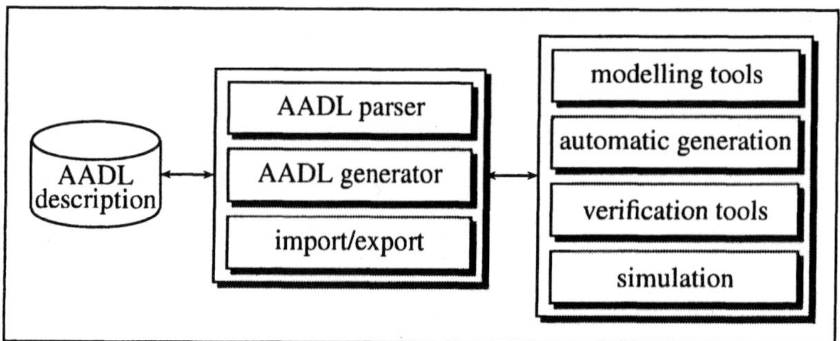


*Figure 2.* Possible organization of an tool suite supporting AADL

The first objective of an AADL parser is to read the AADL descriptions and to build in memory a data structure which will be manipulated by tools. Such a parser can be applied on textual AADL descriptions or their equivalent XML format, but also on XMI format when using graphical AADL descriptions based on UML. Depending on the context of its use, it can provide several other services:

- Detection of all the syntax and semantics errors. This is useful when the description is written by hand or by a tool which does not correctly manage all the semantics rules of AADL;
- Creation of error messages explaining the detected errors. This is useful when using the textual AADL format in a description written by hand.

Another similar module can be shared: the AADL generator. This module is able to produce an AADL description from a memory representation of the architecture. Of course, these two modules have to work together to share the same memory representation. They constitute a single software library for the tool developer.

**Modelling.** Many modelling tools exist and are used for system and software development. Some of them are based on UML [uml], others on HOOD [hood], other on different standards. They enable the description of an architecture by combining elements and assembling them. Introducing AADL in the system development process strongly requires such modelling tools. This requirement can be fulfilled either by specific tools developed to support AADL, or by existing ones where some import/export functions are added to read and write AADL descriptions. A graphical version of AADL is currently under definition. This graphical AADL is based on UML 2. This choice will help in the reuse of existing UML modelling tools in this context.

Just using existing modelling concepts is not enough to take completely advantage of AADL. The first AADL descriptions of a system under development can happen in the very early stages of a project, for example during the capture of the needs. And the classical modelling tools are not able to take these aspects into account. Some tools exist to support requirement engineering (Doors [doors], Catalyse [catalyze]) and could also be interfaced with AADL. Innovative methods also exist to deal with this problem with formal approaches and proofs of consistency. For example, TRDF [GLL1996] defines how to rigorously lead the first phases of the development to capture all the requirements and to produce complete and consistent specifications. Since these methods are not yet supported by tools, new ones have to be invented. They will enable the production of AADL description during the application of these methods.

Examples of possible tools are given below:

**Requirement capture** this tool will help in the capture of the need of the client and its formal expression in the highest levels of an AADL description;

**System design and validation** this tool can help in the description of the specifications of the system and the reuse of already existing building blocks with formal verification of their compatibility with the architecture;

**Feasibility and dimensioning** this tool will ensure that the already described architecture is feasible, and will complete the description by giving values for the pending properties.

**Generation.** During a development process, many parts can be automatically generated instead of being fastidiously hand coded. This is the case for the source code itself. This function is now well masterised by tool vendors and is often associated with modelling tools.

Automatic test generation is also possible in this context. Some of these tests are based on the low-level aspects of the develoment. Unitary tests are related to the source code and the detailed design results. A lot of research is led to better cover this activity [inka, danocops, agatha]. By choosing a single formal description language for the whole development cycle, we enable the use of this language to contain what is needed to generate these tests. Moreover, in such a description we also have a lot of information to generate higher level tests for integration phases.

**Verification.** Since we use a formal means to describe the system architecture under development, many formal verifications can be processed. For example, it is possible to *prove* real-time properties: Is it possible to always execute the tasks and meet their deadlines? Is it possible to communicate all the data through the connections? Such verifications will take place after a detailed design phase because they need precise information about the organization of the system and its parameters.

Another type of verification can be performed during the first phases of the development (capture of the needs, specifications, design). Any of these phases will produce and refine the AADL description of the system architecture. Provided that the development method keeps all the needed information in the description, it is possible to check by tools whether the architecture resulting of each phase is consistent. It is also possible to check whether all the requirements resulting from a given phase are taken into account in the next one.

**Simulation.** Verifications can also be performed by simulation of the execution of the system architecture under development. If we have all the interesting information in the description, it is possible to simulate the behaviour of each element and get a good evaluation of the global system. As presented previously, ADeS is an example of such a tool and illustrates the capability of AADL to provided the needed information to perform such a simulation.

The simulation can also provide an evaluation of the behaviour of the architecture during each step of its development. This is useful for a rapid prototyping of the system during its specifications or at the beginning of its design. As the design is refined, the simulation can be used to evaluate its consequences on the behaviour of the system.

## 4. Conclusion

We have seen that ADLs are more and more considered, and particularly in avionics and automotive domains. Among these ADLs, AADL seems to be an interesting one, and the development of a tool suite supporting this language is now necessary to promote it and enable its easy use by industry. Bases exist to ensure the feasibility of these tools and to build them by reusing some components.

Tools supporting AADL can provide services in several categories: A set of parsers and AADL generators can help in the manipulation of the language, modelling tools can help in the creation of architecture descriptions and provide support for innovative formal design methods, automatic code and test generators can take advantage of the information contained in the description, verification tools can check the consistency and completeness of the designed architecture, simulation tools can give an assessment of the behaviour of the system architecture during its development.

Since the use of AADL in system engineering may be very large, a complete tool set must be composed by many more or less independant tools, developed or adapted by their own specialists. The difference with the current situation will be the interoperability capabilities, thanks to the international standardization of AADL which enables these tools to share the same language.

The development of innovative tools and methods in relation with research projects, like ASSERT, will provide improvements for AADL. The standarization committee has already planned a new version of the standard to take into account these inputs.

## References


[aadl] Axlog ingénierie, "AADL (Avionics Architecture Description Language)", 2003, http://www.axlog.fr/R_d/aadl/aadl_en.html.

[metah] Honeywell, "MetaH Evaluation and Support Site", 1998, http://www.htc.honeywell.com/metah/.

[aee] AEE, 2002, http://aee.inria.fr/.

[ES2002] Jean-Pierre ELLOY, Françoise SIMONOT-LION, "An architecture description language for in-vehicle embedded system development", 2002.

[east] "EAST-EEA – Embedded Electronic Architecture", http://www.east-eea.net/.

[ades] Axlog ingénierie, "ADeS", 2003, http://www.axlog.fr/R_d/aadl/ades_en.html.

[objectgeode] Telelogic, "Telelogic ObjectGeode", http://www.telelogic.com/products/additional/objectgeode/index.cfm.

[simulink] Mathworks, "Simulink", http://www.mathworks.com/products/simulink/.

[scilab] Inria, "Scilab", http://scilabsoft.inria.fr/.

[uml] "Unified Modeling Language", http://www.uml.org/.

[hood] HOOD User's Group and Jean-Pierre ROSEN, "HOOD, An Industrial Approach for Software Design", 1997.

[doors] Telelogic, "Telelogic DOORS/ERS", http://www.telelogic.com/products/doorsers/index.cfm.

[catalyze] SteelTrace, "Catalyze suite", http://www.steeltrace.com/products_catalyze_suite.htm.

[GLL1996] Gérard LE LANN, "Proof-Based System Engineering and Embedded Systems", invited paper, European School on Embedded Systems (Veldhoven, NL, Nov1996), in Lecture Notes in Computer Science nř1494, Stringer-Verlag Pub., Oct 1998, pp. 208-248. http://www-rocq.inria.fr/reflecs/publications_fr.html.

[inka] "Projet InKa", http://www.axlog.fr/R_d/inka/inka_cadre.html.

[danocops] "DANOCOPS : Détection Automatique de NOn-COnformités d'un Programme vis-à-vis de ses Spécifications", http://www.telecom.gouv.fr/rntl/projet/Posters-PDF/RNTL-Poster-Danocops.pdf.

[agatha] "Atelier de génération de tests de spécifications industrielles AGATHA", http://www-drt.cea.fr/fr/prog/list/systemes_embarques/list_outils_atelier.htm.

# AUTHOR INDEX

# Author Index